AFTER OXFORD

Getting in. Fitting in?
Standing out.

Daniel Stone

DANIEL STONE

Copyright © Daniel Stone 2020

All rights reserved

To contact the author, email: afteroxfordbook@gmail.com

AFTER OXFORD

Dedicated to my mother

Millicent Janet Stone

My first and my best educator

Table of Contents

INTRODUCTION: GRADUATION DAY

"For we drink deeply from wells of freedom and opportunity that we did not dig." - Cory Booker, United[1]

I had undertaken this journey countless times before - sometimes in sunshine, and occasionally in snow, but mostly with the dreary overcast backdrop that so often accompanies English mornings. However, this journey was unique. It was the conclusion of two weeks of final year exams, three years of studying, a lifetime of dedication, and the fulfilment of a legacy of hopes and dreams. The weight of this moment followed my every step. My time at Oxford had come to an end. I thought of the friends I had made, the campaigns I had fought, and of life beyond the classroom. And I thought of my grandparents, who had allowed waves of hope and ambition to carry them across the ocean: away from the familiar warmth of the Caribbean and into a cold and unknown land.

My paternal grandparents, Selvin and Brynel Stone and my maternal grandparents, Joseph and Phyllis Williams both moved to the UK in the early 1960s at a time where men and women from across the Commonwealth had been invited to contribute their labour to rebuild British industries after World

---

[1] Booker, C. (2016). *United: Thoughts on Finding Common Ground and Advancing the Common Good*, Ballantine Books.

War Two. They settled in Handsworth; an area three miles away from the centre of Birmingham. Some Caucasian inhabitants welcomed these new arrivals with written signs: *No Blacks, No dogs, No Irish.* Others moved en masse from inner city areas into suburbs that were outside of the financial and cultural reach of most emigrants. Overt racism and structural inequalities quickly taught my grandparents not to aspire too high or to expect too much. Britain was not their home. They were guests who, according to some, were overstaying their welcome.

In those early years, my grandparents spoke only of defiance and survival. My father's father told me about the journeys he had taken in the long English winters; walking to work because the snowfall was too heavy for buses to traverse. His family was depending on him to provide for them, so he walked. He walked for miles until his toes had become numb and it was difficult to breath. He walked without ever considering stopping. In those difficult times, it may not have seemed feasible that their family could thrive in the UK, and that one of their kin could graduate from the most prestigious university in England. But in this moment, here I was, giving voice to that which had been unspoken, and credence to the impossible.

Unlike most other universities, the University of Oxford is made up of 38 independent but interconnected Colleges. I studied at St Peter's; one of the more inconspicuous of the 38, despite its prominent green doors and the a-frame protruding out onto New Inn Hall Street in an attempt to lure tourists inside. In the more popular Colleges, hundreds of cameras would be readied on a daily basis to capture a snapshot of a dining room or the entrance to a place of study. Eyeing a tourist in St Peter's was a rare occurrence and one that I was always curious about. To me, Colleges were the places where I had classes, met with friends and attended parties. The sum total of these activities had given me an undeniable source of identity, friendship and community but in isolation, they were of little meaning - like seeing a tenth of a painting or hearing a few seconds of a song. After the tourists had walked around the three main quads in St Peter's and taken their fill of pictures, they would head out onto New Inn Hall Street and continue with the rest of their day. I would return to my room, surrounded by Oxford in all of its dimensions.

Today, New Inn Hall Street had come to a standstill as a hundred or so undergraduate and master's students walked through the large green doors on their pilgrimage to the Sheldonian Theatre. Like all graduates, I was dressed in the mandatory 'sub fusc' attire; a dark suit, a white shirt and bow tie, and a flowing black gown. The white fur-like trim that ran from the top of my shoulders down to the centre of my chest and the mortar board perched delicately on my head were special additions for graduation day, and gave me a sense of regality.

As a student of Economics and Management, I passed the Sheldonian at least twice per week on the way to lectures. The large raised courtyard surrounding the theatre was separated from the street below by a metal wrought iron fence, which was supported every few metres by an imposing stone pillar. On top of each pillar was the stone carving of a head. All of the heads were male, bearing European features and an array of magnificent beards. I had wondered who these men were and what they were guarding. But the Sheldonian seemed like a place where one had to be invited to enter and that its wrought iron fences had, at one and at every point in time, been designed to exclude people like me.

Observing this spectacle were hundreds of onlookers. There were tourists; cameras flashing as they sought to capture their personal encounter with the University of Oxford. But the majority were families and loved ones: bemused by the ostentation of proceedings and the fact that their relatives were central to it all. As we continued on the procession towards the Sheldonian, I thought back to the drinks reception that had taken place earlier that afternoon.

It felt like a short time ago that parents had trudged back and forth from car to front door, balancing cardboard boxes full of prized belongings in their arms while trying to introduce themselves to their children's friends. Today, cardboard boxes had been swapped for glasses of champagne. Their broad smiles relayed the fact this milestone also meant the end of a journey for them.

Conversations began to follow a familiar pattern: "Three years already! Can you believe it? What will you do next?"

By the date of my graduation, Friday 22 July 2011, I had already begun work as the Vice President of Charities and Community for the Oxford University Student Union, which gave me an easy, but perhaps unexpected answer to that question.

My parents, Mark and Millicent were with two of my friends from university, Tendai and Dan. "Finance, sounds interesting." I overheard my dad say. "So are you the guys who are going to cause the next financial crash?" My dad began to laugh while Dan looked nervously towards the ground. Dan's dad came over and shook my hand: "I can't believe three years have gone by so quickly!"

My parents were born 12 days apart in the latter months of 1963, in Handsworth. Both were the first of their siblings to be born in the UK and were from large families. My dad has seven siblings and my mum has eight. The Handsworth my parents experienced was different to that of my grandparents. As more families poured into Handsworth from countries like India and Pakistan, more white families moved out.

My parents' childhood represented the richness of the cultures around them. They watched from their bedroom windows as kaleidoscopes of fireworks shot into the night sky in celebration of Eid, they ate sweets - whose names they couldn't pronounce - for the festival of Diwali, and they received Christmas cards that featured images of black Marys, Josephs and Jesuses. But diversity was also accompanied by an uneasy tension brought about by differences in culture, religion and language that often left groups competing to build *their* community in the belief that this could only be achieved at the expense of others.

Competition may have seemed necessary because without the legacy of wealth afforded to antecedent populations and still faced with unbridled prejudice, the opportunities afforded to my parents' generation were severely constrained. My dad told me that he knew of only one of his peers - out of a pool of hundreds of friends, relatives and acquaintances - who had left school and attended university. The contradictions of seeing wealth that you're unable to touch along with the degrading and oppressive effects of racism, sometimes led to anger spilling over into riots. In such volatile times, solidarity with people you could trust was essential and valuable. And who better to trust than people who shared your religion or culture or skin colour? My parents would often tell the story of their wedding, complete with several hundred guests, which had been able to happen without either of them having any savings. They managed because people in their church community and family had so generously taken care of everything: they cooked food, sewed outfits and provided gifts. That was the power of community.

AFTER OXFORD

Early in their marriage, my dad worked as an artist for the Yellow Pages phone book, and my mum was an office administrator, before giving up paid employment when her first child, Selina was born. I was born just over a year later in the summer of 1989. My brother Matthew arrived in September 1991 and the last of my parent's children, Joanna, was born in July 1995.

My parents presided over a house that was full of creativity. In school vacations we would build 'pirate ships' in our bedroom and paint masks in the living room. We would take regular weekend walks to the library and were given diaries as gifts to encourage us to pen our thoughts. As devout Christians, my parents set down clear spiritual and behavioural guidelines. Swearing was not tolerated. Slips in behaviour were met with an icy glare or a cutting remark. Open defiance would be swiftly returned with the swish of a belt or the back of a slipper. But my parents were fair. They were always quick to let us know when we had done well. When I was commended for my achievements at school or at church, I most looked forward to telling my parents, who would proudly shake their heads in disbelief at what their child had accomplished.

The multiculturalism of my parent's youth was also our experience. Within my circle of school friends was a mix of heritages sufficient to form a United Nations. My classmates could trace their roots to India, Jamaica, Pakistan, Vietnam, St Kitts, Bangladesh, and occasionally to the Midlands.

In the 1990s and 2000s, there were a number of high profile gang-related incidents involving the Handsworth-based Burger Bar Boys and the Johnson Crew from a neighbouring inner city area, Aston. This led to the enduring perception that Handsworth and Aston were unsafe for anyone who was brave enough or poor enough to live there. But Handsworth was the place where I went to school, where I played outside with my friends, and where I belonged. Sure, you could find trouble if you were looking for it, but that was also true in suburban life and in the cities that escaped the mistrusting glare of the national press.

I

The limited seating capacity of the Sheldonian amphitheatre had restricted admission to the graduation to three guests per family. I allocated two tickets to my parents. To the impartial observer, Matthew would probably be the favourite to get the third ticket, owing to the closeness of our bond as brothers; Selina was the eldest child, so could arguably claim the ticket as her birth right; but then perhaps it was more important to use this moment to inspire Joanna, who was in the process of applying for university?

Given that there were already three deserving candidates for the final position, it was met with confusion when I decided to put an additional member of the family into the mix. From my observations, it seems that grandparents and their grandchildren have a variety of complex and unexpected relationships. Some grandparents shower their grandchildren with love and affection that they were too exhausted to give to their own children. Others are able to play freely with their grandchildren because they are safe in the knowledge that they can hand them back to their parents in a few hours' time. And there are some who develop a resilience and inner strength that only comes when you've lived in this world for decades and realised that you still have the power to smile.

My grandad Selvin and my late grandma Brynel had an incredibly close relationship with my cousins, Jessica and Bria. My cousins lived with their mum, Andrea, around the corner from my grandparents' home in Kingstanding. They would see our grandparents almost every day; after school, at church and on weekends. On our occasional visits to see our grandparents, Jessica and Bria were usually there. This was great, because we then had three teams to participate in the garden wheelbarrow race. I observed the ways in which Jessica and Bria interacted with my grandparents. They spoke easily with them, and knew what jokes they would find funny. They could trace the disciplinary line, and knew when not to cross it. And most importantly, they also knew where to find the Ribena and the biscuits with chocolate on them.

I respected my grandparents, and knew that I should trust them as I did my parents, but our interactions weren't frequent enough for me to know them and for them to truly know me. Their ornate plates set in a high cabinet in the front room of their house confused me, as did the black and white photos of people with stony expressions rather than the smiles I thought were mandatory in front of a camera. Nevertheless, I considered my grandparents to be kind people. Our grandma would always ensure that we were well fed, usually by the plums and other fruits grown by my grandad in his wonderfully kept garden.

Only when I was much older would I learn that my grandad had been born into a farming community in Jamaica. As a boy, he had learned to milk cows, break in horses and grow fruits and vegetables. I wondered whether my grandad's commitment to horticulture was his way of remaining connected to the life he had in Jamaica.

My interactions with my mother's mother Phyllis Williams, had been even less frequent. My grandma and late grandad, Joseph Williams, had spent most of my childhood years living in Jamaica. Following the passing of my grandad in 2009, my grandma had sold their property in Jamaica and permanently relocated to the UK, where all her children and grandchildren were based. By this time, my grandma was well into her seventies. Our conversations were always pleasant enough, although they often revealed the gap between our generations: visits to see my grandma often became tutorials in the use of the iPhone, the DVD player and the answering machine.

All the same, I enjoyed these visits, and my grandma remains someone I like spending time with. I have a hunch that the condition of someone's soul can often be observed in the way that they laugh. My grandma's laugh is free, light and child-like; her head tilts back and there is an audible chuckle usually followed by a playful push on the arm of the person delivering the witty remark. I knew that my grandma had endured tough times during her life: material poverty, a demanding rural upbringing, and a husband who wasn't always supportive of her Christian faith. But she had always chosen forgiveness and gratitude regardless of the situation she found herself in, and I felt great respect for that.

As I thought about who to give the final ticket to, I sensed that it would mean a lot to my grandma; perhaps more than it would mean to my siblings. I thought of the selflessness and the ambition that had brought my grandma to the UK; where she had raised nine children, forming for them a nurturing home, in which my mother's character had been able to flourish. I recognised that this was an opportunity for me to say 'thank you'.

I called my grandma to tell her the good news. "Ooooohh, dat's nice," she exclaimed. "I had *heard* but me no-know if…" My grandma intentionally leaves sentences unfinished, but only when she's said enough to leave the speaker with no doubt as to what she means. After I had made the decision to give the ticket to my grandma, I remember my mum knocking on my door while I was alone in my room: "You've done a really good thing Daniel."

And so it was that my mum, my dad and my grandma were sat in the rafters of Oxford's Sheldonian Theatre as the Vice Chancellor invited forward the first set of graduands to complete the formalities that would mark the end of their time at the University of Oxford. The vast majority of the ceremony was in Latin, and without the assistance of the ceremony brochure - translation enclosed - the meaning of the words would have been lost to all. Row by row, we were called up to respond to an oath that binds all graduates to be loyal, obedient and faithful to the University and its interests. On taking the oath, we could legally graduate and receive our degree certificates.

Our response was two words in Latin, but as the moment drew nearer, I suddenly became unsure of whether I had learned them correctly. I looked up towards the ceiling, hoping that my eyes would be able to locate the part of my brain where this crucial bit of information was stored. In doing so, I saw the theatre's magnificent ceiling; the pink cherubs darting through a pale blue sky to attend to a fiery chasm that was above the heads of those seated below. Or perhaps I had interpreted the painting incorrectly, and the angelic creatures had in fact emerged out of the void with no intention of going back?

The time was now upon me to say the words. I stood up and nervously walked towards the platform. The Vice Chancellor was waiting.

What were those two words again?

Vos dabitis fidem ad observandum omnia statuta.

What was the correct order?

Privilegia, consuetudines et libertares istius Universitatis.

How loudly should I say them?

AFTER OXFORD

Quantenus ad vos spectent.

He was now looking at us - "Do Fidum!"

And just like that, I had graduated.

DANIEL STONE

BEFORE OXFORD

HARD LESSONS

"I like school because of the challenges I face" - Daniel
Stone, 1999, End of Year Report, Class 5C, St James
Primary School.

It's 7.48am and I am watching a pot of milk. The pot is around two-thirds full and sitting atop a live flame on our gas-fired cooker. Oranges and blues lap against the bottom of the pot, willing it to get hotter and hotter and hotter. The day before, I had been caught out reading a book while on duty and the milk had escaped over the curved brown edges, vanquishing the flames below and condemning my siblings and me to a breakfast of Weetabix without enough milk. Even the extra generous teaspoon of sugar hadn't been enough to ease the tastelessness, so each mouthful was forced down my unwilling throat in a glacial manner.

A series of tiny milk bubbles were gathering towards one end of the pot, and I waited expectantly for the inevitable eruption. At that moment, I heard a click at the kitchen door. In came my younger brother Matthew, midway through his own morning task, which was setting the table for breakfast.

"Watch the milk. Don't let it spill over again!" Matthew teased. "Shut up," I muttered bitterly as I went faithfully back to my watching brief. It stung that my mum had reacted with annoyance at my lapse in concentration and that a day later, Matthew was reminding me of how I had failed.

Matthew reached into the cupboard for the Weetabix, corn flakes and an unopened box of rice krispies. I always felt that these cereals worked best in combination. The crunchiness of the rice krispies were a good foil to the stodginess of Weetabix and the delicate wafer-thin corn flakes that would seemingly disintegrate under the power of hot milk.

Whooosh!

In a flash, the milk was stretching and rushing towards the rim of the pot. I responded instantly, turning the dial on the stove anti-clockwise until the flame subsided. The milk settled down to a restful state, masked with a layer of thick cream. I smiled, vindicated.

"Breakfast is ready!" I yelled.

Having positioned the cereal on the table, Matthew had taken his place in front of one of the spoons. Selina marched in importantly wearing a well-ironed green pinafore and matching cardigan. She sat down and began to examine the back of the box of rice krispies. I'd looked at the box a few days ago and knew that they had enclosed toys from the latest Disney film.

"Bagsy the toy!" I shouted.

"You had it last time!" responded Selina.

"No I didn't, it was your turn."

"No, I gave you the toy. It was one of those football things…"

Indeed Selina was right. The previous rice krispies box held a set of football pencil-tops. Selina who didn't care much for football had given a green and white t-shirt-shaped pencil top to Matthew.

"You gave it to Matthew not me," I countered. "So it's my go, and you can have Matthew's toy."

"I don't even like Celtic!" Matthew protested.

AFTER OXFORD

The conversation got louder and louder and no closer to a solution.

"Unu, be quiet and bless the food," said my mum, who had just come in with my younger sister Joanna. Joanna was at nursery and was dressed in a bright turquoise sweater with an image of the Teletubbies gaily leaping through Teletubbyland.

We immediately fell silent, heads bowed and eyes closed. A moment or two of silence passed. I cracked open my right eyelid a millimetre or two and peered in the direction of my mother. Through a slight blur as my pupil readjusted to the light, I could see her firm stare directed straight towards me. I jammed my eyes shut again. I wondered if I was still in her bad books on account of yesterday's indiscretion.

"Dear Lord." I began. "Thank you for this food that you have provided. I pray that you bless it into our bodies. In Jesus' name."

"Amen" we all chimed in.

While we began pouring out the cereal, my mum turned on the radio and adjusted the dial to 96.4 FM, BBC West Midlands. The familiar voice of Ed Doolan reverberated around the room. The local news was a valued source of information for me. On weeknights I was often forced to go to bed before the conclusion of critical European football matches, and was reliant on the news reader to provide the vital information that the rest of the country had found out the night before.

On rare and magical occasions, the radio would also announce schools that had been forced to close because of snow. I would sit in agony as the list of closed schools was reeled off in alphabetical order: "Abbey Catholic Primary School. Acocks Green Primary School." After what seemed like an eternity... "St George's Church of England Primary School," and then finally, "St James Church of England Primary School..."

It was at the behest of the newsreader - who had forecast rain for later - that we left the house that morning wearing waterproof coats and hats, alongside our lunch boxes and book bags. Our book bags were green satcheleque waterproof bags with a large St James crest printed on the front. On the back was written our name and class number to prevent mislaid bags going home with the wrong child. Enclosed was a disorderly assortment of workbooks, homework sheets, stationery, football-shirted pencil-tops, small figurines, sweets and pogs. Pogs were thin circular discs of various colours and designs that formed the basis of a game everybody was obsessed with, and served as a valuable currency amongst my friends.

Book bag in hand, Selina, Matthew and I began the walk with mum, while Joanna was pushed along in a buggy. St James Primary School was located at the top end of Westbourne Road, our street, and was perhaps no more than 500 metres from our house. With short legs and youthful impatience, the uphill walk seemed to go on for miles. It wasn't helped by the fact that our mum would stop frequently along the journey to talk to neighbours on our road. On this occasion, Mr Lee had just opened the front door of his house and was ambling towards the gate. He smiled widely: "Marnin'."

"Morning!" my mum responded brightly, and they began a familiar neighbourly chat.

We were taught that, as children, we were not to enter into conversations with adults unless invited. Sensing that this exchange wasn't going to require my input, my mind drifted off into the day's upcoming activities, namely, lunchtime. On Wednesdays Year 5, and Year 5 only, were allowed to use the football pitch. In reality the 'pitch' was a tarmacked area no larger than a regulation penalty box. Our 'footballs' were sponge to minimise the possibility of injury. Despite these limiting factors, the pitch had chalked lines and a goal, and to us, it was as good as Wembley.

This game was also on my mind because of what happened last Wednesday. On the journey home, I had told my mum about a new student, Luke. Luke had recently started at St James and wasn't very good at football. With the guile and precision of Alan Hansen, I had relayed the facts of his missed shots and aimless passing. My mum had stopped me and asked me to reflect on how I would feel in his position. Had Luke been sad? Yes. So, what would a good friend and a good person do to help Luke? I hadn't been able to produce a definitive answer to this question, but I recognised her point. I had been self-centred and had failed to look at the situation from Luke's perspective. I resolved that at this lunchtime, I would do better.

"Daniel, come."

My mum had concluded her conversation with Mr Lee and I was lagging behind my siblings. When we had reached the end of the steep climb up Westbourne road, there were only a matter of minutes to go before the bell to signal the start of the school day. My mum had stopped at the large green gates to speak to the teacher on duty, but given that we were in safe and familiar grounds, we were allowed to leave the gaze of my mother and escape into the freedom of the playground.

Towards our left was the junior playground for pupils in reception class up to the end of Year 2. Selina, Matthew and I continued straight and onto the Secondary playground where the majority of the older students were already amassed. Coming into the playground, there was a large open tarmacked area with the faint markings of running lanes, due to be repainted in advance of this year's sports day. This area was filled with groups of students shrieking gleefully, running without restraint or playing football, with jumpers as goal posts. Behind this open expanse was a raised area that could be reached by climbing a set of wooden steps towards the right or the left. Once at the summit, you could survey the playground below. To the left of the main playground was our own Wembley, in all of its glory, and to the right a white wall faced the playground, which could also double as a makeshift goal.

It was in front of this wall that I saw a group of my friends on their haunches, undoubtedly playing pogs. As I walked towards the group, my friends Richard, Vy-liam and Samuel moved over so that I could plant myself in between them.

"Deepak is going to win this one," said Richard. "Subhag is next, then it's me, and then you."

I nodded and turned my attention to the game. I was always interested in seeing how other people played; how flicking the discs at a certain angle or with the right strength would lead them to victory. I could see that Deepak was on the brink of winning, having collected all but three of Sam's pogs. A minute or so later and, sure enough, Deepak held his arms aloft, a broad smile stretching across his face amid shouts of encouragement from the circle.

There were rumours that pogs would follow the way of stickers and yoyos in being banned from our playground. It seemed like bans were always imposed at the height of the latest craze, just to stop us enjoying ourselves. Or perhaps some unfortunate soul in Dundee got hit in the eye in a freak accident, causing parents and school officials to deem it unsafe for children.

Subhag stood up and readied himself for the game. As Deepak and Subhag crouched down and began to build the pillar of pogs. I heard in the distance the faint rattling of a familiar sound. Within seconds, a clanging sound of brass was resounding through all corners of the playground. Groans. "We'll continue later," I said. Deepak and Subhag began to return their pogs back to the safety of their book bag; Deepak, delighted with the knowledge that he was taking with him a greater number than he had left the house with this morning.

We stood in single file outside the classroom, waiting for our teacher to emerge. "Did you see me win?" Deepak asked excitedly, still beaming.

"Only the end. After Subhag, it's Richard and then me."

"I can beat Subhag and then if I beat Richard, it'll be Double D, Double D."

'Double D' was the name that Deepak and I called our duo, for the perhaps unimaginative reason that both of our names began with the letter D. We had, however, shown enough creativity to come up with a catchy song that was sure to be aired on Top of the Pops:

Double D, Double D. Who are we? Double D, Double D.

It would be at least another year before we realised that our ingenious name was already being used by shops around the world as a measurement for a part of a woman's anatomy. In blissful ignorance, we began another rendition of *Double D, Double D.*

AFTER OXFORD

After a few moments, the door swung open and our teacher, Ms Chanda ushered us into the classroom and began the register. My 'S' surname placed me towards the bottom end of the roll call, but I knew that I couldn't afford for my mind to drift away from the task at hand. A few months ago, I had lost concentration and to the amusement of my classmates had answered "yes, Mum" rather than "yes, Miss." This wasn't my only concern, either.

I had a stutter. It wasn't always obvious, but it was present and I was conscious of it. Like an energy-saving light bulb or an engine left out in the cold, once I was running, my speech was fine, but it was always the start of a sentence or an interjection that held the most fear.

As we drew nearer through the Samras and Scotts to the Sophals and the Stirlings, I felt as though everyone's eyes were on me.

"Daniel Stone."

"Yy-yyes miss." A slight hiccup, but I had survived.

Formalities completed. At this point in proceedings we would usually start to open our exercise books and write the date neatly in the top right hand corner of the page. But this morning Ms Chanda again drew our attention. "From this lesson forward, the following pupils will be joining the set 1 Mathematics class for years 5 and 6: Richard Caddle, Aneeka Masih, Vy-liam Ng, Shona Robinson and Daniel Stone. Bring your pencil case with you and your maths exercise book: you're going over to class 5S."

Class 5S was taught by Mrs Spooner, a larger than life character who always wore leopard print and who once sang *Wind Beneath My Wings* at a school talent show while holding a framed picture of Michael Owen. Visits to other classrooms had historically been done at the behest of my class teacher who wanted a trusted pupil to deliver a message in the form of a folded written note. I loved the responsibility associated with this task. I would knock at the door, patiently waiting for a response.

Thirty sets of eyes would look in amazement to see that the person at the door was not an adult, but a pupil like themselves who was now commanding the time and attention of their teacher. If Selina or Matthew was in the class, their classmates would instantly turn to them to see if they had realised that it was their sibling at the door. I would flash them a quick smile before continuing with my duty.

However, coming to a foreign classroom and staying for a lesson was different. And as I entered the unfamiliar territory with my four peers standing sheepishly by my side, I was grateful to see that Selina's affectionate smile had already found me from the other side of the room. There were five empty desks dispersed around the room and Mrs Spooner beckoned us to take one of the empty seats, booming "Welcome aboard!"

I chose a desk towards the front of the classroom on the right hand side.

"Welcome to our friends from Class 5C" beamed Mrs Spooner. "You are most welcome."

After reviewing the class rules, Mrs Spooner explained that we would start the class with a game of time-table shoot-out. To play, two students on opposite sides of the room would stand and face each other, and the teacher would issue a random multiplication sum, say, five multiplied by six. The most committed students would make a gun silhouette with their fingers as they stood, cocking back the revolver and firing the answer, followed by the word 'bang' in perfect unison with when they verbally delivered the decisive blow. Whoever lost would sit down and another would stand in their place.

Maths was one of my favourite subjects, and I would practice my times tables religiously, even in my free time. I would often lie in bed in the dark, rehearsing the combinations of numbers that I found most tricky. 2, 5 and 10 could be recalled without any thought. 3, 4 and 11 were only marginally more difficult, although 11 could pose a problem once it had progressed past 10 multiples of 11. The times tables that I hadn't quite mastered were 7, 9 and 12. I also knew that certain teachers would throw a curveball by asking a calculation from the 13, 15 or 20 times tables.

I had by far the quickest hands amongst my Year 5 classmates. Interestingly, my stutter never seemed to surface while I was involved in a shootout. It was as if my lips had realised the importance of the moment and had agreed to surrender their independence for a greater cause. However, I was now stepping out into the unknown: an older year group who may also have fearless gunslingers amongst them. The shootout began on opposite ends towards the rear of the classroom. Although I would only be permitted to observe the first half-a-dozen encounters until it was my turn, I answered along in my mind to warm up.

My turn came quickly, and I stood facing my opponent, fingers pointed out from my body, ready for the opening salvo. "3 times 7" Mrs Spooner said. "21, bang!" My reflexes were on my side, and my opponent sat down dejected. Another of my classmates would soon be seated too, followed by a second, a third, a fourth. By the time I had beaten my ninth or tenth opponent a murmur was building around the classroom. When I was more than halfway through the class it dawned on me that I was three or so victims away from Selina. Perhaps it would be better to lose now, I thought, rather than face my sibling. My pride wouldn't let myself do it, and before I knew it I was standing face to face with my sister, albeit separated by at least a dozen tables, populated with at least two dozen eyes curious to see which Stone would triumph.

The moment hadn't been lost on Mrs Spooner who gave this showdown a bigger build up than usual. Her feet moved shoulder width apart, she crouched slightly and rolled up her sleeves: "6 times 15." A curve ball. I knew that 3 multiplied by 15 was 45. 6 multiplied by 15 would be double that. "90, bang!"

A smile broke out across my face. I liked winning. The adulation of classmates and teachers left me feeling happier and more confident; I would sit taller in my chair and look forward to the rest of the lesson. This was in contrast to the emotions I felt after a defeat, when I would find it impossible to shake feelings of shame from rising in the pit of my stomach. So I always pushed myself to win. But I was learning not to allow my personal success to make me blind to the fact that in becoming a winner, I had also created several losers. It was my parents who began to cultivate this way of thinking within me; through quiet conversations after school football games and through lessons taught on a Sunday morning.

I

"Daniel, get Selina" my dad whispered.

It was a Sunday morning, and like every other Sunday morning, we were in Mount Zion Community Church in Aston. The final song before that morning's sermon was building to a crescendo, and the outbursts of *Hallelujah* and *Thank you Jesus* were already beginning to echo around the auditorium. I had sat down at the start of the final song, and was relieved that my dad hadn't instructed me to get to my feet. Selina was sitting next to me; I nudged her gently and pointed in the direction of my dad, who was walking towards the back of the church.

He hadn't turned back to face us or given any further instructions, but I had picked up on some clues: he had taken his coat, which meant he was going outside, but he had not taken his bible, and, most importantly, he hadn't mentioned Matthew, Joanna and my mum, which meant that he surely wasn't going home. I motioned to Selina, and we both stood up to walk towards the exit.

I could feel the inquiring gaze of my friends following my footsteps as I moved closer to the exit. They were hoping for a signal from me to indicate that they should now attempt something audacious to escape their parents and reach the freedom of the minor hall, where we could play football with a tennis ball until the end of the service. But I would not be offering a signal today.

Besides, our parents had become wise to our escape strategies - they no longer bought that we were all desperate to use the toilet at the same time. If we did manage to evade our parents, we also had the ushers to contend with. The ushers were members of the church congregation who would regularly volunteer to stand towards the back of the church hall, welcoming visitors, collecting the monetary offering and preventing sly children from leaving the room. They would firmly ask where we were going, and if the child being questioned gave an unconvincing answer or had developed a reputation for crying for the toilet, only never to return, you would quickly be returned to your parents. On this occasion, the usher on duty had seen my dad walk past a few moments earlier, so no explanation was necessary.

My dad was waiting in the foyer as I turned the corner with Selina. He seemed slightly annoyed that he had to pause his journey out of the building in order to wait for us.

"Where's your coat?" He snapped.

"Ermm… Oh! It's –" I had left my coat on my seat, and quickly turned to go back inside and retrieve it.

But my Dad stopped me with his hand: "Leave it. It's not raining." The three of us strode outside, and it felt wonderful to feel fresh air on my face again. Pentecostal church services are distinctive for two reasons: the particularly vibrant, energetic singing of their church choirs, and the notorious length of their services. Sunday morning services at Mount Zion lasted a minimum of two-and-a-half hours. I was delighted to walk out of the service early and onto the streets of Aston.

Selina and I turned the corner, following closely behind my dad. He suddenly came to a stop, seemingly deep in thought. We stood in silence, awaiting further instructions. The breeze pushed past my body and rustled the leaves in the tree above. I began to regret not having my coat with me.

"What do you see?" He said, finally.

I began to look around me, unsure as to what my dad was referring to. A bus drove by, leaving a swirl of dust behind it. Across the road, I could see an empty packet of ready-salted crisps. Next to it was a crumpled Twix packet, and some greasy paper that once contained a fish and chips. On the far side of the pavement was an abandoned shopping trolley filled with large black and blue plastic bags of unidentifiable contents. The bushes next to the trolley were unkempt, and craned over the pavement, partially blocking the path. My eyes scanned back to the side of the road that I was stood on.

I watched Selina, looking to see if she'd gotten any further than me. Her gaze was fixed further down the street, on the house of a Somali woman who was in the midst of a heated conversation with another person, whose head was poking outside of an upstairs window.

"I see anger," Selina murmured.

"Good," my dad replied. "Daniel?"

"Rubbish… There's a lot of rubbish and the area isn't being looked after."

My dad looked across the road and saw the abandoned trolley and litter. He nodded. "And what would Jesus say about this?"

I was surprised by the question. We were taught that Jesus had been on the earth over 2,000 years ago, and had spent his days teaching the multitudes, healing the sick and feeding the 5000. Would he really be concerned with such mundane issues like litter and neighbourhood disputes?

As I thought about the stories of Jesus that I had read in the bible, a passage in the book of Matthew came to mind:

> [31] *"When the Son of Man comes in his glory, and all the angels with him, he will sit on his glorious throne.* [32] *All the nations will be gathered before him, and he will separate the people one from another as a shepherd separates the sheep from the goats.* [33] *He will put the sheep on his right and the goats on his left.*
>
> [34] *"Then the King will say to those on his right, 'Come, you who are blessed by my Father; take your inheritance, the kingdom prepared for you since the creation of the world.* [35] *For I was hungry and you gave me something to eat, I was thirsty and you gave me something to drink, I was a stranger and you invited me in,* [36] *I needed clothes and you clothed me, I was sick and you looked after me, I was in prison and you came to visit me.'*
>
> [37] *"Then the righteous will answer him, 'Lord, when did we see you hungry and feed you, or thirsty and give you something to drink?* [38] *When did we see you as a stranger and invite you in, or needing clothes and clothe you?* [39] *When did we see you sick or in prison and go to visit you?'*
>
> [40] *"The King will reply, 'truly I tell you, whatever you did for one of the least of these brothers and sisters of mine, you did for me.'*

"I don't know what Jesus would say," I began, "but I think he would speak to that woman. And I think he would care enough to clear away the rubbish".

II

As the boys from classes 5C and 5S approached the pitch, Ms Chanda was waiting there with a sponge football. "Have you boys eaten your lunch?"

"Yes miss."

She smiled, and handed over the treasured ball.

Luke was standing sheepishly by the side-lines, not sure if he was still welcome to play after his less-than-assured debut the Wednesday before. I beckoned to him and told him my plan. Out of the first three chances I teed up for Luke that lunchtime, only one ended up threatening to trouble the person in goals. On the first occasion, I skipped past a defender and pulled the ball back to Luke, who had oceans of space around him (clearly none of the other defenders had taken seriously the idea that someone would consider passing him the ball). Despite our earlier conversation, this also seemed to take Luke by surprise and he failed to control the ball and it ran away from him.

The second time, Luke did shoot, but the goalkeeper easily kicked the ball away. The less said about the third attempt the better. But by now, Luke was getting used to the idea that chances would be presented to him, and so several minutes later, when the opposition keeper had saved a shot, Luke was on hand to kick the ball into the empty net. Luke ran straight to me and we jumped in delight. My other team mates who, by now, had recognised what I was trying to do, were also ecstatic and ran to Luke in celebration.

What struck me about this encounter was that scoring goals was something that I did so frequently - either during school, after school or on weekends - that it had lost most of its meaning, but to Luke it meant everything. And because it meant so much to Luke, it had meant so much more to my team, and to me.

III

My parents' requirements were based on the question; "Did you try your best?" If I replied affirmatively they were always content. But I demanded more of myself. I wanted my best effort to be rewarded with the best outcomes. And I could see no reason why this wasn't possible.

The report card I received at the end of my time in Class 5C proved that I was on track to achieve my goal. Every tick was confirmation that I was doing well. Really well.I didn't know where I was going with this need to achieve, but that didn't in any way diminish my ceaseless work ethic.

Saint James C. E. Primary School

Report for the School Year 1998 - 99

Year Five

Pupil *Daniel Stone*

Class *5c*

This report is a summary of your child's progress and achievements during this year. We will be pleased to discuss it with you at the Parents' Evening which will be held on Monday July 12th 1999. We welcome your views on your child's progress and on this report. A form is enclosed for your comments. Please return it to the class teacher before the Parents' Evening. Thank you

Key
A = Achieved   W = Working Towards

English *(includes Speaking/listening, Reading, Writing, spelling, Handwriting)*

	A	W
Can participate confidently in oral activities	✓	
Can read aloud expressively, fluently and with confidence.	✓	
Demonstrates a developing use of inference, deduction and previous reading experience.	✓	
Can use appropriate study skills to research information.	✓	
Can write independently in a well organised way for a variety of purposes using clear sentence structure and generally accurate punctuation.	✓	
Can discuss his/her writing and redraft as appropriate.	✓	
Can spell correctly in the course of writing, words that conform to regular patterns including more complicated words.	✓	
Can produce generally fluent joined up writing in independent work.	✓	

Mathematics

	A	W
Can select and use appropriate materials for solving mathematical problems.	✓	
Uses knowledge from different areas of mathematics during investigations and to solve problems.	✓	
Can use the four rules of number.	✓	
Can use co-ordinates.	✓	
Understands reflective symmetry.	✓	
Understands rotational symmetry.	✓	
Can talk about the properties of 2D and 3D shapes using mathematical vocabulary.	✓	
Can construct and interpret a range of statistical diagrams.	✓	

Knows the following multiplication tables:

2x	3x	4x	5x	6x	7x	8x	9x	10x	All Tables
A W	A W	A W	A W	A W	A W	A W	A W	A W	✓

Science   *Topics covered - The Body, Forces, Sound, Light, Electricity.*

	A	W
Can plan a scientific investigation which is logical and progressive.	✓	
Understands the principles of fair testing in investigations.	✓	
Knows that sounds are created when an object is vibrated and that sounds can travel through a variety of materials.	✓	
Knows about the main parts of the human body and their functions.	✓	
Understands the need for a healthy diet.	✓	
Knows the force of friction causes an object to slow down.	✓	
Knows that forces act in a particular direction.	✓	
Understands the main principles of light including that it travels from a source and can be reflected.	✓	

Technology *(includes Information Technology and Design Technology)*

	A	W
Can investigate and evaluate products.	✓	
Can make a design based on knowledge of skills and materials, reviewing and amending designs to overcome problems.	✓	
Can choose and use materials appropriate to the task.	✓	
Can review the final product and the development of the design.	✓	
Has begun to use information technology independently to retrieve, develop, organise, save and present work.	✓	

Geography *Topics covered - Weather Patterns, Maps, Communication.*

	A	W
Can make a range of maps using symbols and keys.	✓	
Understands map scales.	✓	
Can use map co-ordinates.	✓	
Uses appropriate geographical vocabulary when talking about maps & the weather	✓	
Can describe weather patterns around the world.	✓	

History *Topics covered - Tudors, Victorians*

	A	W
Makes deductions by putting together information drawn from primary and secondary historical sources.	✓	
Recognises that over a period of time some things have changed and others have stayed the same.	✓	
Understands the characteristics of life in Tudor times.	✓	
Understands the characteristics of life in Victorian times.	✓	

Art

	A	W
Uses ideas, feelings and imagination within their art work.	✓	
Identifies different kinds of art from different periods, cultures and traditions, in particular the Pre-Raphaelites.	✓	

Has worked well in the following areas:

Painting		Drawing		Printing		Clay		2D/3D		Textiles	
A	W	A	W	A	W	A	W	A	W	A	W
✓		✓		✓		✓		✓		✓	

Music

	A	W
Can perform in a group, maintaining a part independently from another.	✓	
Can devise and develop musical ideas within simple structures.	✓	
Can listen attentively to music of various kinds recognising the main musical elements.	✓	

Physical Education

	A	W
Can practise and improve more complex sequences of movement.	✓	
Can respond safely to given tasks.	✓	
Works cooperatively as a team member during games	✓	
Can evaluate their own and their peer's performance.	✓	

Religious Education

	A	W
Has studied aspects of Judaism, Sikhism and Christianity.	✓	
Has begun to question their faith experiences and how they respond.	✓	
Has shown a growing respect for the faiths and beliefs of others.	✓	

AFTER OXFORD

Personal Development	A	W
Is a confident, mature and sensible class member.	✓	
Shows a mature attitude to work.	✓	
Works co-operatively within any group.	✓	
Has developed greater self discipline when working independently.	✓	
Can concentrate on a given task for over an hour.	✓	
Is prepared to listen to and act on constructive criticism from others.	✓	

General Comments

Daniel is a polite, well behaved and hard working boy who can be depended upon to do his best at all times. He has a vigilant and enquiring approach to learning and will very often take the trouble to work things out for himself. This has made him very self-reliant, confident and self-sufficient. Daniel is very quick to grasp new ideas in all subject areas and explores new concepts tirelessly to fulfil his craving for knowledge. Daniel's work is always impeccable as he has set very high standards for himself. I am very pleased with Daniel's achievements and his eagerness to learn. I wish him every success in his final year next year. Well done Daniel!
Miss Chanda.

Attendance

Headteacher's Comments

Daniel, an outstanding report! Your excellent attitude to work and learning should lead to great success.

Pupil's Comments I am very pleased with my results and I can't wait until I'm in Year 6, I hope that I can carry on my work and my aim is to get into grammar school.

I like school because of the challenges I face.

31

The sentence that stands out to me was the comment that I wrote at the bottom of the final page: *I like school because of the challenges I face.*

Who writes that as a ten year-old? To *like* something because it challenges you and pushes you out of your comfort zone and forces you to learn and improve? Most children and many adults don't have the foresight to recognise that challenges experienced in the short term can often hold the key to future success. But here I was, in Year 5, having internalised this process; and I *liked* it. This mind-set perhaps helped to relieve the pressure that can sometimes haunt high achievers. When I attained a goal, it was empowering and would propel me towards further success. If I fell short, it was a challenge that I needed to work to overcome.

Coming towards the end of Year 5, the challenge that began to occupy my mind almost entirely was that of gaining a place in grammar school. The national debate on grammar schools has raged for decades. Those in favour tend to point to the benign effects that grammar schools may have on the most able children from less affluent backgrounds, whose abilities may not be 'fully developed' in a comprehensive system. The counterargument is that these students perform equally as well in the comprehensive system and also have a positive influence on their 'less academically-able' peers.

While national discussions persist, Birmingham has had a long history of selective grammar schools that have educated students for well over a century. The most famous brand of Birmingham-based grammar schools, King Edwards, has schools across inner city Birmingham as well as in the more affluent areas of Camp Hill and Sutton Coldfield. The boys' school in Aston and the girls' school in Handsworth were established in the Victorian era before decades of immigration transformed these once exclusively Caucasian and middle-class areas into districts almost exclusively belonging to working class families from the Commonwealth. The grammar schools in Handsworth did at times try to provide opportunities for students in the local area - although their generosity may have had commercial as well as philanthropic motives.

This explained why, on a number of Saturday mornings at the beginning of Year 6, I found myself taking a ten minute bus ride to King Edwards VI Handsworth School for Girls. I had enrolled into the Children's University, a programme designed to expose young people from local schools to experiences and ways of thinking that they wouldn't encounter in their everyday lives. It sounded challenging and so I signed up without hesitation.

The school was magnificent. From the outside it consisted of an impressively large stone building surrounded by several football pitches covered in grass, complete with painted markings and nets - actual nets! The interior had long corridors, imposing halls and science labs full of equipment. Classrooms were not the colourful domain of young children but seemed to emphasise purposeful cogitation over aimless fun. Teachers at the Children's University expected more of pupils; to think deeply, study faithfully and respond creatively. I could feel myself learning, expanding and improving with each lesson.

My time as a student in the Children's University had convinced me that I wanted a place at grammar school, but to get into grammar school I would have to perform well in an entrance exam, the 11+. My parents were supportive of my wish to go, and bought me some revision guides to help me prepare.

I was unfamiliar with the comprehension questions for the verbal ability test, and some of the mathematics for the numerical ability test, but I was certain that I could make up for any gaps in my knowledge with hard work. However, I was concerned by the non-verbal or logical reasoning test, which on the face of it seemed to be anything but logical. The shapes, colours and configurations were unlike anything I'd seen in school. At times it would feel like I understood the general feel and rhythm of the questions, but then I would be subsumed by confusion again. I urgently set about the task of preparing for the exam; working through the numerical and verbal guide twice, and the non-verbal guide three times.

The day of the 11+ exam came and my dad dropped me off in the car park of King Edward's in Aston. Earlier in the morning we had said a prayer together as a family, and now he wished me a final good luck as I pushed open the car door: "Just do your best Daniel, that's all you can do."

I took my seat in the exam hall, taking my neatly sharpened pencils out of the clear pencil case and laying them on the desk. When the exam started, it proceeded in a similar vein to my practice sessions. The verbal and numerical reasoning tests were difficult, but I felt that I was engaging positively with the questions in front of me. However, the non-verbal reasoning test was monstrous. I remember sinking into a black and white spiral of unfamiliar shapes, guessed answers and seemingly illogical sequences. I came out of the exam devastated. I felt sure I couldn't have passed.

But as time went on some confidence returned, I had never failed before, and the notion felt so alien that I was sure it couldn't happen to me now.

Several months later and the envelope enclosing my fate finally arrived. My parents called me into the front room of the house and closed the door. I saw the unopened letter in their hands. "Here you go Dan," my mum said warily. I peeled back the fold of the envelope and took out the single sheet of paper. As I grew older, I would learn that single sheets only ever possessed enough space for disappointment.

The letter said that I had performed well in certain aspects of the assessment, but had received a poor score in the non-verbal element. My score was enough to give me a decent position on the waiting list, but I would not be given a place by any of my chosen grammar schools. I couldn't contain my dismay any longer and burst into tears. My parents had undoubtedly seen the dejection etched onto my face as I read the letter. "Never mind" said my Dad, going down onto his knees to enclose me in his arms. "It's their loss," Mum whispered.

For a number of days I was inconsolable. As someone who had placed enormous value on objective measures and the need to succeed, my biggest test to date had been a failure. On Monday morning, I returned to school to find that several of my friends and classmates had passed and would be going to grammar school. This felt like a second loss: I would be separated from some of my best friends and would have to face secondary school without them.

My teachers told my parents that they were surprised to learn of some pupils, who they considered less-academically able, gaining a place, while I had not. My mum spoke to some of the parents of successful children, to offer her congratulations and to find out how they did so well. Parents who a few months ago had been tight-lipped about their child's preparations for the 11+ were now overflowing with information about tutors and revision tools. I know that my mum left some of those conversations feeling betrayed. People who she considered to be friends had chosen to hold back information that could have benefitted her son.

This was the first time I recall feeling disadvantaged. As children, we didn't grow up with plenty (by UK standards). My dad's annual income was stretched to breaking point to cover a mortgage and four children. My mum supplemented this income by taking whatever part-time roles she could find to fit around the needs of her children.

She worked a number of years for the Avon home-to-home beauty company; on evenings and weekends we would assist with the task of splitting the large deliveries of creams, lipsticks and other beauty products, and would then help to hand-deliver orders to customers in the local area. My parents managed a strict budget, and from time to time we would have family meetings to discuss cost-cutting measures and pocket money (which did not rise with inflation, or anything else for that matter). When other kids did well in school, their parents bought them gifts or gave them money. My trophies were never monetary.

Nevertheless, I felt loved and supported, and I had never felt poor. But in this moment, I felt impoverished. There was information at my fingertips that could have helped me to perform better in the 11+. I was unable to grasp it because my parents and I did not possess the knowledge, resources or social capital. With more knowledge of the 11+ admissions test, we may have invested in a tutor. With more resources, I may have attended a primary school in a more affluent part of the city where entry exams were discussed freely with parents. And with better social capital or community support, parents may have chosen to help their neighbour and friend rather than being caught up in a competitive, illogical and, for me, destructive mind-set.

I entered the final few months of primary school knowing that what lay ahead was not King Edward's or Handsworth Grammar, but Hamstead Hall School. My best friends had either successfully applied to grammar school or lived outside of the likely catchment area for Hamstead Hall, meaning that we would be scattered across a number of schools in and around Handsworth.

When our allocated schools had been announced, we made a pact to continue to see each other on evenings and weekends. Reducing the amount I would see my friends seemed unimaginable given that we spent most of our waking hours together. We were either together in the classroom or playing together outside: kicking a football across the street while keeping an eye out for advancing cars or racing Wickes' trolleys down the steep hill in Sandwell Park. At weekends and during school holidays, where time was at less of a premium, my friends would spend hours on end playing football at Oakland's Community Centre. To arrive at Oakland's, we could either walk fifteen minutes or so to the main entrance or take a perilous shortcut over a wall, through an alleyway and between a jagged partition in the fence.

We always chose the shortcut. And we always made sure that everyone made it across unharmed.

One of the last times my group of primary school friends shared together was my 11th birthday, which was on the 3rd of June. It always seemed to rain on my birthday and, like clockwork, when the third of June came around again in the summer of 2000, so did the rain.

This didn't stop my closest friends Deepak; Vy-liam; Subhag; Richard, and his twin brother Vincent; Luke; Samuel and several others; making their way to my house to play pass-the-parcel, and a number of indoor games that my mum had planned in anticipation of the rain. And of course, we had food. Lots and lots of food. Chocolate fingers, party rings, chicken, burgers, and cherries impaled onto cocktail sticks with small cubes of pineapple and cheese.

As I blew out the candles on my birthday cake, I wished that the rain would stop, that one of my presents would be a Game Boy, and that the people standing around me would stay my friends forever.

THE STAIRS

"I had gone from being ignorant of being ignorant to being aware of being aware" - Maya Angelou, I Know Why the Caged Bird Sings[2]

Selina had started at Hamstead Hall School the year before. I remember being in awe of how smart she looked on her first day of school. The Hamstead Hall jumper was navy blue with a gold H.H.S. logo on the left breast and an impeccable navy-blue and gold tie. Gone was the book bag, and in its place was a Reebok satchel that hung smartly off her shoulder. Instead of joining us in our short walk up Westbourne Road to St James', Selina headed off alone to catch the school bus at the bottom of the road. Everything about secondary school seemed to be better and more grown up.

Then during the first fortnight of Selina's time in secondary school I began to notice a pattern. While Matthew, Joanna and I were lounging around in the front room, watching cartoons, Selina would walk in. Without acknowledging us, she'd walk straight through the room and into the kitchen or upstairs. Over the noise of the TV, we'd hear Selina crying and my mum offering words of support.

---

[2] Angelou, M. (1979). *I Know Why the Caged Bird Sings*, New York: Random House.

From what I heard of the conversations, her distress centred on name-calling, difficulty fitting in and the notorious high school mean girls. But a year had passed since those first traumatic weeks of school, the tears had dried and her muffled complaints had been replaced by cheery tales of school trips, close friends and academic success.

Selina's present optimistic state meant that I was looking forward to my first day with confidence. As I looked in the mirror, I couldn't believe how much I'd matured in the space of a few months. "Daniel, say cheese!" I turned to stand in front of the fireplace and smiled proudly.

"Have you got your change?" Selina asked as we began the walk towards the bus stop.

"Yes". I murmured. "What time does the bus come?"

"10 past 8. It's the same time every day. If you miss Pete's Travel another bus comes five minutes afterwards."

"What's your first lesson?"

"I don't know," Selina answered. "It's a new year so we'll have a new timetable."

Selina was a valuable source of information. She explained that only Year 7s and Year 8s would be in school today to give the new students time to settle in. Registration would take place at the beginning of the day, and after lunchtime in form groups. Selina was in Stour. She listed the other five form groups, which were apparently all named after rivers in the UK. I only retained the name Avon because it shared it's moniker with the company that dropped beauty products at our home on a weekly basis.

There were four other children waiting at the bus stop at the bottom of the road when we arrived, along with an elderly Indian man and two middle-aged black women. After waiting a few minutes, a yellow bus became visible on the far end of Rookery Road and the adults shuffled backwards to allow us to pass. "That's Pete's Travel," Selina confirmed. A yellow bus was a rare sight in Birmingham – usually buses were blue and white - and I was fascinated to see how different it might look inside. I had already taken my bus fare out of my wallet in preparation, and after mounting the two steep steps onto the bus I handed it to the driver. The interior was disappointingly similar to all the other buses I'd been on, and probably could have done with a lick of paint.

I reached the stairs and turned to Selina. Without speaking, she knew that I was enquiring as to whether we should sit upstairs or downstairs. The top floor of a double decker bus was a status symbol in regular public transportation. While the lower deck was largely occupied by the elderly or parents with young children, the upper level was filled with teenagers and young adults. Whenever my mum had taken us on a bus, she confined my siblings and I safely to the lower deck. We would hear music blaring loudly from upstairs, often featuring the expletive lyrics of the latest hip-hop artist or vibrant dancehall rhythms.

As we grew older, my mum gave into our harassment and would allow us to venture temporarily from her sight to sit at the very front of the top deck. From here we could look out across the street below and experience every swerve and acceleration of the bus. We also had the prime people-watching position, and could witness everyone queuing to get onto the bus with shopping bags and pushchairs or hurriedly trying to take the last few puffs on their cigarettes.

While sitting on the top deck, I became accustomed to its unwritten subculture. It seemed that those children who had strayed above the lower level were allowed upstairs, but only in front of the point where the barrier protecting the staircase was. After this point, the bus was the possession of the true upper-deck dwellers, who sported varying degrees of unfriendliness. The most unsavoury looking characters tended to congregate towards the back, and they were the ones playing the deafeningly loud music; laughing boisterously at their own conversations and smoking cannabis.

It was this knowledge of bus hierarchies that made me certain that the cool older kids in Hamstead Hall would sit upstairs, in all likelihood at the very back.

Selina shook her head, and we took a seat on the ground floor.

I

I had been allocated to class 7 Rea. Our form tutor, Mrs Richardson led us through a series of induction activities which included being handed a class timetable and a planner for homework. Mrs Richardson reassured us that for the first few days, someone would help to guide us around the school from one lesson to the next. A guide was essential because Hamstead Hall was a large school, and it took me months to become fully acquainted with the place in its entirety. Our form class was in Craythorne Block, which housed the mathematics, science and IT classrooms, as well as the administrative offices, the main school hall and the head teacher's office. 'Woodend Block' was towards the furthest end of the school and was a rectangular two-story building for art, music and design and technology. In-between was another large block of classrooms called Parkside, where the humanities subjects were taught and the canteen and food hall were housed. Hamstead Hall was one of a select group of government-sponsored Sports Colleges, and boasted a proud array of sporting facilities, including indoor gymnasiums, an impressive grass-covered sports field and a multi-million pound sports hall (although that wasn't completed until midway through my time as a student).

As a result of its spaciousness, Hamstead Hall also had an abundance of areas to explore during breaks in teaching. The sports field was big enough to fit two full-sized football pitches and a running track on it. Behind the sports field was a wooded area that was officially out of bounds, but which would provide adequate cover for students seeking to engage in activities they'd rather the teachers didn't see. As well as the grass pitches, there were several tarmacked areas for playing football, including a caged area close to Woodend Block and another marked football area known as 'Top Playground'.

A message was sent around that we would be playing football on Top Playground at lunchtime. I made the walk from the lunch hall with two boys in my form class, Paul Spence and Richard Singh. Paul had a number of unusual features: a ginger and grey tuft of hair sat just above his forehead on an otherwise black head of hair. He also had darker brown freckles scattered unevenly across his light brown face. Paul was a similar height to me but was slightly bulkier. Richard was stockier still and was significantly shorter. Richard was Sikh and wore a top knot to keep his hair - uncut due to religious beliefs

- bundled neatly at the crown of his head. Seating in our form class had been organised alphabetically according to surname, placing Paul, Richard and I in close proximity. It turned out that we had a lot in common; including our interest in football.

The warm autumn sunshine shimmered on the path underfoot as we trekked nervously on the unfamiliar route towards Top Playground. Out of the three of us, I was by far the most cautious. Paul and Richard knew that several of their friends from primary school would be there. Paul also knew the names of the best football players, including someone called Tobias who, rumour had it, was being scouted by Birmingham City FC.

"Yeah, I played with him in Little League. He was better than a lot of the older boys. I think he finished top scorer last season." Paul reported. He explained that a lot of boys in the local area played football on Saturdays for local little league teams. These matches were often scouted by the main local professional football clubs, such as Aston Villa, Birmingham City and West Bromwich Albion.

My parents had never considered professional football to be a viable option for me. It wasn't that they disapproved, they were just external to the networks of parents who knew about these opportunities for their children to participate in sports.

My nerves multiplied. I knew how important it was to make a good first impression. But what if everyone was so much better than me? And if our ability levels were similar, surely the fact that they had played together before would give them a significant advantage?

I knew that if I was unable to play well during this first lunchtime, I was likely to be excluded; forbidden to speak to certain people in my year group or to access certain areas of the school grounds. Being deemed 'good enough' to play football on Top Playground would give me the keys to the city. It was my latest challenge; succeed, and I would be validated, accepted and free.

"What position do you play?" I asked Paul.

"Whichever I wanna." Paul replied, laughing. We turned the corner and saw Top Playground around 10 metres or so in front of us. "How about you?"

"I prefer playing on the wing or as a striker." Both roles were attacking positions on the football field and carried the expectation of creating chances and scoring goals.

We approached the gate to the playground. On the far end was a high iron fence with thick blades that separated the playground from the car park behind. To the right was a mesh fence around waist high that shielded a disorderly area of trees, bushes and weeds that ran down a steep slope. On the opposite side was a small grassy area with a gentle incline that lay outside of the four corners of the playing area. Closest to the gate were two basketball hoops.

It was here that I sat down to replace my school shoes with the Nike R9 astro turf trainers that I had persuaded my parents to buy for me over the summer. I rustled through my rucksack, pushing aside my school planner and Lynx canister to pull out the trainers.

Paul was already wearing black trainers that had passed under the radar of our form tutor, who must have assumed that they were shoes. He walked over to the thirty or so boys who had gathered at the far end of the car park and was already busily chatting away to two people. Richard finished putting on his trainers before me and headed over to someone he knew. I stood up, lifted my jumper over my head, unloosened my tie, and pondered my next move.

I decided to hang back. Paul and Richard were deep in conversation and I didn't want to disturb them. There were a number of other boys who also appeared to be on their own, including one person I recognised from the bus stop in the morning.

I observed that we had a football and more than adequate numbers to start a match, so why weren't we organising ourselves into teams and starting the game? The desire to ask this question burned in my chest. I knew it was the sensible thing to suggest but what if I was ignored or ridiculed? What if my voice didn't carry when I opened my mouth to speak? And what if I began to stutter? As I thought all of these things, my heart filled with doubt and the desire to speak was quelled.

After a few moments, a boy called Ashley called us to order: "You lot go off and pick numbers. Me and Sanjay are captains." The majority of the group trudged obediently over towards the basketball hoops, leaving Ashley and

Sanjay leisurely kicking the ball to each other until we announced that we were ready.

I was happy about this decision to pick teams by numbers. For people like me, who didn't know many of the other boys, it was by far the most egalitarian way of assigning players to teams. Everyone was guaranteed to be chosen and there was no shame in being picked last, as this would be the result of fate rather than perceptions of your ability.

"Are you lot done yet?!" Ashley shouted from the far side of the playground.

We had organised ourselves into a closed circle and a boy called Riyomi had assigned everyone a number, counting up from one in a clockwise direction.

"Yeah - You're choosing between 1 and 28," Riyomi replied.

"One." Ashley fired back. Riyomi left our ranks and stood behind Ashley. Sanjay responded with "12." They went to and fro three times before it dawned on me. All the boys who had been chosen had known each other prior to Hamstead Hall. I eyed my peers more closely and recognised the subtle movement of fingers resting closely next to the owners' thighs and forming unmistakably into fives, fours and threes to signal their number to the beady-eyed captains. So much for egalitarianism!

For what it was worth, I was number 22. Both teams began to assemble themselves into an impression of a team formation, with defenders, midfielders, attackers and a goalkeeper.

The more confident boys immediately moved towards the attacking positions and waited for the rest of us to fall in. I hung back in defence. As the game began, I was astonished by the chasm between the football I had known at St James and that which was unfolding before my eyes. Players stood in space, passed the ball accurately over great distances and there were a handful of players with incredible skill.

When the game started all eyes were on Tobias and he didn't disappoint. The subtle touches. The control. Stopping. Starting. Twisting. Turning. Shooting. Scoring! He was the best footballer I'd seen, and was thankfully on my team.

My debut was less spectacular, but I did make a number of good tackles and driving runs: setting up two goals for my teammates. Towards the end of the lunch hour, Ashley and the other self-proclaimed Football Lords of Top Playground decided that the area could no longer accommodate a match of 15-a-side, and several boys were told to leave. Paul and I had done enough during those initial exchanges to make the cut. But Richard had not. He trudged off top playground with his head hung low. I took a step towards him, then paused.

I had sought out the culture of the back of the upper bus deck. Now that I had found it, I would have to learn how to live within it.

II

My dad passed on the majority of perceptions that I held about masculinity. He was the main breadwinner in our household. Although our mum would sometimes (for good reason) have to be firm, my dad always seemed sterner and more aggressive with his words. As boys we were encouraged to show physical and emotional strength. Not to cry without good reason, and not to turn down the opportunity to participate in 'men's work': stacking chairs, mixing cement, or assisting with the church moving team.

My church had a monthly rota for teams of 5-8 men who would help to transport sound equipment from our permanent but small building in Aston, Birmingham, to the Great Hall in Aston University each Sunday. When my dad's name was on the rota, Matthew and I were also enlisted by default. Every four weeks, we would be woken from our sleep at around 7 in the morning and would begin the process of ensuring that the church was set up for testing at 9. We didn't complain about the task because our father's conception of men did not allow for it.

Men turned up and fulfilled their duties. The other enlisted men would congratulate my dad on the effort and dedication shown by his two sons: "Your boys are hard workers," they would say, chuckling. On overhearing these comments, I would smile at Matthew, and our backs would straighten as we wheeled out the sound equipment from the elevator into the auditorium.

The ideal masculinity I had been taught was primarily based on sacrifice. Mount Zion wasn't divided along gendered lines as was common in a number of more traditional churches. We had female church leaders and women carried out most of the same functions as men, usually in greater numbers. But there was an acceptance that men had to step up in situations where others couldn't (at least not with greater difficulty). As boys, we were being prepared for the roles that we would assume more fully as men. A process that was to do with the development of our attitude as much as it was of physical strength.

Central to this development was the role of the Youth department at Mount Zion, led by Pastor Errol Lawson. Errol was over six feet tall with broad shoulders and an even broader smile. His autobiography *From the Postcode to the Globe* had told the story of his troubled youth and the role that faith played in helping him to turn his life around. Errol was visiting schools around the world as a motivational speaker while setting up mentoring and youth leadership programmes. He channelled this passion into his role at Mount Zion; telling us all as young people that we were leaders.

The Daniel in the context of Mount Zion was different to the Daniel in Hamstead Hall - and I was conscious of it. At Mount Zion, I would readily put myself forward to take on additional responsibilities such as managing the tuck shop during live music events, volunteering as part of the security team and leading small groups of my peers in times of prayer or reading through the bible. Like all young people, I had a mentor, Aaron Thomas. But I had also been trusted to have two mentees; boys who were younger than me and who it was felt could learn from my example. However, in school I was still nervous and unsure about myself. I was uncomfortable operating within a version of masculinity that was hell-bent on asserting its dominance; and where a poorly-judged comment or misplaced glance could turn into a testosterone-fuelled battle to prove one's strength.

Aaron's advice was that I should pray for these boys: "You don't know what their home lives are like," Aaron would explain. "You have an opportunity to be a positive influence."

I initially dismissed this advice as wishful thinking - I reasoned that certain people would always act this way regardless of their background. But I pondered Aaron's words on the journey home and the following morning I began to pray for them. As children, our parents had encouraged us to develop a 'personal relationship' with God, which involved spending time daily in prayer and reading the bible, usually first thing in the morning. My prayers focused on the events and people I was likely to encounter in the day; writing any recurrent themes onto a list to ensure that I didn't forget them.

To this list I added the names of my friends and of the boys on Top Playground. Most days I would read the list verbatim until I had reached the bottom of the page. But on other days, I would have specific requests: "Dear God, thank you for Ashley. I thank you for all that you have blessed him with and that he is a leader. I pray that you would fill his heart with compassion and that he would be a good example to all those who look up to him. In Jesus' name, Amen."

In the jungle of the playground, the older boys were determined to cement their place at the top of the food chain. The football cage adjacent to Woodend Block had 8-foot-high metal gridded walls with a single point of entry. We would often play football against year 10 and 11 boys in this cage, mindful that, at a moment's notice, the following chain of events could be triggered.

First, someone would lock the cage door. Second, a signal would be passed between the older boys who would try to catch any younger ones who hadn't noticed the first event. Third, there would be a mad rush to climb over the fence to safety, while those who had been too slow to react and were trapped in the cage would be punched repeatedly, until the assailants grew bored. Eventually muscles regained feeling and bruises healed. No-one I knew was ever seriously hurt, but the playground fostered an environment that kept us rooted firmly to the base of Maslow's hierarchy of needs. The playground was about survival.

Despite the very real threat of physical and emotional harm, there was something seductive about this culture. The older boys seemed fearless and respected. I saw this confidence bristling in boys like Ashley and Riyomi, and it was infectious. But I also knew clearly the difference between right and wrong. And so I stood on the stairs of the bus; trying not to be associated with the bottom deck, but unable to participate in the culture of the top.

AFTER OXFORD

III

By Year 9, I had learned how to survive as a quieter creature in this unstable environment. My footballing ability meant that I was known by the popular boys in my year group and could venture fearlessly onto Top Playground without fear of reprisals. But I wasn't a prisoner to the hierarchies of popularity that tried to divide the playground. I was happy to speak to anyone in my year group, whether they were sporty, academic, popular, or none of these.

Richard and Paul were among my closest friends; we spent hours laughing together at the start and middle of every school day. I would be left breathless by Paul's impersonations of our P.E. teacher, Mr Clarke; sticking out his right hand, palm facing upwards, mimicking the way that Mr Clarke would shake hands with students who performed particularly well.

I was also good friends with Chris Howe, who I recognised during that first lunchtime on Top Playground. Chris lived on the road parallel to mine and like me, he was a quieter character. Our friendship began at the bus stop; the sight of the yellow vehicle pulling around the corner would bring our conversation to a hold. When the school bus stopped running - due to persistent vandalism by students - Chris and I walked to and from school together. The journey would last for about 45 minutes and we did that walk twice a day; Monday to Friday; for around five years. On our trips to school we would discuss the previous evening's football match, wrestling and general school gossip. It always seemed to go by quickly.

Another friendship group I belonged to was made up of those pupils who had been given labels such as *bright* and *gifted and talented*. I would often ponder what this meant for the students who were not part of this exclusive group. Were they *dull* and *talentless?*

Hamstead Hall was a multi-cultural multi-ethnic school. Students from British Black Caribbean and British Indian backgrounds were in the majority but there were a significant number of White British and other ethnic groups. It was noticeable that out of the dozen or so gifted and talented pupils identified in my year group; around a quarter were Indian girls like Jade and Nisha; a similar number were black girls like Natasha and Aleisha; Sunil,

47

Pardeep and Sundip were of Indian heritage; Sean and Holly were white; and Aaron was of mixed white and Asian heritage. The black boys in my year were nowhere in sight.

But I couldn't argue that this categorisation wasn't reflective of what was happening in the classroom.

The major academic subjects were organised according to academic ability. I was a permanent fixture in the top sets of all subjects along with the others in the gifted and talented cohort. Around us, a carousel of our peers would drop in and out of the top set, depending on the subject matter. I tended to sit next to one of the boys from Top Playground: Tobias in English, Riyomi in Maths and Chris in History.

Classes tended to follow a similar pattern. After hearing the school bell, I would trudge off to my next lesson, usually accompanied by someone who I knew was walking in the same direction. Arriving at the classroom, the door would be open and the noise of students busily unpacking their rucksacks or talking loudly about the day's activities would fill the corridor. If the class was after lunchtime, the unmistakable whiff of Lynx Africa would greet every new arrival into the room; the slightly spicy aroma lingering until the end of the school day.

My Maths teacher, Mr Mortimer, would always put an activity on the board; a brain teaser or a countdown conundrum. While other students leisurely removed their pencil cases from their bags and continued their conversations, I would take my seat and begin working on the problem. If I reached the solution before Mr Mortimer had returned from his break time duties, I would put down my pen and see if I could follow the train of whatever conversation had been going on around me. Then we would hear the door slam.

"Good afternoon class. There's a question on the board - if you've not got to the number 731, you shouldn't be talking."

Teachers like Mr Mortimer commanded immediate respect. Conversations would draw to a close and any students who were still upstanding would take their seats. At this point, while Mr Mortimer took off his coat and confirmed that his notes had remained in order, I would hear hushed conversations taking place all around me. Sometimes they were about sports or about video games or about a rumoured fight that was going to take place at the end of the school day.

After a few moments, Mr Mortimer would draw the attention of the classroom: "So, who has the answer?"

In the early years of my time at Hamstead Hall, my hand would shoot straight up, but over time, I had become more hesitant. But maybe not for the reason you might assume. Yes, I was aware of not seeming overly keen in front of my peers, but within the context of the top set, the plaudits of getting a tough question correct far outweighed any drawbacks associated with seeming to be *too* intelligent.

Instead my hesitancy came from the skills of observation that I learned as a boy - walking around Aston and helping Luke to score a goal. My experiences had taught me that in any given lesson, a moment would come where I was able to offer a unique contribution or a correct answer to a difficult question. This moment was usually preceded by a few seconds of silence while the teacher searched desperately on the faces of their pupils for even the faintest glint of understanding. There would be an instant look of relief when I raised my hand. So, I kept my hand down to give others a chance to answer; to score a goal and to feel the elation of the teacher's affirmation.

Pardeep raised his hand:

"25 multiplied by 9 is 225;
8 minus 5 is 3;
225 multiplied by 3 is 675;
8 multiplied by 7 is 56;
675 plus 56 is 731."

I looked at the 731 underlined on my paper, content that I had also found a solution. I glanced to my right to see that Riyomi's page was blank. I found this attitude to be common among my peers. Many of the black boys in particular had a work ethic that ranged from doing nothing to doing the bare minimum. I thought that perhaps the demotivating effects of being in a lower set or the fact that they had been unable to understand the question had accounted for this behaviour. But neither of these points were true for students in the top set who had both the affirmation and the ability.

I never asked my peers publically why they failed to apply themselves fully in lessons - that was likely to end with me in a headlock. Occasionally, and usually following parent's evening, my friends would seek out my advice on how best to get ahead in the classroom. The amount of time that they followed my instructions would vary from a week to three days to a single lesson, before they inevitably slipped back into their old habits. I would sigh ruefully before turning back to my exercise book to find a solution to the conundrum.

IV

I was 13 or 14 when I was stopped and searched for the first time.

I was with Chris. We turned the corner onto Craythorne Avenue to begin the walk towards Hamstead Hall. As I looked ahead, I saw the backs of two fluorescent vests emblazoned with the words 'West Midlands Police'. A number of students had already passed them, but I could sense that we were occupying the gaze of one of the officers. As I approached the policeman, he stretched out his arm.

"We've had a number of burglaries in the area," he started, "and you fit the description of the perpetrators. Would you mind if we searched your bag and person?"

Chris and I nodded our heads and stood in stunned silence. We had nothing to hide. But it was demeaning to have to stand by and watch a complete stranger rifling through my possessions. I watched as the officer aggressively moved my trainers to one side, lifting the pencil case to see if it carried an unnatural weight. The other officer barely looked at us. Other pupils were walking by, glancing sympathetically at Chris and me.

After a few moments, the search was over: "Thank you. You can go on your way." I snatched my bag out of his hand and continued on my way to school.

In conversation with Chris and in the days following, I would replay the incident over in my head repeatedly, questioning the logic of this whole approach. How many burglaries were really committed by school children on their way to school? What were they really hoping to find in my bag that would link me to a potential crime? And why, of at least a dozen children who passed by within the space of a few minutes, were Chris and I the only ones who were stopped?

Sadly, this was a common occurrence for the black boys in my school. So common in fact, that some boys had started to collect the pink slips you were given after each stop. There was a rumour that you would get some form of prize for collecting 20. Several of my peers surpassed this mark but I never did find out if the rumours were true.

I told my dad about the incident when I got home: "How can his foolishness still be going on in this day and age?" He exclaimed; his eyes enraged behind his thick rimmed glasses. "I'm sorry you had to go through this Daniel." His expression remained steely as I looked up to him.

My dad told me about the stories that he'd heard about as a boy of police beating up black people for minor infringements: "Daniel, if you see a policeman, always cross over to the other side of the road," he had ordered. "A lot of racists join the police as an excuse to beat up black people. You can't trust them. When they look at you, they see the enemy."

I enjoyed the conversations that I had with my dad about race and culture. They usually followed a TV programme we were watching as a family, such as *Roots* or a book that my dad had seen me reading. The books on our shelves at home were mostly my dad's books and featured historical figures like Jack Johnson, Malcolm X and Nelson Mandela. I enjoyed learning about the different contexts in which black people throughout history had fought for justice, equality and visibility. I was inspired by their courage and motivated to avoid their flaws.

I particularly enjoyed some of the deeper musings of authors like W.E.B. Dubois, who described the natural tension that he says must exist within black people who are forced to inhabit two conflicting identities: one based on the way that they see themselves, and the second based on other people's perception of them. My experience of Britain, almost a century after *The Souls of Black Folk*, was that my Jamaican-ness and Britishness were relatively comfortable bedfellows. I didn't see a contradiction in cheering for the Jamaican relay team, while supporting England in the football World Cup; or

51

listening to Bob Marley in the kitchen, while singing worship songs written by white composers in a black majority church.

I think this was because, in many ways, the tenets upon which contemporary Jamaican and British societies functioned were the same. This could partly be explained as a symptom of colonialism, which had cemented in the Jamaican psyche the principle that Britain was the social, economic and moral pinnacle. Not only did Jamaicans believe that the streets of Britain were paved with gold, many also thought that British culture was superior, godlier and more 'civilised'. In practice, this meant that British morals and principles were at the centre of many Jamaican households. The two foremost ideologies were to act according to a Christian morality (or at least keep up the appearance of doing so) and the belief that society was fair: if you worked hard and honestly, you would do well.

However, it soon became apparent that these opportunities would be accompanied by a caveat: Jamaicans were black. And because they were black in a country where the majority of institutional leaders and structures had been built and maintained by people who were white, they would have to endure racism and the humiliation of being pigeonholed into jobs deemed to be 'good enough' for black people.

"That's really good Daniel. But you know you're going to have to work twice as hard."

This was my dad's response when I told him about some of the early aspirations I had to apply for university. He hadn't said it to dissuade me from applying but, on the contrary, to encourage me to work harder to achieve my goals.

As a teenager, I began to grapple with these ideas myself. I could not ignore the struggles that previous generations had faced; my parents were intelligent, hard-working people but were in jobs that were a source of frustration rather than fulfilment.

My dad would come home from work just before 6pm on most evenings. If I was watching TV, I knew that the sound of the key turning in the lock, was a signal for me to change the channel to BBC One in advance of the start of the six o'clock news, and to put the kettle on for his cup of tea. I learned quickly not to ask my dad any questions about his day: he would only sigh heavily or begin describing some aspect of his work that had annoyed him. He would end the narrative looking even more dejected. My mum was a teaching assistant at St James, a job that she enjoyed but that didn't make the most of her abilities. I knew that things had been hard for my parents. But surely things would be different in modern Britain? Surely my race wouldn't count against me when it came to applying for jobs and universities?

I resolved that the answers to these questions, at present, were out of my control, and too far in the future for me to worry about. However, I took comfort from the fact that my dad's solution, the thing that he had identified as the magic potion that could right the wrongs in the world, was *hard work*.

I could do that.

In the Year 9 SATs, Mr Mortimer had entered me, Pardeep, Sundip, Sunil, Jade, Nisha and Aaron into a non-compulsory examination that, if we passed, would give us a Level 8 in Maths (the highest level available). Several other students had turned down the opportunity to take the exam; it would mean extra classes after school and an additional examination to take. But I trusted Mr Mortimer when he told us that it would be a useful stepping stone going into our GCSE years; an early introduction to content and the opportunity to familiarise ourselves with a higher level of thinking.

On results day, Mr Mortimer had taken the unconventional decision to stand in the classroom corridor holding the brown envelope with our results enclosed. We were told to go into the corridor one at a time, following the well-rehearsed order of the class register. When it was my turn, I pushed back my chair and walked nervously towards the door, my head bowed slightly towards the ground. In the corridor, Mr Mortimer stood with a neutral expression on his face. As I approached, he turned the page that was resting above the lip of the envelope, to show me the result. I had been given a Level 8, and by a single mark. "Smile Daniel!" Mr Mortimer exclaimed, shaking my hand. "You deserve this. Keep this up and you'll go far in your GCSEs." Comments like these meant a lot and it was energising to know that my teachers believed in me.

Driven by its black head teacher, Mr Morris, Hamstead Hall had made raising the attainment of black boys one of its top priorities. But reversing societal expectations that black boys were more likely to be criminals and troublemakers than gifted and talented was an uphill battle.

Mr Clarke was a teacher who understood that this conflict would have to be won internally before improvement was going to be visible in the classroom. He would push us towards faster times and more accurate execution but he also demanded better attitude and character. Only if we attained both was it rewarded with a firm handshake.

V

I was in Craythorne Hall at the beginning of Year 10. Our head teacher, Mr Morris, had chosen to use this assembly to remind us that we had just begun the most important year in our lives. I was experiencing a peculiar feeling of deja vu having been told something strangely familiar a year earlier in the lead-in to our Year 9 SATs. Come to think of it, we had been told that the way that we performed in Year 7 was likely to have implications for the rest of our secondary education. And wasn't Year 6, with its SATs and 11+ exam, the most pivotal period of my life to date? I rolled my eyes impatiently, wondering why teachers felt it was necessary to bookend every academic year in this way.

But then something that Mr Morris said caught my attention: "Unlike your SATs results, your GCSE results will be on your university application. Your GCSE results will be on your CV when you apply for a job. Your GCSEs will follow you wherever you go." My eyes widened. Perhaps teachers had exaggerated the importance of past exams, but there seemed to be a seriousness in Mr Morris' expression which told me to take heed to whatever he said next: "The coming ten months could change the course of your life."

At that time, I knew that I wanted to apply to university but my thinking hadn't matured enough to have a preference for specific higher education institutions. Buoyed by the previous year's SATs results, I thought that I might like to study Maths; I was good at Maths and enjoyed finding solutions to challenging problems. But I hadn't researched any Maths courses or looked up their associated grade requirements - that all seemed too far in the future. I decided to focus my attention on maintaining the work ethic that had served me well. Across all subjects I threw myself into the new topics that were introduced in Year 10.

I noticed a change in attitude of some of my peers, which lasted way beyond the customary week-long honeymoon period. My classmates rarely failed to complete their homework and the usual hubbub at the start of lessons was replaced with an expectant hush. Perhaps Mr Morris' speech had worked?

Gaining the Level 8 in Maths had made me one of the pacesetter among the gifted and talented cohort. I was increasingly used as a yardstick against which other students measured themselves. If a teacher had graded my assignment with a B, the class would infer that the marking had been harsher than usual. And sure enough, no-one else in the class would be graded above a B.

I initially embraced this added responsibility but as time wore on, I became increasingly unnerved by the fact that I was no longer allowed to keep any of my grades private. Before I even had the chance to read my teacher's comments, those sat around me would lean over to my desk to enquire how I had done. Occasions such as these were frustrating because I cherished feedback. My teacher's comments either held the affirming words of validation or the manual to future success.

An important feedback mechanism were the predicted grades that were given to students a few days prior to the first parent's evening of Year 11. My predicted grades were well above the average of the school but were lower than what I considered to be possible; there was only one A* in Maths and a variety of As and Bs.

The rationale that a number of my teachers gave to my parents was that *If Daniel applies himself, the A / A* will be within his grasp.* I didn't know how to do anything else but *apply myself,* so for me, this confirmed what I already believed to be true. But it was also great to receive an A* prediction. It supported my belief that I was good at Maths, and had consequently made me more energised for classes and lessons.

Many of my friends had predicted grades that were much lower than what I had received. On reflection, I can see why it could have been difficult for some of my peers to remain optimistic, while being shown in black and white that their teacher didn't believe that they could pass or realistically hope for a higher grade.

I thought of the crushing blow that must have landed on their self-esteem, and the embarrassment they must have felt that parent's evening. I also reflected on the fact that while my trajectory since the start of Year 7 had been one of relatively high expectations and exclusive gifted and talented groups, many of my classmates had endured five years of low sets and low expectations. Was this the norm across all schools? Surely some schools had been able to successfully indoctrinate their students from Year 7 to believe that success was the only option? And perhaps in these same schools there was a culture of predicting higher grades at GCSE and pushing their students to achieve it?

I set about the task of putting myself in a position to perform at my best. My most potent weapon was a handwritten revision timetable. Working backwards from the first day of examinations, I would insert time for practice exams, practice questions and revising content. My tactics would vary from subject to subject. For Maths, once I had learned the content, I would practice question after question and past paper after past paper, seeking to identify and then eradicate any gaps in my knowledge. For essay-based exams, I would write out stories and arguments act by act, to ensure that I had the logical process correct in my mind, then I would practice essay questions.

Once I had the timetable and my approach set, I was determined to stick to it. And boy did I stick to it. My dedication to after-school football was restricted to make more room for revision and exam practice. And if I was too busy to revise for a day, I would do twice as much the day before. I sustained this work ethic for more than 3 months before the start of the first examination. I much preferred a gentle incline towards my examinations rather than a steep cliff of last-minute preparations.

GCSE results day was in late August 2005. I walked to school with Chris and entered Craythorne Hall. I was standing in the same spot where Mr Morris had delivered his speech two years earlier.

I was handed a large brown envelope and pulled back the seal. I brought the paper above the lip and kept pulling. I read and re-read.

AFTER OXFORD

According to the sheet enclosed I had achieved As in English Language, French and Food Technology, and A*s in English Literature, History, Mathematics, Religious Education and Statistics, and two A*s in Science.

Overall, 7A*s and 3As.

GETTING INTO OXFORD

"Achievement is talent plus preparation." - Malcolm Gladwell, Outliers

The first meaningful conversation I had with somebody about the University of Oxford came at the age of sixteen. I was speaking with an alum of the University, Mr Rogers, who was my teacher for A level Further Maths. Mr Rogers was employed by King Edward's Grammar School, but a partnership programme had been developed between non-selective secondary schools in Birmingham, such as my own, to offer students an opportunity to study Further Maths.

Initially, when Mr Mortimer asked me if I was interested, I politely declined. I had already committed to four A levels I really wanted to study and was concerned that a fifth would stretch my time too thinly. He implored me to reconsider, explaining that studying Further Maths would help to consolidate knowledge learned in the standard Maths A level.

He also reasoned that studying a fifth subject (alongside Maths, Sociology, History and English Language) would give me room to manoeuvre when applying to universities. I knew that university offers tended to be made on your three best A level results. If I took 5 AS levels, I could drop the AS level I performed the worst in after the first year and carry four subjects forward to A level. This would then mean that if I did poorly in one of the four, it wouldn't adversely affect my chances of getting into a top university.

The two-hour classes in Further Maths took place on a fortnightly basis at Cadbury Sixth Form College in South Birmingham. The journey to the College took around half an hour, but on the return journey, we would always get caught in rush hour traffic, and it could easily take more than three times as long.

For the first lesson, I was accompanied by six others from the group of gifted and talented students: Nisha, Jade, Sunil, Sundip, Aaron and Pardeep. There were an additional eight students from neighbouring schools and two from Cadbury College. By the second week, our numbers had fallen by two. I responded to these announcements with surprise; surely it was too soon to throw in the towel? But as the term wore on, I began to surmise that these early drop-outs may have seen the writing on the wall. By the end of the first term, there were only six people still standing on the entire course; Pardeep, Sundip and I being the representatives from Hamstead Hall.

Studying Further Maths was a chastening experience. I rarely put my hand up in classes; not to defer to others but because I only occasionally understood the question well enough to offer a reasonable answer. I felt completely out of my depth and thought that I had perhaps taken on one challenge too far. On top of the difficult content was the time spent waiting in endless lines of traffic. When I finally made it home, I would spend the next two weeks alone with my textbook, struggling through its contents until the trip to Cadbury College came around again. I was certain that I was going to quit. But not yet. I'd already invested time and effort into the course and was determined to get at least *something* out of it. I resolved that, all being well with my other four subjects, I would quit after the AS year.

Mr Rogers understood the predicament that we were in, given the lack of classroom time and support. He was a patient and jovial teacher who would laugh sympathetically when we struggled to grasp concepts or gave answers that were embarrassingly wide of the mark. He also seemed to know everything about everything. During a short snack break between the first and second hour, Mr Rogers would join us in the canteen and chime in with our conversations. Towards the end of the first term, I mentioned to Mr Rogers that I had recently joined the Labour Party:

"So you've joined Keir Hardie's ranks," he chortled. "What do the cards look like nowadays?"

I inferred from this that he had previously been a member and proudly took out my crimson red membership card. One of the corners had become slightly frayed but it was otherwise in pristine condition; the red rose bloomed high in the top right hand corner, and below 'Mr Daniel Nathan Stone' was written in sharp white lettering.

Mr Rogers took the card out of my hand, examining it carefully. "I hear there has been trouble in some local CLPs?" I stared blankly. Noticing my expression, he offered an interpretation: "Have you been to a meeting yet?"

I told him that I had. The meeting had been held in Laurel Road Sports Centre, a 15-minute walk from my house. Around forty people had attended. The Chair opened the meeting and welcomed the members, commenting that it was good to see some new and younger faces, with a wink in my direction (the only member who seemed to be under the age of 40).

There had been a promising start to the meeting, with verbal reports given by the three councillors and the MP, Khalid Mahmood. But during the question and answer sessions that followed these reports, the mood of the meeting changed. Voices became raised, short discussion points became hostile orations, and there was no mention of action. I was astonished to find a confrontational attitude among a group of people who, I had assumed, were all gathered for the same cause. Instead, it appeared that they had met for the sole purpose of talking *at* each other, and would continue to do so on a monthly basis.

Mr Rogers listened intently, cheerily humming at the humorous parts of the account. "Looks like nothing has changed then!" From this point onwards, we would often speak about politics; the battle for leadership of the Labour Party between Tony Blair and Gordon Brown, the focus of debate in the latest Constituency Labour Party (CLP) meeting and my experiences of campaigning on the doorstep. It was always a shame when our discussions had to be halted for the actual business of the evening.

It was during one of these break-time conversations that the subject of universities came up. "What universities are you thinking of applying to?" Mr Rogers had asked the table.

"I want to do Maths at Birmingham," Pardeep had responded.

"A fellow Mathematician!" Mr Rogers had beamed. "You've definitely got it in you."

Liam, a student from Cadbury College was next: "Engineering."

"Another fine subject," Mr Rogers nodded affirmingly. "Where do you want to study?"

"Dunno," Liam shrugged. "Maybe Manchester or somewhere in London."

"Daniel?" Mr Rogers turned to me.

"I'm thinking of applying to Oxford," I muttered nervously. This was the first time I had said these words to anyone. My thoughts were still unformed - like dough that hadn't yet been put into the oven, they needed shaping and warmth.

As Pardeep and Liam were giving their answers, I had contemplated whether or not this was the best setting to make this declaration. But I trusted Mr Rogers. He seemed like the kind of person who would know things about universities. If he advised me not to apply or if his facial expression betrayed his doubt, I may never have attempted to get into Oxford.

Mr Rogers' eyes widened and a large grin stretched across his face. "I'm an Oxford man myself, St John's College." I detected no doubt or hesitation in his voice. "Do you know what subject you're going to apply for?"

"Maths, I think. Or maybe Economics, but I haven't decided yet." Economics had only recently come onto my radar as a possible option for a degree. I had recently read a book called *Capitalism and Slavery* by Eric Williams, which had opened my eyes to the role that numerical analysis could have in explaining and bringing light to social phenomena, both progressive and deplorable.

"There aren't any pure Economics courses at Oxford." Mr Rogers said - meaning that you couldn't learn Economics as a stand-alone subject, only when combined with other disciplines. "Have you heard of PPE? It could be a good fit for you, because I know you're interested in politics. Have you looked into that as an option?"

That evening, I went online to research the three-year degree in Politics, Philosophy and Economics. I excitedly read through the descriptions of the Politics and Economics modules, which promised to give me the tools I needed to understand society and to influence it for the better. But Philosophy was a mystery to me. I had only rarely encountered philosophers in the classrooms of Hamstead Hall. Karl Marx and Friedritsche Nietsche had featured heavily in a History module on totalitarian governments but the consequence of their writings seemed to receive more attention than the original texts. We were never given copies of *The Communist Manifesto* or *Beyond Good and Evil*. Our exposure to these texts was reduced to soundbites.

I decided to purchase a book on philosophy entitled *The Great Philosophers from Socrates to Turing*, which introduced me to the ideas of Socrates, Plato and Kant. Much of their language seemed dense and inaccessible, and it would take me an age to read through the chapters. But every now and then, I would encounter something profound, such as Plato's *Cave*, which tells the story of a man who becomes so accustomed to living and surviving in darkness that when he finally attains freedom, the bright lights of the world are too much for him. With my budding interest in politics and social issues, it hadn't occurred to me that liberty and prosperity, without adequate support systems and self-development, could expose people beyond what they could handle and enjoy. I could see why Mr Rogers had recommended PPE to me.

A few months after this conversation, I visited Oxford for the first time. As I alighted from the coach, I breathed in what seemed to be two distinct, but interlinked Oxfords: the 21st Century city, and the historical market town. High-walled old stone buildings towered above the streets, with streams of ivy running from the ground, up the wall and into the unseen vacuum behind. The roads were impressively wide compared with Birmingham and on either side, familiar shop front names were taking on a different air. Signs bearing the names Waterstones, WHSmiths and McDonald's were set in grand buildings, next to pedestrianised walkways and adjacent to quaint locally-owned businesses and coffee shops.

Oxford was different to anywhere else I had visited. It seemed to have a maturity and intrigue to it. I walked around like a wide-eyed tourist; my head swivelling and inclining to take in as much of Oxford as I could.

The trip had been organised by Mr Booth, a deputy head teacher at Hamstead Hall. His son, Tim, worked in an administrative role in one of the Oxford colleges, and had arranged for a dozen students to visit for the day. The whole gifted and talented cohort had surpassed expectations during the previous year's GCSEs and it was hoped that we might add to the two students who had gone to Cambridge over a decade ago, or produce our school's first student at the University of Oxford. This trip was designed to provide us with the information and inspiration we would need to make an application.

After confirming that all students were present and accounted for, Mr Booth led us along the edge of the wall until we came to an opening, marked by a folded wooden sign that read *Welcome to St John's College, founded in 1555*. Tim Booth worked in St John's College - the same college that Mr Rogers had attended - surely this had to be fate?

Stepping into the threshold of the College was like entering Narnia. Behind the high walls and the foreboding wooden gate were immaculate gardens and grand buildings. Stone archways separated one part of the College from the next and it felt like I was constantly discovering St John's; some of it was glistening and modern, other parts bore the stony weight of history, but everywhere I turned there was a magical atmosphere of serenity. Despite being situated only a matter of feet away from a busy thoroughfare, the noise from the cars outside was seemingly unable to penetrate this man-made haven of thinking and reasoning.

Tim explained that the college was organised in a system of 'quads': square courts with grass or paving in the centre and rooms on all four corners. I couldn't help staring at the students who knew these paths well, and were hurriedly walking along them with an air of business and importance. A feeling was rising within me that these paths were not beyond my grasp.

At lunchtime, we ate in the main hall of St John's College; I was now unquestionably on the set of a Harry Potter film. Long wooden tables stretched in five rows from the main entrance to a raised seating area. We sat on long benches that could only be edged forwards or backwards when all the students perched on it decided to stand and shuffle with it in unison. Individual table lights in the shape of candle stick holders were placed on the table after every eighth person or so, and chandeliers stretched down from above on huge chains.

The academic tutor we met in the afternoon reminded me a lot of Mr Rogers. He asked us to introduce ourselves and to say which subject we were interested in studying. After each response, he would smile broadly and begin a conversation about our chosen subject, inquiring about the books we were reading and if we had read the recent article on the matter in last week's Guardian or the previous month's Economist. When it was my turn, I stated my subject of interest as PPE. I was halfway through *The Great Philosophers*, but wasn't confident enough to test my knowledge against an academic, so I steered the conversation towards politics.

The visit had the desired effect. I left Oxford with a canvas bag bursting at the seams with prospectuses and information on the application process. I rifled through the pages, pointing out facts to my classmates: "Did you know that you can make an open application to Oxford?" Aaron shook his head and I pointed the open page in his direction. I could see other conversations taking place on the coach: Nisha was speaking to Jade and Natasha about the societies you could join, and Pardeep and Sunil were in the seats behind me comparing the notes they had hurriedly jotted down. It seemed as if everyone on the coach would apply - but I wondered how many would get in?

"Stone." Pardeep called out, leaning between the seats. "Are you going to apply?"

"Yes, I think I will." I responded, looking earnestly down at the prospectus which was open on the pages belonging to St John's College.

I

Many of my closest friends continued into Hamstead Hall Sixth Form and were preparing their university applications. I was still walking to and from Sixth Form with Chris who was intending to study Sociology and Criminology at Coventry University. Richard was applying to study Business Management at Birmingham City University. Paul had begun in Sixth Form but dropped out after the first term; Richard told me that he'd stormed out of a lesson vowing never to return. In the following days, Paul refused to reply to texts from anyone at school and we eventually lost contact.

Paul had been a good friend but a noticeable chasm had formed between us as we approached the business end of school. I was more focused and driven than ever but Paul was still seeking the enjoyment that came from making people laugh. He didn't buy into the urgency of Mr Morris' speech and he didn't believe that he needed to change. I tried to reason with him but to no avail.

For those who remained in school, there was an expectation that we would all attend university, regardless of what our experience of academic life had been to date. Parents, teachers and communities were united in their belief that higher education provided the most secure foundation for a future career. My parents were less prescriptive: higher education was largely an unknown entity to them and they were happy to trust me to make sensible decisions. They knew that I enjoyed learning and probably assumed that I would naturally want to take this course without the need for any further encouragement.

I began working on my university application in the summer of 2006. University applications in the UK are processed through the University Confirmation and Application Service, or UCAS for short.

The rules regarding UCAS applications have varied over time, but the core principles are that students have the opportunity to apply to multiple higher education institutions - I had six options. Of those which offer you a place, one is listed as a firm choice and the other, an insurance. Most universities accept applications on a rolling basis, so there has never been an official deadline to finalise your UCAS application. That is except for applications to study Medicine, and applications to the Universities of Oxford and Cambridge, which have their own early submission deadline, before the end of October.

The first section of the form required me to insert my GCSE results from Year 11 and the AS level results that I received earlier that summer. Overall, I was thrilled with my AS results.

I was on a very high A in Sociology, a comfortable A in History, and a borderline A in Maths. I was astonished to discover that I had been awarded As in all three of my Further Maths modules. This meant that my overall score in Further Maths was currently higher than in the standard Maths A-level. The only disappointment was in English Language, where I had been given a C overall, following an exam where everyone in our class had been given a U grade. Our English teacher was stunned into silence when he realised that *everyone* had been given the lowest possible grade, and vowed to demand a remark.

My decision to take five AS levels had proven to be an astute one and my initial fears of being stretched too thinly had proven to be unfounded. I had fewer free periods than many of my classmates, and during breaks in teaching I would always be found in the student common room with my head buried in a textbook. I was pleased that I could now reap the rewards of my hard work. I would drop English Language and proceed with four A levels that all had the possibility of returning As.

My classmates from the trip to Oxford had also received their AS results. For some, the dispiriting English Language results had proven to be a death knoll in their Oxbridge admission hopes. Without at least three strong AS levels, they would be unable to make a competitive application. Some dropped out of the race immediately while others were unwilling to give up on their dreams and soldiered on.

As the student with the best AS results, I had become the school's best hope of breaking their Oxford duck. But it was still hope rather than expectation. My teachers supported my ambition by predicting me to get 4As but their language was often restrained. They would make comments such as "you've done really well Daniel, but you know how tough it will be..." Their hesitation betrayed their fears that I would ultimately fall short. Fears that were founded in the belief that pupils from schools like Hamstead Hall had little chance against the private and grammar school juggernauts.

After all, there had been nothing in the history of the school to suggest otherwise.

This was the relatively straightforward section of the application. Much of my concern and time was spent constructing the shape and content of my personal statement; prose of no more than 4000 characters. Our teachers encouraged us to think of an original opening salvo that would draw in the reader and share something of who we were. I eventually settled on an opening sentence about sharing a box room with my younger brother Matthew and how this had made me inquisitive about the different ways in which people lived and experienced life.

I went on to discuss *The Great Philosophers, Capitalism and Slavery,* and to quote Adam Smith's *The Wealth of Nations.* Sticking closely to the rubric, I added a paragraph on my A levels and the topics that I was enjoying the most, ensuring that there was a clear connection to my interest in PPE. I added a section on my involvement with the Labour Party and a few lines on the practical ways that I had seen economics and politics in action at the places that I had worked.

My closing remarks expressed my hopes of being able to pursue my passions at St John's. I lost count of the number of times that I checked and rechecked, edited and re-edited my personal statement. Eventually I was happy that it was coherent and engaging, free of grammatical and factual errors, and most importantly, that it told the reader who I was.

Alongside my personal statement, I submitted one essay apiece from both Sociology and History, and requested a reference from the Head of Sixth Form. Our teachers were delighted to help where they could, although they often apologetically admitted their lack of familiarity with the Oxbridge application process.

There was, however, an unmissable buzz in Year 13 classes as we approached the submission deadline. Nisha, Jade, Sunil and Aaron were all in the process of writing applications. The end of October quickly arrived, and the applications had been submitted. All we could do now was wait.

II

The PPE interviews were to be held in the first week of December, and I had spent the weeks following the submission of my UCAS application improving my knowledge of current affairs, and revisiting the texts that I had cited in my personal statement. By mid-November some of my classmates had received letters inviting them to interview, and some received the disappointing news that they had not made it past the initial sift of applications. I was still waiting on my letter from St John's.

Ten days before the scheduled start date of the interviews and I still had not heard from them. Nine days. Eight days. Then in the week before the interviews were due to commence, a letter came through the post inviting me to interview. The letter included information on what day and time to arrive (Sunday by 4pm), the duration of the interview (until Tuesday), what to wear (anything you're comfortable in) and what to do beforehand (read up on current affairs, but apart from that, you can't prepare).

I took the train down to Oxford on Sunday afternoon, pulling into Oxford shortly after 3pm. I had packed the only suit I owned, a chocolatey-brown colour that I paired with a creamy shirt and brown tie. Unusually for me, I'd spent hours over the course of several shopping trips trying to pick out a suit that I could wear both at formal interviews and celebratory occasions. I was delighted with my choice and proudly wore it on only the most important of days. There was a bitter chill in the air as I exited the train station. I took a deep breath in and pressed ahead purposefully, knowing that on the other side of the journey would be a warm meal and my date with destiny. The sun was beginning to fade as I dragged my suitcase behind me on the tarmacked road. But I felt calm and hopeful. I watched the shadows of passers-by stretch behind them, suddenly covered by a passing vehicle before re-emerging unharmed. And I was reminded that I had nothing to lose. If I didn't get through the interview, there would be no inquest or inquiry. Disappointment, but perhaps not surprise. My teachers had warned me how tough the process would be and my dad's words that I would have to *work twice as hard* still echoed in my mind.

Failure would only confirm what people had suspected all along: Oxford wasn't for people like us. I hoped that I could prove them wrong.

I crossed the road and once again traced the high walls to the entrance. The wooden door was open and I could see the figure of a suited man waiting on reception to welcome the new arrivals.

"Welcome to St John's. Can I have your name, and the subject you're interviewing for?" The man didn't look much older than me, but seemed to carry the weight, in his intonation and body language, of a maturity I knew I did not yet possess.

"Thank you. My name is Daniel Stone, and PPE," I responded, taking care to sound out my words.

"Was that Stone?" He echoed.

I hung my head slightly, "Yes."

"Splendid. I'm reading PPE too. In my second year," he remarked, while scanning the register below for my name. "Here you are." Another two hopefuls arrived behind me accompanied by their parents. Our host repeated the routine: name and subject. Once our numbers had swelled to around seven, roughly half of the group were led off towards the right of the quad and the other half towards the left.

I was in the right-hand group, and nervously tried to make eye contact with an applicant who had also made the journey to St John's without his parents. He smiled back and I took the few steps over to where he was standing. His name was Simon and he was from North London. He supported Arsenal, and was also a member of the Labour Party. He had a thick North London accent and used terms like *geezer*. It was such a relief to meet someone so early into the interview ordeal who I could relate to.

Simon and I followed our tour guide under an archway and towards the glass-fronted building that I recognised from our school trip. On that day, our tour had veered off towards the left and into the dining hall. But today we had been given permission to go inside, to climb the steep staircase and to stay for two nights in the room of a student. I agreed to meet Simon at the foot of the building at 5.45 to go to dinner, giving me roughly an hour and a half to settle into my new surroundings. I turned the key in the lock and entered my room.

Growing up, I always shared my bedrooms with one or more of my siblings. Initially it was Selina, before Matthew joined to make it a three. Then Selina got too old to share with her two brothers and was given her own room, which was later also occupied by Joanna. I was used to cramped living spaces, compromise and bunk beds. But in this room I would have my own space to live: my own writing desk, my own wardrobe and chest of draws, and my own bed that was only one storey high. I walked over to the window that was looking down on the quad below; another group of students were being escorted towards another accommodation block. I closed the curtains and walked over to my bed. I lay back, looking up to the ceiling and began to pray; "Dear God, thank you for bringing me this far and thank you that you will be with me in tomorrow's interview. I pray that your will be done. Amen."

I met with Simon as planned and we walked over to the dining hall together. There were only a handful of people in the queue so we were able to walk directly towards the kitchen staff with our trays; I selected the chicken with potatoes, carrots and green beans, and cake and custard for dessert. We scanned the dining hall to select an appropriate place to sit. There were five rows of tables. The two farthest rows were completely empty, awaiting the arrival of more applicants. I wanted to suggest to Simon that we sat there, away from everyone else for at least another few moments. But I reasoned that this would be antisocial and a missed opportunity to make friends like I had done with Simon.

There were two larger groups in deep conversation, who I thought it best to avoid. Instead, I nodded to Simon in the direction of a small huddle of three boys who were sitting towards us in the middle row of the five. As we approached, two of the boys shot friendly smiles in our direction while the third, who was talking at the time, stood to his feet so that we could slide onto his bench.

The three introduced themselves to us as Peter, Jack and Michael. Once the introductions were over, Peter continued where he left off; monopolising the conversation and barely pausing for breath. He spoke about his rigorous interview preparation schedule and rattled off the list of books that he had brought with him to Oxford. He asked us pointed questions about obscure current affairs, so that when we didn't know anything about them he could give detailed answers that would make us feel inferior. He also memorised historical facts about St John's College, including naming the people in the portraits hung in the main dining hall.

Through our collective will, we were able to wrestle the conversation away from his grasp and turn it to other subjects such as the North London derby that had taken place the day before and our plans for the Christmas break. Simon and I were spending time with our families in London and Birmingham respectively, while Peter, Jack and Michael would be travelling overseas.

We also discussed what we were planning to wear to the interview, all of us looking for reassurance from the others. Simon said that he had packed a smart shirt and tie.

"I'm wearing a suit," I chimed in. "That should be OK, shouldn't it?"

"Yes, I've got a suit too," replied Peter. "A suit is fine, as long as you don't wear anything hideous like brown." My heart sank, but I resisted the urge to let out any emotions that would betray the embarrassment I was feeling. I ate quietly for the remainder of the dinner.

Afterwards, I ventured into the common room with Simon. Over the course of the next hour or so, I beat Simon at pool, I lost to Simon at pool and we watched an uneventful re-run of the Everton vs West Ham match that had been played earlier that afternoon. I felt relaxed and at ease as I walked back into the bedroom to read through my notes a final time before bed. As I entered the room, my brown suit was visible through the half-opened wardrobe. I trod over solemnly and pressed the door shut. "Just do yourself justice Daniel. Just do yourself justice."

I had two interviews at St John's. The first was overshadowed by the second to such an extent that I have no recollection of how the first interview went. The second interview was so bad and so traumatic that I can recall every question asked by the interviewer, every hesitation, every scrambled answer I offered up, only to witness the eyes of the interviewer sinking further and further into disappointment.

The second interview exposed the shaky foundations of my knowledge of philosophy, which I had hoped might be stabilised by *The Great Philosophers*. It seemed like I was in the interview for an eternity, as I responded to question after question with either a blank expression, or a variation on an answer I'd given before.

"Is scarlet really red" "Can you provide an explanation of what Descartes meant when he wrote 'I think, therefore I am?'" "Why is it wrong for a consenting adult not to wear a seat belt?" The interview was a literal car crash.

In defence of the interviewer, he only asked the Descartes question after I had quoted the famous maxim with the hope of proving that I was at least marginally competent. I had also mispronounced Descartes' name to the annoyance of the interviewer who had interrupted: *Day-car*.

The interviewer who sat opposite me on a large oblong table had initially been quite supportive; encouraging me to think carefully about my answers and looking intently in the hope of teasing out some interesting insights. But halfway through the interview I could see that he had given up. His remarks were more impatient and his eyes often looked past me, possibly to the clock on the wall or out of the window opposite. At the end of the interview, he offered some conciliatory thoughts: Oxford interviews were difficult; I had done well to make it to interview; and I would learn the outcome in a few weeks.

I called my mum after the interview: "It was horrible mum. I couldn't think and the questions were really hard."

"But you know Dan, if you found it hard, everyone would have found it hard. You never know."

"Maybe," I grunted disconsolately. But I knew that I hadn't given a good account of myself, and I hadn't done myself justice.

I gave a similar summary to my hopeful teachers and friends when I returned to school on Wednesday morning. They would have seen my gloomy expression from a distance and their *How was it?* was already tinged with melancholy. It was difficult having to retell and relive the second interview over and over and over again, and to witness their disappointment. I carried their hopes, as well as my own, for months and months. I knew the morale boost it would have given the school to have a student get into Oxford. It would have been the zenith of the school's rise from being a troubled school to being one that was sought after by local parents. But I knew that our dream was over.

In the fortnight following the interview, I had taken the view that I had performed so poorly that if I got in, there was clearly something wrong with the process. I played the interview over and over again in my mind; with each iteration, I would provide better and more intelligent answers. But the moment to do so had passed. I put my poor performance down to subject choice (I didn't know enough about Philosophy to be interviewed on it), execution (I didn't do well enough in the moment) and preparation (I didn't know what, but there surely could have been more that I could have done beforehand).

It came as no surprise to me when the letter informed me that I had been rejected. Again, it was written on a solitary sheet of paper. My family were waiting in the front room to console me but this time, there were no tears.

No-one else from Hamstead Hall had been made an offer and my failure had deflated any remaining hope that my teachers and peers were clinging onto. Everyone was disappointed. Richard had responded by saying: "If you can't get in, where's the hope for the rest of us?"

After I received my letter, I sent a message to Simon. He had been unsuccessful too. Our silver lining was that both he and I had put the University of Warwick as our insurance choice. I felt content with Warwick as a consolation prize. After all, it was a prestigious university with a good PPE course. I hadn't gained a place at Oxford but I had ultimately landed where I most wanted to be, in a good university - and I'd already made a friend before starting there.

Assuming that Simon and I both made the offer of AAB, we would be studying PPE together in the new academic year.

DON'T MIND THE GAP

"We know the reality of our struggle but instead of being consumed by despair we must be prisoners of hope" - Dr Cornel West

In the spring of 2007, an alternative course of action was presented to me. The provocateur-in-chief was Bernardine Evaristo, the Booker Prize-winning author of fiction books including *Blonde Roots*, *Soul Tourists* and *Girl, Woman, Other*.

I met Bernardine on an English writing retreat organised for students who had taken the infamous AS English Language. Our English teacher had successfully applied for some funding to take the whole class - around 20 students - to a farmhouse in the middle of the English countryside. We had participated in workshops led by Bernardine, written our own poetry and critiqued each other's work. I really like Bernardine. She was honest, intelligent, and wrote majestically about some of the issues of belonging and identity that I was experiencing in my own life.

Bernardine visited our school several months after the residential trip, and although by this time it was my A2 year and I was no longer studying English Language, we arranged to meet in the school canteen. I updated her on my progress, and informed her that I had been rejected by Oxford.

"Why don't you apply again?" She said. So matter-of-factly that it made it seem as if that should have been my first and natural response.

AFTER OXFORD

"Apply again? But I have a place at Warwick."

"Yes, when you get your 4As, you could reject your place at Warwick and then reapply to Oxford next year."

I liked that Bernardine had said *when* rather than *if.*

But I wasn't convinced that rejecting my offer was the best course of action. It would mean falling a year behind my cohort who were mostly going onto university. And if I did reject my place, what would I do during my gap year? And how would I tell my dad? He believed that gaining a place at the University of Warwick was a tremendous achievement and that it was probably the best I could hope for given that I'd tried and failed to get into Oxford.

His view was that Warwick was my reward for having worked twice as hard throughout my time at school. Rejecting my offer would make no sense at all.

I listened to Bernardine's advice and kept it stored away in the back of my mind. In the short term, I decided to focus on what was in front of me. I needed AAB to get into Warwick. Miss that, and I would be in complete limbo, without a place at any of my preferred university destinations. I was most confident about getting an A in Sociology after a strong set of results in my AS year. My other subjects were less certain. History had an unpredictable coursework module and I had only scraped an A in Maths. Then there was Further Maths.

After the AS results had been announced, Sundip and two others left the course. Another pupil left at the beginning of the A level year and as the spring term approached, Pardeep, my only classmate, decided that he wouldn't continue. It wasn't surprising, as he had been falling behind with some of the assignments and was coming to lessons unprepared; something that couldn't be hidden in a class of two. I was now taking the journey to Cadbury College on my own and having one-on-one lessons with Mr Rogers. Hilariously, I would still travel to the College in an otherwise empty minibus. On the way back, the courteous bus driver would drop me directly at my house, rather than back to Hamstead Hall, as per the original arrangement.

The final module was Further Pure Maths 2, which began to introduce in more depth some of the approaches and theories that would be explored in mathematics at university level. It was hideous, and I would come to lessons perplexed and desperate for Mr Rogers to help me to understand. But I was relentless in my determination to learn the content, and would spend hours working through problem sets trying to arrive at the solution.

On A level results day, I once again entered Craythorne Hall and retrieved the A4 envelope with the name 'Daniel Nathan Stone' written on the lip. The results were displayed in alphabetical order, meaning that the first result belonged to Further Maths.

The far corner of the paper flopped loosely as I tried to make sense of what was written. I read it again just to make sure. Not only had I got an A overall, but I had received As in all six of my Further Maths modules. I shook my head in disbelief and imagined Mr Rogers' reaction. He would raise his fists triumphantly and pronounce *Wellll done Daniel!*

I steadied myself and kept reading. History - A. Maths - A. Sociology - A. I walked over to the raised platform in Craythorne Hall and laid the envelope down. I placed my hands on top of my head, interlocking my fingers while my head tilted up towards the sky; I closed my eyes and sighed.

When I opened my eyes, the paper was still on the stage, untroubled. And in black and white were my four As. I had done it and my reward was the power of choice.

I

I told my dad that I was thinking of taking a gap year one evening after he'd come home from work.

"Why do you want to do that Daniel?" He exclaimed, staring at me with thundering eyes. "Your mother and I know how hard you've worked, so why would you throw it all away? There's a lot of people who talk about doing gap years and never end up going to university."

He didn't wait for my answer: "You're good at studying, stick to it." Then he turned back to watch the TV, as though the conversation had ended.

I didn't know which point to respond to first. My dad was from a generation in which most decisions were black and white, and where rules were to be obeyed. From his perspective, if I was fortunate enough to have been offered a place at such a prestigious university, why would I ever risk losing it?

My argument was that a lot had changed in the year since I first applied to Oxford. My predicted grades had become a reality. While my dad saw my offer as being fortunate, I knew the value of my 4As. Warwick weren't *doing me a favour*, they were in the market for the best students in the same way that I was in the market to get myself to the best possible university. I earned my place and was in no doubt that I would be able to successfully reapply to a top university. A gap year would also give me time to evaluate my subject choice, and to decide whether I really wanted to pursue a course with a large philosophical element. The idea of a gap year was growing on me, but I needed to come up with a plan for how I would make the best use of my year out.

An attractive option had been presented to me by my local Councillor, Paulette Hamilton. I met Paulette at the end of a Labour Party meeting. I was still being mentored by Aaron at Mount Zion and he had encouraged me to think of someone who would be a good professional mentor; a person who was working in a field or industry that I might one day like to work in. The idea of being a politician really interested me; it seemed to be a role where you could make a difference and improve the way that society worked. I had gone online a few days before the meeting and read Paulette's biography. She'd grown up in Handsworth - and her biography said that she was passionate about education and health. I sent Paulette an email to ask if she would consider being my mentor.

At the end of the meeting, I made a beeline towards Paulette. She was reaching for her coat, but greeted me warmly when she saw me walking towards her.

"Hello, young man!" A beaming smile immediately springing across her face.

"Hello, Councillor Hamilton…" I faltered. Paulette was still smiling, so I continued. "I sent you an email about the possibility of mentoring…"

"Ah! Yes. You're… was it Daniel?"

I nodded.

"I received your email, but I've been really busy with Ward duties the past few days. I was hoping I would see you this evening. Can you meet this week?"

"No problem, thank you. Yes, I can do any day except Wednesday."

Paulette paused for a moment, I could sense her visualising her diary and commitments for the week. "Look, I'll give you my number," she said, gesturing for me to hand her my phone. "Send me a message tomorrow and we'll confirm a time and place. And please, call me Paulette."

"Thanks very much Paulette, I will do that."

"How did you find the meeting?" Paulette asked. I looked towards the ground, unsure about how honest I should be.

Paulette interpreted my response without me verbalising it: "I know, but stick with it."

This would be the first of many times that I would surrender my natural instincts in order to follow a piece of advice from Paulette. I can't think of a single time when her suggestions have led me astray.

Following the meeting, Paulette agreed to become my mentor. When I mentioned the possibility of the gap year, Paulette had indicated that I could shadow her for two days a week. She had contacts in the City Council departments responsible for education, children's services and health. I could spend time with the heads of these departments, learning about their jobs and the magnitude of the challenges facing the city.

AFTER OXFORD

Errol Lawson was now the full time Youth Pastor at Mount Zion. He said that I could assist the youth department with administrative tasks and contribute to school visits. And I found a job advertisement for night shift workers at Wilkinson's, a DIY and homeware shop, which would allow me to build my savings before going to university.

This still didn't convince my dad, who remained anxious that I could waste my academic potential. Exasperated, he concluded our conversation by telling me to pray about it. I thought that I was right and that my dad was wrong, but his anxiety troubled me. I knew that I was unable to see the different turns my life would take if I accepted or rejected my place at Warwick. So perhaps my dad was right and I shouldn't deviate from the track I was on? I followed his instruction and prayed. My prayers were simple: "Have your way God. Lead me, guide my feet, and give me peace in whatever decision I make."

To help with the decision making process, I also fasted for a week. As children we were taught that denying our natural urges for food would help to heighten our spiritual sensitivity. As we grew older, our fasting progressed from skipping breakfast to refraining from eating for the 12 hours between 6am and 6pm. I found fasting to be a helpful exercise. The time that I usually spent eating was repurposed for prayer. And my refusal to give into feelings of hunger kept my thoughts about university firmly at the front of my mind. As I got towards the end of the week, the uncertainty that clouded my mind had slowly lifted, and I knew that I wanted to turn down my place at Warwick. But I was still nervous at the thought of defying my dad.

I ended the week of fasting in a half-night of prayer held by Mount Zion on the last Friday of every month. This was a collective time for prayer, beginning around 7pm, and ending at midnight. To my immediate left stood my dad who, along with many other people in the church, raised his voice and shouted his petitions to God. The noise began to build, voices bouncing and colliding around the room, then I heard a whisper in my left ear: 'Take a gap year.'

I turned to my Dad: "What did you say?"

He glanced at me with irritation, then carried on shouting his prayers. When the collective clamouring had finally died down, I tugged on my dad's sleeve and got him to sit.

"What is it?" He said, frustrated.

"What did you say to me?"

"Say about what?" He was bristling now, annoyed that he was missing the information being provided from the stage.

"I heard you say that I should take a gap year."

"Look, this isn't the time for this. I've already told you my views on this. But it's your life."

I kept seated during the next two prayers. I had a lot on my mind. Maybe the lack of sustenance over the past few days had made me hallucinate the voice? Or I had made it up out of a desire to have this finalised once and for all? Part of me believed it was the manifestation of my heart and soul, telling me what I knew all along.

Regardless, the most important thing was my decision.

As the last prayer ended and a hush filled the auditorium, our Pastor asked whether anyone had a word or prophecy for the congregation. Prophetic words were thoughts, ideas or facts, said to be transported straight from God to the minds and hearts of people. In reality, it seemed to be more complex than this. Not everyone who claimed to be a prophet showed evidence of any prophetic ability, and those who claimed they were able to prophesy varied in their accuracy and the ambition of their statements. I knew some people who unmistakably had a gift. They could reveal specific predictions about the future that would come to pass. On the other end of the spectrum were people who gave very generic statements that, while perhaps true, could never be verified or proven to be so: "If you're going through a tough time, God is with you."

I was listening carefully as the speakers began. The first prophecy was about the growth of the church and the church building, which received hearty 'Amens' from the assembled crowd.

The next message was about Jesus winning the victory and a coming revival that was going to sweep through Birmingham and lead thousands upon thousands of souls to faith. To this, people stood to their feet, waving their hands and shouting 'Hallelujah, thank you Jesus!' The church was now alive with energy and expectancy, but I remained rooted to my seat.

The third speaker began with a tone that was out of kilter with what had gone before. It was a sober message about the work that was required to create an active church: "I feel that God would challenge us. We come to church every Sunday, looking our best and driving in our nice cars. But all around us people are poor and suffering and lost. There are people here tonight who have businesses, ideas and projects in their heart that will help PEOPLE. But you're allowing these THINGS - cars and clothes - to get in the way of your calling."

Smatterings of applause began. "And one more thing. There's someone here who is trying to decide whether they should give God their time. I think it's a year the person is thinking of giving. God is saying to take the time out and to trust him."

I had no doubt in that moment that the message was for me. I turned to my dad, whose face remained expressionless. He then looked at me and smiled.

That evening, I logged onto the UCAS website, and rejected my place at the University of Warwick. I would have started in ten days' time.

II

The first few months of my gap year were a whirlwind of activity. Paulette had been true to her word and I spent Mondays and Wednesdays shadowing her and meeting with service leads based in various departments across the City Council. I spent a day with the Head of Children's Services who told me about the crisis facing children in care.

There weren't enough foster parents in Birmingham, especially for black children and children of mixed heritage. He told me that there were likely to have been children in care in my secondary school and that schools were expected to support the attainment of young people in care. None of my peers had openly declared this, but as I thought about the boys on Top Playground, I wondered how many of the boys with the latest trainers or the most expensive shoes had been given these items by foster parents.

In November, Paulette sustained a leg injury, so I began to take a 45 minute bus ride to her house in North Birmingham for mentoring sessions and conversations. As we spoke, Paulette began to notice my eyes looking down at the ground or up at the ceiling or outside of the window; anywhere that would prevent me from making direct eye contact with her.

"You're a shy young man." Paulette would laugh.

"I suppose I am," I responded. My eyes temporarily making contact with Paulette's before wandering off again. I thought that my reluctance to make eye contact was because my mind was working and searching for answers. It would take a certain amount of self-assuredness to trust my brain to work while staying focused on the person sitting opposite me.

"But you're also a very intelligent young man with a lot to share with the world. Have you done much public speaking?" Paulette asked.

I explained that I had done a few talks at Mount Zion and that I had recently chaired the inaugural forum of the *Let's Talk* initiative, a regional programme designed to provide a safe space for young people to discuss and debate the important topics of our time. The theme for our first meeting was climate change. As Chair, my task was to keep the event and discussions running on time, to introduce the main speakers and to facilitate the feedback from group activities.

On these occasions, I prepared and practiced my contributions in advance of the events to the extent that I would be able to speak comfortably and without notes. But I rarely sought out speaking opportunities. This was partly because I was still fearful of my stutter, and the risk of having a verbal meltdown in front of a large crowd (despite the fact that this had never happened before). But it was mainly because I didn't believe that I had much to offer a room of strangers. I was an 18-year-old who, while having some good exam results, really hadn't achieved anything. I had done nothing to fix our broken society, to raise the spectre of poverty or to awaken consciences to the seriousness of climate change; so what could I really hope to teach others?

At the end of one of our mentoring sessions, Paulette said that she wanted me to prepare a 10-minute speech for the next time we met. It could be on any topic I liked, but I needed to plan the speech and pretend that I was delivering it in front of a large crowd. I had seen Paulette speak at multiple community meetings and she seemed completely at ease, her eyes fanning across the assembled crowd while she answered questions and provided updates on council business. I thought this would be a good opportunity to get feedback on my public speaking from someone who I trusted and respected.

The next day I began to think about the topic I would talk on, and finally decided that I would do a speech on Nelson Mandela. I had recently finished reading *The Long Walk to Freedom*, and it had made a great impression on me.

In the pages of the book, I read about a man who showed the skills and character traits I aspired to call my own. He had shown tremendous perseverance to withstand 25 years in prison without allowing his hope to fade; unwavering discipline to begin each day in his prison cell with press-ups and sit-ups in order to maintain his physical and mental agility; and uncompromising wisdom to seek peace and reconciliation rather than revenge.

I delivered my speech to Paulette. She said that, as expected, the content was good, and had pulled out some interesting lessons from Mandela's life. I had maintained good presence and eye contact when speaking, and had barely used my notes, which enhanced my ability to connect with the audience. However, my pace was rushed at times and my delivery was generally quite flat. I needed to think about how I could keep my audience engaged.

"But overall, it was fantastic." Paulette had said. I smiled and looked away. "What are you doing next Wednesday evening?"

I rarely had anything booked on evenings now. I had successfully applied for the job at Wilkinson's and was working full time; shifts began at 9pm and finished shortly after sunrise, but I had next Wednesday off: "I'm free."

"Good. I want you to speak at an event I'm attending at Aston Villa Football Club."

Paulette reassured me that I would not be speaking in front of a 43,000 capacity crowd, but that my audience would be a group of students in years 11 and 12 who would be attending a careers event in one of Aston Villa's hospitality suites.

In the days leading up to the event I planned the structure and content of my talk. I knew that a strong start would endear me to the audience and give me confidence for the remainder. I rehearsed the opening sentence in my mind: "Good evening. My name is Daniel Stone, and I am here to tell you my story..."

As I rehearsed, I pictured the reaction of the audience in my mind. I expected they would listen intently as I introduced my primary education at St James, and the experience of secondary school in Hamstead Hall. I hoped they would move towards the edge of their seats as I discussed my GCSE years and my predicted grades, the climax coming with my GCSE results. Once the 7A*s and 3As had captured their attention, I would go on to talk about my A level results and the importance of maintaining high standards. My closing message would give the three tips that helped me to succeed: resilience, discipline, and the pursuit of excellence.

But I was unsure about what would happen next: Would they applaud or would there be an eerie silence? Perhaps I had been obnoxious to think that people would find my story to be interesting and relevant? Instead of moving towards the edge of their seats, perhaps they would be impatiently waiting for this imposter to come off stage so that Paulette or one of the real guests of honour could speak?

Feelings of self-doubt began to consume me but I thought back to the talks I had given before. "People are generally nice." I told myself. "The worst thing that you'll get is a polite round of applause and if it goes badly, except for Paulette, you'll probably never see these people again!"

AFTER OXFORD

The suite was an impressive room covered in a burgundy carpet, which featured blue roaring lions at each point of the embroidered diamonds that spanned the floor. On the cream walls were portraits of Aston Villa legends and some of the club's greatest moments, including the 1995-96 League Cup triumph, and the European Cup victory of 1982. Rather than taking a seat amongst the crowd of around 60 students and parents, I was ushered to the front row to sit with Paulette.

As I replayed the speech over in my mind, Paulette was called to the stage. After a warm round of applause, she began discussing her own career journey. It was the first time that I heard certain aspects of her career as a nurse: how she had served some of the poorest communities in Birmingham and eventually decided that she could affect more lasting change by standing for election. She spoke about becoming a mother and balancing family alongside a desire to progress in her career.

In our mentoring sessions, Paulette had told me about the racism and sexism that being in public office had brought her way. I could see the pain of these experiences in her eyes as she spoke about the "opportunities and challenges" of a life in politics. But she told the audience that she loved her job, she loved serving people and that they had to believe in themselves. I was so entranced by Paulette's talk that I had forgotten that I was about to be called to the stage.

"And now, I'd like to bring to the stage a young man who is from Handsworth," Paulette sent a smile in my direction, and I began to rehearse the first line. "He went to Hamstead Hall School and did extremely well in his exams. Getting... How many A*s?" Paulette paused, waiting on me to answer. I gestured the number 7 with my fingers, distraught that the structure of my speech and my big reveal were now in tatters. "7A*s!" She continued. "Aaannnd he's going to Oxford University next year!"

I almost jumped out of my seat. Paulette knew that I hadn't even reapplied to Oxford yet, but in front of this audience she had made it sound like I had been given a place. I was truly perplexed. "Please welcome, Daniel Stone."

As I took to my feet, I was deep in thought. How would I start? Should I correct Paulette? What she said wasn't true, and I couldn't deceive the audience. But then, why had she said it? There must be a lesson she wanted me to learn? But if I went along with the story, wouldn't people ask me questions after the event that I didn't have the answer to? No, I would have to make the correction. So how could I reverse the damage without shaming Paulette or myself? The applause died down.

"Good evening, my name is Daniel Stone…" I paused, giving myself more time to formulate the next sentence. "I haven't quite made it to Oxford yet, but will be applying in October." I hesitated, peering up, expecting to see disappointment sweep the faces of the children and their parents, but they were still smiling and hanging on my every word. I readjusted, and instead used the 7A*s and 3As as the beginning of my story.

I explained that my GCSE results would have meant nothing if I had stopped working hard, showing discipline and pursuing excellence during my A level years. I told them that I had unsuccessfully applied to Oxford but that I was learning a lot about myself and my community during my gap year. I encouraged them to pursue learning, to work hard, and never give up on their dreams.

My talk finished, and there was a roar of applause. I was stunned by this reaction and stood for a few moments, politely holding up my hands to thank the audience for their kindness. I gradually moved towards the row of chairs and collapsed into my seat. As the applause continued, Paulette leaned over and whispered, "You know you're going to Oxford, right?"

III

When Selina turned 13 she was old enough to get a paper round, and would deliver papers weekly on two streets parallel to ours. The papers would arrive on a Thursday morning in large separate bundles of newspapers and flyers. If it was raining, the papers would usually be dropped into our porch, but occasionally it would start to rain only after the papers had been deposited outside our house, and when Selina opened the front door to retrieve them she would be greeted by a large mush of soggy dark grey paper, no longer fit for reading. On Thursday evening, the work would begin. To save on delivery time, Selina would put the leaflets into the inner page of every paper. When only two or three leaflets were delivered, this wasn't a problem. But in some weeks there could be over a dozen leaflets that all had to be separated from their respective piles before being stacked into the paper, covering every inch of lino on our living room floor with colourful promotions from local supermarkets. The upside was that the more leaflets Selina was given, the more she was paid. At the time, the 10 pence per paper seemed scant consolation for hours spent shovelling leaflets into over 300 individual newspapers.

At the age of 13 my dad stopped giving me pocket money, which was a clear signal that he expected me to follow in Selina's footsteps. By now, Selina had gotten tired of the Friday evenings trudging along the streets of Handsworth, and was happy to hand over the reins. I took over the paper-leaflet production line and gave Matthew a cut of my weekly wage in exchange for help with preparation and delivery.

As the older sibling, I took on more of the work and a greater proportion of the pay, but having Matthew around made the job quicker and more enjoyable. We would each take a side of the road, racing each other to see who could complete their allocation the quickest. Strategies for saving time involved jumping over low walls and walking over front gardens, rather than taking the proper, but more time-consuming route, that involved opening and closing a gate.

Matthew and I remained in the joint-enterprise of newspaper-delivery until I turned sixteen. While Matthew continued the paper round, I successfully acquired a weekend job at McDonalds. Once there, I was quickly allocated all the tasks that no-one else wanted.

My first responsibility was to build Happy Meal boxes. At the start of my shift I would be placed in an office at the back of the building, alongside hundreds of flattened Happy Meal boxes and a huge pile of Happy Meal toys. My task for the next 6-7 hours was to form the flattened boxes into a cube, place a toy in the middle and then stack them. Every few hours my supervisor would come in to take the completed boxes onto the shop floor, and would find me in the middle of a carefully-constructed Happy Meal fortress. It greatly surprised him to find that, rather than storming out or giving up, I had built hundreds and hundreds of the boxes.

Several weeks later, another 16-year-old was hired, and I was promoted to front of house. My task was to keep the large ice bin topped up and to pour adequate amounts of large, medium and small soft drinks, so that the busy cashiers could quickly fulfil their customer's orders. As time went by, I developed a knack for knowing how many of each drink to pre-prepare; medium Cokes went like hot cakes, but preparing too many large Sprites was always a mistake.

The next month I was promoted again, this time to my own till, where I learned the art of convincing customers to upgrade to an extra value meal rather than having a burger alone, and of making an ice-cream with the perfect amount of swirls. I kept my till up until the age of 18 when I left McDonald's in order to focus on my upcoming A level exams.

Being in paid employment was an expected part of my life for a number of years. It allowed me to have greater financial independence; to be able to buy video games and clothes when I wanted them rather than relying on my parents. I was always looking for efficiencies in my work; the quickest way to fold newspapers or the optimum number of drinks to have ready at the station. In this way, even the most menial task could become mentally stimulating. And I also enjoyed sharing work with others.

At the end of a long paper round shift with Matthew, we would often share a bag of chips or a King Size Twix. In the staff canteen at McDonald's, I would eat my triple-stacked Big Mac, XL fries and apple pie in the company of colleagues who were a strange array of teenaged crew members and middle-aged managers.

When I began my gap year, I saw it as the perfect opportunity to have my first full time job. I took up a night shift working for Wilkinson's, a DIY and homeware shop. The night shift was a team of six: a man in his 20s called Lee who would begin every shift with a pot noodle and a can of coke – no exceptions. There was also Richard, a retired army doctor, who had travelled all over the world with his work but now wanted a simple and stable job to provide a guaranteed income without much drama. Then there was a middle-aged woman, Ellen, who spoke to us openly about the affair she was having with a teenage neighbour who was thirty years her junior. On hearing this, Richard winked, and warned me to watch my back. The last shift worker was Ernie, a relatively elderly man with a strong Brummie accent. We were supervised by Abdul, a cheery middle-aged man of Bangladeshi origin who always seemed to wear a red Wilkinson's jacket that was two sizes too big.

Abdul had a tough job as supervisor. I would frequently hear cackles of laughter above the shop-floor music. The fact that the laughter was coming from the exact same position was proof that at least two people hadn't moved an inch for at least the past 30 minutes.

Abdul wasn't blind to the fact that people were slacking off but he struggled greatly to assert his authority. After a few weeks, I noticed that my colleagues had the tendency to take breaks that were longer than the allotted 45 minutes. Abdul would burst into the staff room at around the 50 minute mark, his eyes flaming but unable to channel his anger in a way that commanded respect and immediate action. I always kept to time, and sometimes would go back out early if I had failed to clear the trolley of items before my self-imposed deadline.

There was no doubt that the rebelliousness of my colleagues was at least partially motivated by race. "He can't even speak English properly, how can he be our supervisor?" They would sneer, sometimes mocking his accent. Pre-shift conversations and break times provided frequent opportunities to criticise Abdul's competence and suitability to manage the team.

I never joined in with these criticisms, but neither did I jump to Abdul's defence or challenge their ways of thinking. Although I was reading books on heroes who had stood up to racism and various forms of inequality, I didn't yet have the confidence to share these ideas with the world. I allowed my fears, insecurities and faltering self-confidence to keep my beliefs and opinions in the realm of my mind.

Abdul became more reserved, and would take breaks less and less. As the only other non-white member of the team, Abdul felt he could talk to me about the attitude and behaviour of the other team members. He felt angry that he was being defied so brazenly, hurt that his treatment was undoubtedly connected to his race and cultural background, and embarrassed that he was powerless to change it. I would try to reassure him that he was being fair and reasonable, but I could see his fight and patience being drained.

I found myself caught between two camps.

Would I side with the British people with whom I shared a Birmingham-based dialect and an interest in football and UK politics, or would I prioritise my identity as an ethnic minority and as someone who in my heart wanted to be responsive to the needs of the weak and the powerless?

I said nothing.

Several days later, Abdul handed in his notice.

IV

The focus of the autumn of my gap year was my re-application to Oxford. I continued to borrow or purchase books that I was interested in, such as *The Shackled Continent* by Robert Guest, and *The Trouble with Africa* by Robert Calderisi. Africa fascinated me. In a world that has so much wealth, I couldn't fathom why - according to what I was seeing on TV - one continent could be so poor. I reasoned that the same forces that drove African poverty would also explain the inequalities that I saw growing up.

As I contemplated these questions, I began to realise that PPE was not the subject that held my passions, strengths and interests. Although I cared about politics, what I really loved was understanding how the systems and organisations that powered society could be made to be more effective. I found a subject called Economics and Management, which I thought was a perfect fit for the way that I was now seeing the world. It combined the discipline and mathematics of Economics with studies into the behaviours and optimisation of individuals and organisations. It promised to teach me about the allocation of resources and how better outcomes could be incentivised through understanding the drivers of supply and demand.

I also decided that I would apply to St Peter's College. Ironically, St Peter's was the next page along from St John's in the prospectus. I first read about St Peter's around the time of my first application, but I was already too spellbound by St John's to seriously consider applying anywhere else. This time around, every word seemed to resonate with me. I read that it had been founded by a former Bishop of Liverpool to extend an Oxford education to people from non-typical Oxford backgrounds. It was friendly, informal, and was known for having excellent relations between students and tutors. I hadn't visited St Peter's, but had no hesitation in putting it as my preferred option to read Economics and Management.

I updated my personal statement from the previous year. It was more polished, read more confidently, and had some additional texts and experiences:

A wise man once said that where a person is today is the sum of the books they have read and the people they have met in the last five years. In that case I have made tremendous progress this year, as I have replaced the fantasies of Tolkien's 'Lord of the Rings' and the influence of school friends, with the writings of Adam Smith and the company of politicians. It was never an easy decision to take a Gap Year, but I am reaping the rewards of choosing to gain experience at this juncture in my life. A year ago after reading 'Success in Politics' by John Murray, 'Economics 7th Edition' by McGraw-Hill and 'The Great Philosophers from Socrates to Turing' by Ray Monk, I was certain that PPE offered the best route into the political sphere. However, after spending time in discussion with MPs and councillors, as well as witnessing the pragmatic nature of policy meetings, I now see economics as the bedrock of politics.

Taking a gap year has fuelled my political ambition. I realise that I am only going to be young once and have consequently directed a lot of my time towards impacting the lives of young people through mentoring, organising youth groups and football teams in inner city areas, trying to deal with the problem of school suspensions, and working to dispel the fear created by gangs and postcode rivalries. Having more free time has given me the opportunity to shadow my local councillor, giving me greater insight into the daily lives of politicians and more opportunities to speak at conferences, connect with my local community and help with canvassing. Over the past year I have become a central figure in the 'Let's Talk' initiative, which has organised forums for young people across the West Midlands to discuss issues such as climate change and racism. I was part of a delegation that introduced our project in Leeds and chaired a meeting of over 100 students in Birmingham Council House.

My attitudes in life have been shaped by my strong faith in Christianity and the desire to strive for excellence in everything that I do. Coupled with the skills I have acquired in maths, sociology, history and politics, I feel that I possess the abilities and character to excel in economics. I have taken on positions of responsibility. As a youth leader in my church I have planned various events and initiatives, as well as being in charge of security and catering. I have also taken on voluntary placements at a Salvation Army centre, an accountancy firm and a local primary school, which provided me with an invaluable insight into everyday life for ordinary professionals. As well as volunteering, I have enjoyed paid employment working for the Birmingham Mail, McDonald's and Wilkinson's.

The most recent books I have read have revolved around black history and economics. After being entranced by the biographies of Malcolm X, Muhammad Ali and Nelson Mandela, I completed 'Small Island' by Andrea Levy and ''Capitalism and Slavery' by Eric Williams. The economic heartbeat of 'Capitalism and Slavery' introduced me to the link between black history and economics, which was confirmed when I read 'The Shackled Continent' by Robert Guest and 'The Trouble with Africa' by Robert Calderisi. I then began to discover classical economic theories through reading 'The Wealth of Nations' by Adam Smith.

I am a keen sports fan and will take part in any sport that doesn't involve being submerged under water. I enjoy going to the cinema with friends and playing computer games on my PS2, but I have little time with all the commitments I have undertaken. My experiences over the last year have taught me that while politics and philosophy can be learnt, economics must be taught and I hope I can do this at your university.

I submitted my application before the October deadline and waited. As mid-November passed by I began to grow increasingly anxious. I inspected the linoed area directly below the letter box multiple times per day: first thing in the morning, after arriving home from work and whenever I heard the clang of the front gate. I couldn't bear the thought that I wouldn't be called to interview - that I wouldn't have the chance to right the wrongs of the previous year.

To my relief, the letter arrived on the last Monday in November. It instructed me to travel down to Oxford on Sunday afternoon. I tried to remain calm. I reminded myself that I wouldn't face any abstract philosophical questions; I reminded myself that I needed to have a clear mind so that I could respond well during the interview; and I reminded myself that I possessed 4As at A level and that my place at a top higher education institution was guaranteed.

St Peter's was much smaller than St John's: It had three quads rather than a dozen. It had a dining hall with long tables and wooden benches, but it was more homely than grand. All of its students had their own bedrooms, but most had shared bathrooms rather than the ensuite facilities I enjoyed at St John's. But I liked St Peter's. It carried the presence of an Oxford college but in a manner that was more reassuring than impressive.

As I went to bed that evening, thoughts raced through my mind about what tomorrow's interview would be like. I pictured the large wooden table at St John's and the tweed-suited academic who was likely to sit opposite. I was in a suit; hoping that the smartness of my attire would make a good first impression and add weight to my answers. The interviewer asked me why I wanted to study Economics and Management. They nodded along when I talked about my interest in social issues and my belief that social issues boiled down to being economic issues. I was pleased with how articulate and logical my answers seemed, and was growing in confidence that I could replicate this performance when it mattered most.

The only part of my mental reconstruction that troubled me was the reasoning behind my choice of attire. Did my ideas really need to be clothed in a formal suit and tie in order to be accepted? I realised that my suit was a mask. It hid my fears about the negative way the interviewer would respond if I mispronounced the name of a notable economist. It disguised my belief that I would once again struggle under the merciless conditions of an Oxford interview. And it camouflaged my insecurity that I would have to change myself in order to belong.

I decided that I wanted the interviewers at St Peter's to see who I was, and that I would aim for authenticity not perfection. The following morning, I left my suit in the wardrobe and wore smart dark trousers and an open collared shirt.

I arrived fifteen minutes before the start of the interview. The room was towards the right of an octagonal hallway with five other doors and a large open expanse in the centre. A note on the door asked candidates to take a seat on one of the chairs placed in the centre of the lobby and to wait to be called in. A few moments later, another applicant entered the lobby and walked to the room on the opposite end of the arc. After reading the note on her door, she also took a seat.

We exchanged names: she introduced herself as Fran Hadley, a History hopeful from London. Fran was friendly and very well-spoken; she was certain to make a good first impression, I thought to myself.

We continued our conversation, which ventured into our opinions on Birmingham (she had visited two or three times), politics (she had left-wing leanings but I sensed that she came from a wealthy family) and r'n'b music (I can't recall how we got onto this topic); until the door behind me clicked open. An applicant walked out, followed by a gentleman with glasses and a warm smile who stated that he would invite me into the room in a few moments. The conversation with Fran had been a tremendous help. Rather than spending 15 minutes nervously waiting in silence, I had contributed to an engaging conversation with someone who I considered to be close to the mould of a *typical* Oxford student.

The gentleman returned and introduced himself as Dr Massimo Antonini. I followed him into the room where a second interviewer was sitting in one of the three chairs that had been placed around a low coffee table. She stood to shake my hand and introduced herself as Dr Christine Greenhalgh. The room was an academic's office. Large bookcases lined two of the walls and a further pile of books was perched precariously on a wooden table that had been pushed into the far corner of the room. Dr Christine Greenhalgh began: "This interview is not designed to catch you out. We want to hear about your academic interests and see how you approach new intellectual challenges. There's no rush, so take as much time as you need to give an answer."

Dr Massimo Antonini asked the first question: "Daniel, you have a number of interesting topics and experiences in your personal statement. Can you choose one thing and talk about it?"

This question took me by surprise. In none of my scenarios had the interviewer given me a blank sheet on which to pen my own thoughts. I did a mental scan of the contents of my personal statement but was conscious of not taking too long to decide. I glanced towards my two interviewers and saw no signs of impatience on their faces. So I took a few moments longer. Eventually, I decided to speak about African economic development. This sparked a two-way discussion about barriers to development and the potential for future growth. The latter part of the interview touched on current affairs and traditional economic thinking. I left the interview feeling pleased about the answers I had given and the impression I had made.

AFTER OXFORD

The second interview was on Monday afternoon and was led by Dr Robert Pitkethly, who was the College's Management tutor. Dr Pitkethly's office was located in Oxford's Said Business School, a grandiose cream-coloured building around ten minutes from St Peter's. On the way to his office, I walked down an impressive corridor with a shimmering water feature running down the middle, and large windows on either side revealing the stone exterior courtyard. I climbed two flights of stairs and located the room with the name 'Dr Robert Pitkethly'. I was invited into the room after a few moments and Dr Pitkethly introduced himself and the name of another tutor, Dr Taylor, who was going to assist with the interview.

The interview began with a discussion on organisational strategy and operational efficiency. I gave a number of examples related to being a McDonald's employee: the supervisors who timed staff to ensure that we collected food orders within 8 seconds and who monitored the number of swirls that sat atop our ice-cream cones; and the secret shoppers from McDonald's head office who would berate any store managers where employees had failed to ask them if they wished to upgrade their extra value meal. Dr Pitkethly chuckled along as the discussion moved from my lived experiences to the concept of *McDonaldization*; the belief that tasks can be controlled and rationalised to produce ever-improving efficiency.

The second part of the interview was centred on a number of mathematical examples. The subject matter was *'widgets'*, which I was told by Dr Taylor, were small gadgets or mechanical devices. A number of statistical widget-based problems were presented for me to solve in front of the two interviewers. The first few questions were straightforward, but I quickly encountered an unfamiliar problem. I breathed deeply, looking for clues and information that may lead to a sensible answer. I recognised a pattern and offered an interpretation. Dr Pitkethly smiled, and with that came the end of my two scheduled interviews.

I didn't know if I had done well enough to gain a place at Oxford. The interviews were only 20 minutes each and would only provide a snapshot of my interests and ability. I also couldn't control how well others had performed in their interview. In a fiercely competitive process, I could perform well and still fall short.

But I returned to Birmingham satisfied. I felt that I had delivered on my end and that I had done myself justice.

In the week before Christmas 2007, I received a letter with the return address marked as St Peter's College, Oxford. As I held the envelope, I felt the extra weight of several sheets of paper enclosed.

GHANA INTERLUDE

"If you know your history
Then you would know where your coming from
Then you wouldn't have to ask me
Who the heck do I think I am"

Bob Marley, Buffalo Soldier[3]

The email read 'PLATFORM 2 - FREE OVERSEAS OPPORTUNITY - APPLY TODAY!' I was highly sceptical. I had never before seen the words 'free' and 'overseas opportunity' joined together in a sentence. 'Free' and 'opportunity' were sometimes neighbours but this was usually accompanied by an asterisk or further terms and conditions written in the tiniest of small print.

I opened the email and read the text, which explained that Platform 2 was a volunteering programme funded by the UK government. Young people aged 18-25 from financially disadvantaged backgrounds would have the opportunity to travel abroad for ten weeks in India, Peru or Ghana. All expenses would be paid for and the first trips would depart the UK in a matter of weeks, so I needed to apply within the next 24 hours.

---

[3] Marley, B. and Sporty, K. (1983). *Buffalo Soldier.* Island Records.

My initial reaction was that it had to be a scam. I hadn't heard of this programme and couldn't believe that the government would leave a push for applications down to the final day. But the email address did seem official (dfid.gov.uk) and there were no questions in the enclosed application form that would allow the reader to directly access my bank account, so I figured it was worth the risk. When I came to the question about the country that I would like to visit, I immediately selected Ghana.

The continent of Africa had occupied much of my reading and thinking for well over a year. I read about its political systems, its economic challenges and its rich cultural history. I knew that millions of slaves had been traded from West Africa to the Caribbean; slaves who were people, and people who were connected to me through blood, race and culture. I expected the trip to bring me face to face with the reality of material poverty in a manner that would leave a lasting imprint on my current understanding and my future ambitions. Ghana could be a trip of a lifetime, my pilgrimage to my motherland and the perfect end to my gap year.

I submitted my form the next morning.

The Ghana interlude is a series of extracts, copied word for word, from the daily diary entries that I wrote as an 18-year-old. Reflecting on the diary as a whole, three themes stand out: First, my willingness to think critically about the world around me, even those ideologies (for example, faith and capitalism) that I had been socialised into. Second, the value that I placed on relating to people; whether they were from similar backgrounds to me or not, and regardless of whether our relationship lasted for days, weeks or the duration of a bus journey. Third, the effect that being in a new context had on my soul; which was allowed to feel, encounter and examine life from a previously untouched perspective.

Through its joy and fear, wealth and poverty, faith and pessimism, Ghana would change me for the better.

TUESDAY 20TH MAY 2008
WEISZO

AFTER OXFORD

Welcome to Ghana! Today we were fully immersed into the culture of Ghana and our resident village Gbledi Chebi. We had an official greeting at 7am, where all of the village came out to meet and welcome us. We shook hands with the chief and the elders of the village who were all cordial and friendly. I felt special and honoured to be treated so well.

We ate breakfast at the Ghana Wildlife Society, then began our manual labour. Luckily for us it was a cool day, but this didn't prevent us from sweating a bucket load of water! We cleared an area of rubble using picks and shovels, then raked a dirt area. The work must have taken less than 2 hours including regular breaks, but it was still difficult to maintain a certain level of work. At lunchtime we had mango, red red and plantain while talking about films and TV. Annette from Bunac left for England after lunch, having completed her evaluation of the first week. Morale and companionship is very high among our group. We have become more comfortable around each other because we know our characters, likes and dislikes. Martin is hilarious, although Katy is grating on my nerves for taking too much food, especially given that she eats so little!

The afternoon revolved around familiarising ourselves with our bicycles. I carried on in the same vein as yesterday. I read in a local newspaper about the general election in Ghana and the discovery of oil. It seems that Ghanaians desire a better standard of living. After dinner we cycled from Gbledi Gbogame to Gbledi Chebi. I enjoyed the ride which we took at a steady pace, having a first-hand view of Ghana's plant and insect nation.

On my return to the village, I was greeted by a family I had spent my first evening with. I talked and learned how to crush cassava and fufu using the etu and tata. The elder of our village then took us to his home where we stopped to talk and ask questions about the village. I later returned to give him postcards of Birmingham and to show pictures of my family. The children were ready to greet us again with my lethargy turning into compassion. I only wish I had something to teach them.

All day I have been astounded by the level of hospitality shown to us by the local people of Ghana. They are God-fearing people who are full of love for all people. At the moment I am still trying to learn the language. I know akpe (thank you), medekuku (please), nkonye nye (my name is…), ndi / ndo / fie na wo (good morning / afternoon / evening), fika mek bo (I want to buy), va (come), djo (go) and weiszo (welcome).

And we really have been made to feel welcome!

FRIDAY 6TH JUNE 2008
THE EMPIRE STRIKES BACK

Up until today I had been really impressed with how Ghana had fought back against imperialism, building an independence that was moving from physical liberation into the subconscious of ordinary people. However today we travelled to Cape Coast, the poorest Ghanaian region where the spectre of slavery still looms large for all to see.

Our journey to Cape Coast began at the break of a new day (Friday 12.15 am). While others had stayed awake, I wisely caught some sleep before rolling out of bed to shower and eat breakfast. We caught a tro-tro from Chebi to Hohoe where a government coach was waiting. Bad timekeeping meant that we almost missed the bus, but we boarded just before departure. The 5 hour trip to Accra was more comfortable than I imagined, especially given my previous experiences on Ghanaian public transport. I also had the chance to talk to 19-year-old Samuel, an aspiring doctor / pharmacist on a gap year to save enough money for university. The only disappointing thing is that he wants to practice abroad, leaving behind a country that desperately needs his skills. The problem is that England will always remain 'utopia' for many young Ghanaians, even 50 years after independence. The media is helping the West to strike again at the very heart of Africa's well-being, luring away the young men and women who hold the keys to its future.

We arrived in Accra at around lunchtime in what had been a very long morning! I ate sweet cakey snacks and a 'Bread rose' (omelette sandwich), while almost witnessing a fight between a truck driver and the owner of a motorbike he reversed into. Ghana Man Time (GMT), meant that the bus scheduled for 11.30am to Cape Coast came an hour later and we were relieved to finally arrive at around 4pm. Personally I enjoyed the journey as I poured over *The Emperor of Ocean Park*, the rapidly decreasing pages inviting and almost teasing me into reading more

Once we had located our room, our first task was to find some food to sustain us. Our pursuit took us out of the comfort of our hotel and into the reality of the world around us. The village at Chebi was one thing, you could call their life 'different' as 'deprived' seems too harsh an adjective. But there was no escaping the fact that Cape Coast is deprived. Lines of shacks guard the seafront in a line of silver centurions. Local young men run up to you trying to get money for a football team that doesn't exist (unless it has over 50 members), and in the middle of this stands a statue of Queen Victoria. It is astounding that Cape Coast remains so deprived when it attracts so many tourists, but you feel that the mind-set of fishing / coastal communities (also in Accra) is all wrong, almost as if they expect the ships from the 'Motherland' to come from abroad and subdue them once more.

I'm still in Ghana but this feels like a different place, in which the vice-like grip of imperialism is yet to be loosened.

SATURDAY 7TH JUNE 2008
OCEAN

Buki told me today that looking out into the wide ocean blue - from the vantage point safe on a beach - always reminds her of the existence of God: for only he can create something with such simple complexity. For many Africans centuries ago, the ocean was a place of mystery, which carried the white man to their shores and held the uncertain keys to their destiny. However today, even with advances in technology the majority of the ocean remains undiscovered and unreachable. We feel so in control of our world, yet there are many things we haven't even started to understand.

This morning I awoke at 6am. Knox was sleeping gently in the next bed along from me as the weak Cape Coast sunshine peered through the shutters. I fought with the shower until a train of water spluttered out and cleaned me. We ate breakfast (omelette and toast) in spectacular surroundings: waves crashed on the rocks just below the restaurant and the ocean was stretched farther than the eye could see. Deep blue blotted out the horizon and it once again felt good to be in Africa.

We had altered our mode from volunteer to tourist. Armed with my camera, our first visit was to Kakum National Park, famous for its rope bridges made by two Dutch men, which touched only the highest trees. It was a fantastic spectacle of both architecture and nature. I always felt secure in the hands of rope and cracking boards; even looking overboard to catch the full effect of being up so high. At the end of the walk, I was disappointed by what had been a largely pedestrian experience. While waiting for our journey I helped myself to a doughnut and talked to some annoying Americans.

By 2pm we had left Kakum and were on our way to Elmina. On our way we stopped to see crocodiles at a high quality restaurant. Initially they seemed too stiff to be real, but sprang into action as we were leaving. I was pleased to get these visits out of the way, because Elmina Castle was the chief reason I wanted to go to Cape Coast. There was a strange aura surrounding a building which had openly entertained human atrocity in its worst form, a 'trade' which relocated 4 million people from Africa and killed twice as many. Walking around the dungeons and cells, I couldn't believe that man would commit such evils to each other. What shocked me most was the role of Christianity in Elmina Castle. I couldn't believe that there was a church in a building that also condoned rape and murder. Wake up people! How can you justify your acts? I felt a deep sadness, not just for black people, but for the human race - that we had sunk so low.

Britain is an ocean away from Ghana and Africa's past is a long time ago from the present, but the first will always influence the latter and lingers longer in the subconscious.

SUNDAY 8TH JUNE 2008
THE CASTLE

I will never be able to comprehend slavery. I cannot understand how a slave owner could rationalise and justify his actions, usually while 'worshipping' God on the same premises! But more importantly, I cannot try to imagine life for the countless millions of slaves, plucked from their life into circumstances not even comparable to death. I suppose the castles at Elmina and Cape Coast give us deeper insight into the first horrific stage on a perilous journey.

I gingerly took a shower in the freezing water before having toast for breakfast, purely so that I could take my malaria tablet. Waiting around in reception gave me ample time to think about Elmina yesterday and to prepare for the castle today. What stuck out most was how Christianity seemed to collaborate with the slave trade, rather than being the tool to convict consciences of unrighteousness. Religion is so dangerous because it clouds the true reason behind God's love - to change us.

We visited Cape Coast just before 11.30am. The white exterior needed a drop of paint, but architecturally it was much more impressive than Elmina. Walls laden with cannons showed Britain's determination to protect themselves against foreign enemies; playing games with Africa. We were given a tour around the castle, and were shown the place where women were raped, and the church that was located in the castle! Some people will go on this tour and begin to hate white people, I felt no such animosity. As I wrote in the book of comments "It was interesting looking into my past, but it's important that the past doesn't have an adverse effect on our future."

One Nigerian woman should have read my note: when she heard that Zina was mixed-race and English, she exclaimed (in all seriousness) "I'm really sorry for you. You have no roots!" The woman herself was quite light-skinned and probably going through a crisis of identity herself. On the tour a man asked whether anything good ever came from slavery. I found this question interesting - perhaps a positive is that this is unlikely to ever happen again.

After the visit to the castle we took a trip across town to a beach. There was a local beach close to our accommodation but a lack of regular cleaners left it filthy. The second beach was clean, beautiful and surprisingly sparse of Ghanaians'. After tiring myself out playing football and beach ball, I took a long walk to give myself time to reflect.

I will leave Cape Coast with mixed emotions. Kakum National Park and the two castles will be high among the most memorable moments of this trip, but I am relieved to be leaving. I hate being a tourist, when we are here to make a difference. I was disappointed by what I saw in Cape Coast, their attitude was so wrong. They have Ghana's most attractive tourist places but have squandered the opportunity to build wealth. It is almost as if the ships bound for Europe took physical bodies and the spirit of that area.

TUESDAY 17TH JULY 2008
A DAY MADE IN HEAVEN

On a trip of this length it is not always possible to choose a 'best day'. But unless something incredible happens over the next few days, today will take the accolade. It wasn't a perfect day by any means; I had plenty of people asking me to 'remember them' i.e. send them money or a PS3! At times their requests became annoying especially given that I'm a 19-year-old boy with a £10k per year bill to pay to Oxford! But what else would I do in their situation? Hopefully in the future I will be in a position to help them.

With a free morning I decided to do my rounds of the village, possibly for the last time. I talked with the Chebi football team about today's rematch with Gbogame, then went to Bretus' house and talked with him in depth about the PolyTech University and the course of his choice - he wants to do Electrical Engineering in Ho. He has the same fears as all the villagers in Chebi: there are no jobs. All people do is farming; if they have collected enough on previous days they do nothing! For a time this relaxed attitude would be welcome, but as an existence? I felt so sad in a local kitchen watching as young people and women prepared breakfast. But on the other hand, what kind of existence do we have in the West? Living to work, not working to live as people in Chebi do.

It happened today that Bretus' and 'Smiling Boy's' families needed bamboo, so I accompanied them to their farm (agbele). Using my machete I joined them in smoothing bamboo stalks, slicing whole bamboos and bringing them down to earth from lofty and awkward positions. While farming, Bretus told me that he had learnt so much from my life and kindness. I thank God for equipping me with the attributes to be an example to these young men - I know that they will remember me, the words I have spoken and the life I have led.

Just as we were enjoying each other's company Knox came to inform me that we had to begin our evaluation meeting. Evaluations are always a sign of an imminent end which is probably why I entered the meeting in a negative frame of mind. My mood was worsened when Knox told the group that we might not be leaving Chebi on Saturday morning but instead on Monday. However, by the end of the day I began to look forward to two more days in a village I had come to love. The evaluation process was shockingly poor, we were given a questionnaire to complete as a group when the vast majority of questions were personal. The evaluation process had taken us far beyond lunchtime and we arrived at the wildlife sanctuary hungry, but eagerly anticipating the afternoon.

Hanson, the guards, Christina, Faustina and Pearl were seated around a large table. Hanson thanked us for our hard work and discipline; although he and I and everyone present knows that things could and should have been better. Deciding against a public squabble we chose to save points of conflict for another time and enjoy a farewell dinner together. Drinks were on the house and went well with our dinner: jollof rice, fufu, goat and groundnut soup. I used this chance to talk for the last time to the guards: William, Marcel, David, Fred and Geoffrey who all appreciated my hard work and dedication. Togbe spent his time talking to Martin: he finds me boring. With Kerri feeling sick and the kick off for Chebi vs Gbogame almost upon us we returned to Chebi.

Before the game, I prayed to God and asked that he would help me to have a good game. My daily performances in training and games had warranted me a place in attack. I'm not sure of our formation but I played as the main striker with Kosi on the right and Patrick on the left. The first half was relatively uneventful. I won a lot of headers and provided lots of flick ons and had a half opportunity charged down. We wasted a few chances but none was as clear cut as the one Robert blazed over from 6 yards out. At the start of the second half the game was more stretched and I made the vital breakthrough, swivelling onto a loose ball on the edge of the box and sending a curling shot past the dive of the goalkeeper. It felt great! I fell onto my knees and was felled by a crowd of fans and teammates. The goal gave us more confidence and made Gbogame more nervous and hurried. Patrick scored two more goals: the first a tight offside decision, the other when he capitalised on a defensive error - both goals were celebrated by wild scenes which I thoroughly enjoyed. Gbogame were clearly shattered and tempers spilled over into an on field brawl which William did well to control.

Close to the end I sacrificed myself to take on some well needed fluids and to give our team a more defensive outlook. Valiant Khalid who played right wing was also replaced. Gbogame then pulled a consolation goal back to make the result 3-1. Gbogame were gracious in defeat. After the game I presented both teams with a football and William warned them about their future conduct.

After the game I was on cloud nine. I kept my humility by thanking God. When I emerged from the shower some of the team were waiting to interrogate me on why I had given a ball to both communities. I explained that it was not a prize for the winners but a gift for both villages. The talk was peaceful and understood by all parties. Back at the house people were dancing to the Hip Life CD I had bought for Martin. Half of the group had gone drinking; Katy, Martin and possibly Staci were drunk. I almost forgot - Khalid had given a cedi to every child in the village (totalling about 50 cedis!) Khalid is generous and a good person.

So one, maybe three days left in Chebi! Wow! I'll really miss this place.

CHEBI v Gbogame (17/7/08)

Kojo

Bretus	Anthony	Edu	Koku
	Khalid	Kojovi	Alex
	Kosi	Daniel (me)	Patrick

AFTER OXFORD

Goals: Chebi - Daniel, Patrick (2)
Gbogame - Aka

Cards: 0
Attendance: 150
Venue: Chebi Park

WEDNESDAY 23RD JULY 2008
THE END

Everything that begins must have an end. This morning I woke up on a plane, deep into my journey home. Before Frankfurt I sat next to a Nigerian woman who spoke to me about her son and Canada, sometimes in Yoruba even though I had told her I didn't speak it. Somehow I managed to make sense of her words to have an interesting conversation. I enjoyed the plane food and the movie I watched, *Step Up 2*. The plot was predictable (like *Save the Last Dance, Coach Carter etc.*) but the dance battles compensated for the lack of originality. I slept for the remainder of the flight which took me out of the Motherland and back to Europe.

I could immediately tell the difference between Africa and Europe. The airport at Frankfurt was professional but dreary and people walked around with troubled looks on their faces. The steward I asked for help was rude and didn't even listen to my question. Back on the plane I conversed with a German woman who had several children studying in England (she was attending a graduation), and before I knew it, my feet were back on English soil / tarmac after 10 weeks away. We strode in amazement to pick up our luggage and exit the airport. Katy's whole family were waiting with a sign ready to take her home. The whole group wished each other well and said our goodbyes. In WHSmiths Martin bought me a Barack Obama book.

It was hard to say goodbye to people I had come to admire and love. Martin and I were left together as the only passengers taking a coach to Birmingham. The 2.5 hour journey was in tropical conditions thanks to a broken heater and my mind drifted back to the tro-tro experience! But time always goes quickly with Martin: we read a newspaper, discussed our futures and tried to analyse the behaviour of some of our fellow travellers over the past ten weeks. On our arrival I hugged Martin then joined my dad to drive home. Back to reality.

Mum cried when I came through the door. They had put up a sign reading 'Welcome home Daniel.' For the rest of the day I enjoyed food: kebab and chips for lunch; pizza, pies and cake for dinner. In between I watched a rerun of the Man Utd vs Chelsea Champions League final on the PC, beat Matthew 6-4 in a FIFA re-enactment of the game and listened to Sammy G's hip hop / rap album.

I went through the vast array of photos with my family and reflected on a brilliant 10 weeks I will never forget. But I am glad to be back home, in my house, with my family. They were overjoyed to see me and warmly received my gifts and souvenirs. We had a toast for my return before enjoying the all action film *The Bourne Ultimatum*. It feels so strange being at home... It feels like I was never away!

I've had a great 10 weeks full of adventure and experience but alas it has ended. As everything must.

I was born on 3 June 1989 to my parents Mark and Millicent Stone who created a loving household full of laughter, creativity and clear behavioural guidelines. My childhood was full of games and sport taught me some important lessons about getting on with others. but I also developed a strong work ethic and was committed to always giving my best effort with the aim of obtaining the best results.

I struggled to assert myself at the beginning of my time at Hamstead Hall but eventually excelled, gaining 7A*s and 3As at GCSE. Above: At the entrance to Top playground. From left to right: Paul, Richard Johnson, Riyomi, Tobias, Ashley, Nathan and me.

My ten weeks in Ghana were an incredibly transformative period in my life: Eating fufu with Knox; Me with the other Platform 2 volunteers; Organising the community fun day in Gbledi Chebi; Having a time of quiet reflection at Cape Coast Castle.

My mentor, local councillor and friend, Councillor Paulette Hamilton helped me to believe in myself and the ability I had to make a positive contribution to the world. I would go on to become an active campaigner for Paulette and the Labour Party.

My grandparents' generation were notorious for not smiling in photographs. My dad's parents Selvyn and Brynel Stone in a more relaxed mood while my dad played with me.

My grandmother, Phyllis Williams at my graduation; Joanna and Selina on either side of us. Far right: with my parents on my graduation day.

DANIEL STONE

DURING OXFORD

THE FIRST TERM

"If you know the enemy and know yourself, you need not fear the result of a hundred battles. If you know yourself but not the enemy, for every victory gained you will also suffer a defeat. If you know neither the enemy nor yourself, you will succumb in every battle."

- Sun Tzu, The Art of War[4]

I knew how much my acceptance into Oxford meant for my community.

When grocery shopping, I would see someone speaking to my parents while pointing in my direction. My parents would beckon for me to come over and I would reluctantly push my trolley towards them, annoyed that this conversation was likely to add more time to an already tedious shopping trip. However, I was aware of the responsibilities I had to be a good ambassador of this good news, so I replaced my impatience with a polite smile. "Well done!" They would say cheerily as they shook my hand longer than I thought was necessary.

Turning to my parents, they would gush, "You've done an excellent job Mark and Millicent." My parents would respond with a hint of embarrassment: "We're blessed to have good kids. They've always worked hard and we don't

---

[4] Tzu, S. (1964). *The Art of War*. Oxford: Clarendon Press.

know where they get their brains from!" This would always make me smile. I was glad that my achievements had reflected well on my parents and I admired my parents for humbly deferred praise back towards me.

The conversation would continue and if this friend also happened to be a parent, they would introduce me to their children as 'the one' who was going to Oxford. I'm not sure how much sense many of these children made of this fact, but they knew enough to mirror being both shocked and impressed. I was pleased that my achievements were being used to inspire people who were younger than me but I was also wary of the lessons that others had taken from my journey.

I had already been called to the stage several times at Mount Zion Community Church to tell the congregation the name of the university where I would begin studying in the autumn. On every occasion, the Senior Pastor at Mount Zion, Calvin Young, had bookended my story with the rhetorical question: "Can anything good come out of Handsworth?"

It was a question laced with pride and defiance.

At the time black boys, often from inner city areas like Handsworth, were being demonised for being knife-wielding, womanising thugs who were at constant risk of expulsion from school. I was providing a story with a very different ending. The fact that I had been educated in a comprehensive secondary school had added to the narrative that I could have been anyone's son, grandson, nephew or neighbour. But while recognising the significance of what I had achieved, I didn't want my success to erase the struggles of my peers or the failings of the education system as a whole.

If people would use my achievements as a reason to prevent individual soul searching and to ignore the need for reform, then I thought it was better for me to keep silent.

As the time drew nearer for me to leave for Oxford, I began to imagine what it would be like to be a full-time student at St Peter's. This partly served a practical purpose. In order to begin packing, I needed to imagine the scenarios I would be in; playing football required football boots, I would need a new suit for formal dinners and I wondered if I should bring my Xbox 360?

Armed with the memories of my interview, I couldn't help but picture myself in my bedroom or the St Peter's Junior Common Room or walking towards the dining hall. In my imagination, I seemed settled and engaged in activities I enjoyed doing.

A letter from St Peter's had provided further information about what to expect: a demanding workload, high academic standards and an induction week free of classes, which had been given the colloquial term *freshers' week*. There were around five or six non-negotiable activities that I had highlighted prior to my arrival in Oxford. There was a Christian Union meeting on Wednesday, the freshers' fair on Thursday, the mandatory freshers' dinner on Friday, football trials on Saturday and a series of club nights throughout the week including something called a 'foam party'.

A St Peter's freshers' week Facebook page had been set up for all new starters and a number of people were eagerly posting comments throughout the day. I had nothing particularly insightful to add, nor did I have any questions that I thought another fresher could answer. So I stayed quiet.

Someone called Mike Lomas used the page to cautiously ask if "anyone fancied going for a drink" once we arrived in Oxford. The comment was ridiculed by others in the group who were quick to point out the numerous pubs in Oxford as well as the existence of the St Peter's College bar. But Mike's comment revealed the fears that we all had about the hyper-intellectualised culture that we had fought so hard to get into. How high would these *high academic standards* be and what would happen if the ledge was too high for me to climb?

I thought back to the start of my A level Further Maths and reminded myself to remain calm; I would be OK, I just had to work hard and give myself time.

In the week before I left for Oxford, I agreed to meet with some of my friends from Mount Zion Community Centre. We planned to meet in a bar in town to watch football and play pool, but in a thoughtless moment, I'd forgotten my ID. I pleaded with the doorman who had approved the ID of half a dozen young men before me.

The doorman looked me up and down. "Sorry, you're not getting in without ID." I turned away dismayed. I knew that when a doorman said 'no' it usually stayed that way and I had already started wondering if I should leave the guys to enjoy their evening.

As I was contemplating my response, Aaron jumped to my defence. "He's telling the truth. He's going to Oxford University next week!" Aaron smirked, slightly surprised that these words had come out of his mouth.

But the expression of the doorman began to change. "Oxford, really?" I nodded. "Alright, come in."

In the days following, I pondered why the doorman had responded in this way. Perhaps he reasoned that it would be unlikely for someone to think of such an outlandish lie and that it therefore must be true. But connected to this response was the instant association that someone going to Oxford must be worthy of a certain degree of trust and respect. Oxford was already opening doors; in a place where I had least expected it and before I'd even attended a class.

I

My dad helped me to unload the boxes and suitcases from the car into my room in Matthews' Block. Matthews' was the older of the two main first year accommodation blocks in St Peter's. Unlike the glass fronted and contemporary designed New Block, Matthews' was pragmatically designed with a natural brick interior and relatively plain square rooms. While bathrooms in Matthews' had to be shared between three or four users, showering facilities in New were ensuite, which would become a sore point for students over the coming weeks. My bedroom was just above the JCR, the main social meeting space in the College.

After my dad had said goodbye - my mum and siblings couldn't fit in the car alongside all of my belongings - I walked down to the JCR, wearing my favourite outfit; a purple Adidas t-shirt with a fluorescent green trefoil, a bright green Adidas hoodie, dark blue jeans and green Adidas trainers. Most people were fully engaged in conversations; some sat on blue sofa-like chairs, others stood in small groups of three or four. I hung by the door and nervously scanned the room. I noticed that no-one was dressed in sports' apparel; most were in neat sweaters or casual jumpers.

As I looked over towards the large windows to the right of the JCR, I spotted someone standing on their own next to a table. After sidestepping the multiple ongoing conversations, we shook hands and exchanged names.

"What school are you from?" Alex asked.

"I'm from Birmingham" I replied, slightly nonplussed that the conversation had bypassed introductory questions like *Where are you from?* And *What are you studying?* "I went to a school called Hamstead Hall, but you probably wouldn't have heard of it?"

He shook his head. As the conversation returned to more expected topics, it turned out that Alex was a second-year History student who was on the freshers' week committee. Alex encouraged me to mingle with students in my year group and pointed me in the direction of a male student with dusty blonde hair who had just entered the JCR.

"I'm Daniel" I said, stretching out my hand.

"Tom. What school are you from?" There was the question again. After several more school based starter questions, I realised that this was a pointer towards the students who had arrived at Oxford via one of the notable, mainly London-based private schools.

The fact that someone may have come from outside of London or from a comprehensive school was something of an afterthought. But I saw that people had been programmed to start the conversation in this manner, as a warped socially acceptable ice-breaker. So I would move the conversation on swiftly to discuss more conventional things like the week's activities or football.

Halfway through a conversation about Manchester United, a figure standing next to the door of the JCR called the room to order. He introduced himself as Sanjay Nanwani, a second year PPE student, and the JCR President. Sanjay welcomed the new students on behalf of the JCR Committee and invited everyone to go to the white tent on Chavasse Quad after dinner for an evening of fun and games.

As I entered the tent with my neighbours in Matthew's Block, Guy and Richard, we found around a quarter of our year group sat on the floor in rows of eight people about to take part in a 'boat race'. Each member of the crew had a bottle or large beaker of an alcoholic beverage in their hands ready for the starter's pistol.

Once the race began, the first person would guzzle their drink as quickly as possible then the person behind them would commence and so and so on until everyone on the boat had reached the bottom of their vessels. I watched on in fascination as the boat race began. After the first leg, the four teams were neck and neck. The second drinker in, the third boat from the left began to falter and his team mates began to shout and jostle him from behind, hopeful that their efforts would force his oesophagus into submission. Halfway through the race, the boat closest to me was pulling further and further away, each person efficiently 'downing' their drinks in around five seconds flat. I recognised the last person as Fran Hadley. She jumped to her feet and lifted her arms triumphantly; the whole boat shouting in unison.

I rarely drank alcohol at home. Bailey's, Advocaat and mulled wine were Christmas treats and occasionally my mum would bake a cake doused in dark rum that filled my stomach with a warm, comforting aroma. But my parents had made it clear that alcohol was never to be consumed in excess: "You'll lose your senses," they warned. "You could end up doing something you regret or putting yourself in danger."

At Hamstead Hall, some of my peers had taken part in drinking sessions in the woods that had left them temporarily paralysed; unable to walk or construct sentences. I saw no appeal in putting myself in a comatose state; especially not among a group of strangers who I didn't yet know or trust.

"Do you want a drink?" Guy asked.

I paused for a moment. "Yeah, I'll have a J2O."

"A J2O?" Guy echoed, a slightly confused look on his face.

"Yeah, I'm teetotal," I responded. Guy and Richard raised their eyebrows in surprise, then nodded their heads to signal that they understood.

AFTER OXFORD

And so I spent my freshers' week alcohol free. In my sobriety, I had come to the conclusion that the DJs at the student club nights had gone out of their way to select music that couldn't be danced to or enjoyed. I wasn't expecting a full set of r'n'b and hip hop but I had reasoned that they would play popular chart music rather than an endless drone of indistinguishable noise.

Alcohol had removed the inhibitions and reservations from the other freshers. They were talking freely, moving in unsequenced motion to the music and hanging loosely unto each other's shoulders. I was conscious that I was missing out on an important bonding experience with my peers; in the morning they would have tales to tell of *getting with* other freshers or of the pigeon they fought with on the way back from the kebab shop (true story). But if the price I had to pay to have these stories was inebriation, then I thought the cost was too high. There would be other ways that I could make friends. I finished my coke then headed out of the club and into the cold night.

I decided to skip the next club night in favour of playing board games. I recognised some of the faces in the JCR from the Christian Union event I attended earlier in the day. One of the attendees, James, was sitting in front of a blue plastic frame and beckoned to me to join him in a game of Connect 4. I took the seat opposite and picked up a yellow circular counter, placing it carefully and strategically into slots while speaking to James about his background and the church he was intending to attend in Oxford. On Sunday I accompanied James to St Ebbe's, which was a traditional Anglican church with hymn books and pews. The week after, I went to St Aldates, which had a live band and student focused services with bean bags.

In comparison to the Pentecostal church of my upbringing, both were reserved and splintered by moments of complete silence. In Mount Zion, the strumming and drumming of the band and the singing of the worship leaders would get louder and louder in praise to God. The atmosphere of worship was built on a wall of sound. But here, it relied on stillness.

Stillness that forced the believer to respond soberly and consciously rather than being swept along on a wave of emotion. I thought there were strengths to both approaches and concluded that before I chose a church, I would explore other styles and forms of worship.

I visited the Pentecostal churches on the outskirts of Oxford, which provided comforting familiarity. However, attending the church would require me to make a 90 minute round trip every Sunday with a 3-hour service wedged in between. I visited an Elim Church for a number of weeks and a Baptist Church and a Methodist Church.

The most unusual experience I had was in a Brethren's Church, which had a congregation of no more than 30 people. Hymns were sung from a tidy red book, prayers were scattered regularly throughout the service and the sermon was concise and of a similar theme to the songs and prayers that had preceded it. I spoke to one of the members after the service.

"How did you find the service?" Philip asked.

"I really enjoyed it," I began. This was my default answer to anyone who asked me about their church service. "I thought it was really interesting how the service flowed along one theme."

"You know it wasn't planned?" Philip grinned. "Well it was, but it wasn't, if you know what I mean?"

I had no idea what Philip meant. "It wasn't planned?"

"Yes, we all sit in silence and when you hear God speak to you, you can stand up and start a song or say a prayer or read a passage from the bible." I noticed that people had taken their seats in between each song or recitation but I thought that this was primarily to facilitate the silent worship that I had also observed at St Aldates and St Ebbes.

I also noticed another trend: "Do you have to be a man to speak in church?"

"Yes," Philip said. "In accordance with Paul's instructions that *it is shameful for women to speak in church.*" I looked away and Philip could sense my awkwardness. "Will you come back next Sunday?" This was the inevitable conclusion to every conversation I had taken part in at the churches I had visited. I could understand that church members were keen to add to their number and to validate their particular style of worship but I had no intention of returning. I would usually explain that I was touring churches in Oxford and would be in a congregation of a different Christian tradition next week, but I wanted to move on from my conversation with Philip as quickly as possible.

"Yes, I should do," I lied.

II

The next night was the foam party. I intentionally reserved my freshers' week t-shirt for this event, anticipating that any items of clothing worn to the party were doomed for destruction. Our short sleeved t-shirts were bright yellow with green sleeves, a green collar and a green image of the St Peter's College mascot, a squirrel, tattooed on the front.

The start of the foam party had begun in a similar fashion to the club nights that had gone before it; drinking games and awful music. After about an hour or so, a voice on the tannoy instructed us to take our places in the foam pit. To reach the pit you had to walk from the bar on ground level, down four or five steps onto the dancefloor. On opposite corners of the cuboid pit were two large cannons. I stood shoulder to shoulder with my comrades as the countdown began.

"10, 9" the announcer began.

We picked up the theme and chanted along: "8, 7, 6."

"ARREEE YOU READDDDY FRESSSHERS?!" He hollered, while we stuck to the numerical descent. "2, 1."

Suddenly the cannons burst into life and began to rotate, gushing uncontrollable quantities of foam into the pit from all angles. Within seconds my clothes were soaked. I was losing visibility and could only barely make out yellow human-shaped smudges to my right and to my left. Gasping for air, I trod carefully across the slippery floor, levering bodies of foamed mess out of the way until I reached the metal handrail that marked the edge of the dancefloor. I followed it around in a straight line, holding firmly onto it while stepping around anyone in my path. The handrail suddenly veered upwards and I realised that I was at the stairs. I climbed quickly, rubbing the soap out of my eyes and looking down at the mountain of foam below.

I was standing next to Una Kim, the only female in a group of five people studying Economics and Management at St Peter's. Una was over a foot shorter than me and had just escaped being drowned or trampled in the foam induced melee. I was astonished that most people had remained in the pit, gradually getting wetter and wetter, while losing control of all of their senses.

The following day, most of my year group had contracted hives and were complaining about how unhygienic the pit had been. I shrugged my shoulders unsympathetically.

This also happened to be the day of the freshers' dinner. Freshers' dinner was a precursor to the start of academic relationships and academic work, and the real reason why we had applied to Oxford. Our tables were organised by subject meaning that I would be seated with those who were studying Economics and Management, as well as the sole History and Economics joint honours student called Ben. Along with Una and Mike Lomas, the other E&M students were Tendai and Daniel Rozier, who went by 'Dan', which was useful in preventing potentially confusing situations. We identified each other as fellow E&M students on Monday and spent much of the week together.

Una was strong-willed and didn't suffer fools, but we got on really well. Mike was pleased to have found several people who were willing to *go for a drink* and was a down to earth person who I immediately got on with. Dan was initially the quietest of the bunch but over time revealed his dark sense of humour, which would leave us writhing in laughter and pain and disgust, all at the same time. Tendai had an infectious personality and was the life, and invariably the death, of any party.

We were all keen to make a good first impression. Tendai joked that the dinner was our opportunity to prove to our tutors that they hadn't made a mistake in giving us a place. I was less pessimistic; I saw it as an opportunity to interact as people before the dynamic of tutor-student had been set in stone.

Pre-dinner drinks were at 7pm and dinner would be served at 7.30. As the clock ticked towards the hour, I was still agonising over what outfit to wear. I had a dark suit hung neatly in my wardrobe but next to it was a hand-sewn outfit made from the brown cloth with cream emblems that I had picked out in a market in Kumasi, Ghana. This suit carried the scent of Africa; of vibrant colours, warmth and hospitality. It hung perfectly across my shoulders, reflecting the time and attention that had gone into tailoring this suit specifically for me. I walked to the mirror and held both suits up to my neck.

When I entered the dining hall at 7.10, there was a hum of conversations reverberating around the room. Tutors and students were arranged in small circles with slowly emptying glasses in their hands. I tried to locate my course mates among the melee of faces, black suits and colourful dresses. As I scanned the room, I realised that several conversations had halted and that some of the groups were staring in my direction. Some with looks of bemusement and others with smirks on their faces. I saw Dr Antonini towering over a group of suited backs - he was a lot taller than I remembered at the interview. He greeted me warmly as I strode over: "That's an interesting outfit," he remarked. The conversation in the semi-circle had stopped and Tendai shook his head in disbelief. "I bought it in Ghana," I pronounced.

It turned out that Dr Antonini and Dr Greenhalgh had both done significant research into African economic development. They were entertained by my stories of planting cocoa in a Wildlife Reserve and pounding fufu with families in a rural village. I breathed a sigh of relief. My decision to come to an Oxford dinner clothed in the outfit and perspective that I thought represented me best had not backfired. Intellectual curiosity had beaten unwritten tradition.

III

Lectures at Oxford were the rare moment where I would interact with Economics students outside of St Peter's. Hundreds of students would descend on the West Hall of Oxford Examination Schools for an hour long lecture delivered by individuals whose moniker was likely to have graced the spine of renowned textbooks, the Queen's New Year's honours list or the latest copy of the Financial Times. My early lectures were delivered under the shadow of the 2008 financial crash and were often concluded by phrases such as *but the financial crash has shown…* It was fascinating to be in a time where foundational knowledge was so openly and necessarily critiqued.

The first term did provide a significant academic challenge for me to overcome. The quantity of work was fearsome. We had a weekly tutorial in Management and a weekly tutorial in Economics and additional classes in Maths and Statistics. For each tutorial I was required to either complete a question set or prepare an essay of around 2000 words from a reading list of at least a dozen texts. The tutorials were at most three students to one tutor and so any attempts to skirt around the edges of core subject knowledge were certain to be exposed. The looming prospect of my first tutorial meant that I approached my first reading list with a determination to read everything on it. After all, what if my tutor referred to a text or idea that I hadn't read?

I calculated that in order to complete the work required in any given week I would need to spend roughly three days on each essay, leaving the seventh day for Maths or as a cherished day of rest. I was about to enter my third day of Management reading and still had several substantial texts that I hadn't yet begun. I returned to the library after breakfast, hiding myself among a fortress of Management books. Progress was still glacial but I was comforted by the fact that I wasn't alone in my struggles. Tendai and Dan soon joined me in the library and a few moments later, Mike and Una. We agreed to exchange notes on the reading we had done so far and then set about writing an essay.

A few days later, I walked the familiar route to Dr Pitkethly's office with Dan and Tendai. After knocking on the door, I pushed cautiously at the handle, opening the door enough to see Mike and Una picking up their bags and coats and heading towards me. I stood to the side as they walked by, Una sending a comforting smile in my direction.

Three walls of Dr Pitkethly's office were lined with tall bookshelves and exotic plants. If the fourth wall hadn't been a window, I was certain another two bookshelves would have lined that wall too. Dr Pitkethly sat in a high seat facing the door and beckoned for us to sit down. I removed my coat and took the seat to the farthest right of Dr Pitkethly; Dan being in the middle and Tendai to the left.

"So... Welcome." Dr Pitkethly began, shifting in his chair. "I hope you've settled well into life at St Peter's and that you're not too tired from the week's extra-curricular activities." He peered over his glasses, raising his eyebrows in a kidding manner before continuing:

"The work you'll produce at university will be very different to what was expected at A level. Give yourself time and you'll be fine." He paused and looked at each one of us intently, searching for evidence that we had internalised this advice. I nodded my head calmly. "So… How did you find the first week?"

"It was really interesting," Tendai jumped in. "I thought the Mintzberg article was fascinating. You know. I thought his analogy of the left foot following right, and how that links to organisational effectiveness and progress was so insightful." I glanced over to Tendai and could see his brain desperately fighting to maintain pace as he fired out more opinions.

Dr Pitkethly nodded along and after a few more breathless moments from Tendai, interjected. "Thank you Tendai." He looked over towards Dan and me. I was certain that he was going to ask me a pointed question about one of the books I hadn't read. "Now remind me, who is Daniel and who is Dan?"

"I'm Daniel," I responded, relieved to have answered my first tutorial question correctly.

"Thank you, Daniel. Tell me, what did you find interesting about this week's reading?"

I realised that rather than the content of tutorials being dictated by the tutor, Dr Pitkethly would encourage us to lead the discussion and to share the observations and conclusions that had emerged from the texts. Unlike the A level syllabus, which largely required students to fill their brain with prescribed knowledge and then regurgitate it in essay form, studies at Oxford would be a journey of exploring and pursuing my own thoughts and interests and interpreting these thoughts and interests through the language of economic models and management theories. Several days later, my marked essay was returned to me in the St Peter's internal post. I had been given a mark of 62.

I was content with this mark. I understood that marks were normalised differently at university. A first class essay was any submission that was given a percentage of 67% or above. Exceptional essays were graded in the mid-70s and marks of 80% or above were a thing of mythology. 62 wasn't too bad, and besides, I wrote my first essay without knowing the rules of the game.

Over the next few weeks, my course mates and I discussed how we could boost our marks to an upper second class degree and eventually to a first. We worked harder. We included texts outside of the reading list. We revised our essay structure. We were critical and we were reflective. But the threshold of 67% still had not been broken.

The fourth Management essay of the term was on Strategic Management. We had been given free license to interpret the texts on the reading list within the context of a company. I had chosen Nintendo and the Wii console. It had bucked the trend of ever more expensive consoles and had emphasised the joy of playing with others as its unique selling point. As I did the reading for the essay, I couldn't wait to begin writing it. I especially loved the introductory paragraph of an essay. It was always the most liberated section of my 2000 word submission; full of metaphors and wit. After the first paragraph I was instructed to follow the conventional rules of essay writing: argument followed counter argument and assertions followed definitions in a way that cultivated thoroughness rather than originality.

However the Nintendo essay had been different. I enjoyed crafting the substance of my essay while weaving in research and evidence from additional sources. I produced what was, up until that point, my best work; an essay titled *Wii Will Rock You*, which I proudly handed in at my next tutorial.

My essay was returned to me several days later in the internal pigeon post system with 71% circled in red letting.

During the first term, most of my essays hovered around the upper end of the upper second class degree mark. Some of my tutors enjoyed my lucid writing style and would duly reward me with higher marks, while others - usually those external to St Peter's - were exasperated by what they saw to be my lack of structure and cogency.

One of my tutors went as far as to strongly suggest that I purchase a book on essay writing. He would follow each of my submissions with a cutting comment that *he was yet to see evidence that I had adopted the learning in the book*. These comments stung but I had a more balanced view of my progress. I sensed that I was improving and that I was learning how to manage my time more effectively

For example, I learned that the abstract or summary of an article was the best way of determining its relevance and could also provide a fall back option for any texts that hadn't been read pre-tutorial. And as students, we were usually great at covering for each other when we saw our tutorial partner floundering or in need of a new observation to subtly change the topic of conversation.

With the support of Dan, Mike, Tendai and Una, I had successfully made it out of base camp and was ready to continue the ascent towards the expected high academic standards.

IV

I got on well with my course mates but I also knew that my mental, social and emotional wellbeing would be enhanced if I could find people from similar cultural backgrounds to my own. The fact was that Oxford had a culture that was largely built on white middle class values, behaviours and expectations. As someone of Afro-Caribbean heritage, my culture was not the norm. Very few people would understand my cultural references, empathise with my perspective or comprehend my history.

I recall a conversation with someone in my year who asked me why my surname was 'Stone' and not one of African lineages. He was horrified to learn that slave owners would brand their slaves with their surname to reinforce their status as property to be owned and traded.

As a minority in the UK, I had learned how to assimilate into the majority white-orientated culture. I knew how to gloss over my culture, how to suppress contributions that the dominant majority wouldn't be able to relate to, and how to educate my peers on black history in a manner that wouldn't point the finger of blame either for historical events that were outside of their control or for their unwillingness to remove their ignorance since.

But from time to time I would need to allow this part of myself to breathe. It is a concept that is impossible to intellectualise for someone who has never been a minority, but I would need to be around people who would 'get me' without explanation or falsehood. Put simply, for at least some of the time, I needed to be around other black people.

And so when I entered the freshers' fair organised by the Oxford University Student Union to showcase the range of student societies and groups across Oxford, I did so with the intention of signing up for the Afro Caribbean Society. On the way in, representatives from local businesses had lined the streets, giving away student deals to club nights and for Domino's Pizza.

Inside there were hundreds of stalls spread over four or five rooms. As I entered one room, I saw a male student with light brown skin, his arms raised high in a V, looking directly at me. I smiled to indicate that I had seen his signal and strode over towards him. I greeted the male student, meeting the palm of his right hand with the palm of mine before bringing our chests momentarily closer together in a hugging motion. I gave a side hug to the female student on the stall and we were off into a conversation on Oxford, music and food. Our interactions felt free; not stiff or reserved or uncertain but forceful and alive. I asked about a barber shop and was told that it was a 10-minute bus journey to the nearest black barber shop on the far side of the Cowley Road.

Later that day, I explained to Dan why I needed to find a barber who knew how to cut the hair of black people: No, I couldn't use scissors. Yes, cutting the hairline at the right angle and depth was a skill. And yes, it was definitely worth travelling ten minutes to have a good hairline! I was patient with questions and enjoyed crafting honest explanations but I was also resigned to the fact that I would not find many people like me.

You can then imagine my surprise when I met a student at St Peter's College, who was black, of Jamaican heritage and from Birmingham. I met Kaylita for the first time in the porter's lodge, the main entrance in and out of St Peter's College.

She gave me the broadest of smiles and stretched out her hand 'Hello - I'm Kay."

"Daniel" I responded, shaking her hand. "What do you study?"

"Medicine - I'm a third year. What are you studying?"

"Economics and Management." There must have been something in the way that I had pronounced these words; perhaps the 'E' in Economics had a downward inflexion to make the sound 'eh' when other regions in the UK would have retained the 'ee', but a look of surprise suddenly came over Kaylita's face.

"Are you from Birmingham?" I had also noticed something familiar about the way that certain words had rolled off Kay's tongue and now knew why.

"Yes, from Handsworth."

"Handsworth? You did well to get in here!" Kay teased.

We shared stories about Birmingham and freshers' week. Kay asked me if I'd signed up for the ACS and I nodded affirmatively. She then handed me a blue flyer for a student society called Target Schools, who were having committee elections the following Wednesday. Kay explained that Target Schools was a completely student-led access initiative to help inspire and inform school students about applying to study at Oxford. I thought about how pivotal my interactions with Mr Rogers had been in my journey and gleamed at the thought that I might be able to become a role model for someone else.

I went to the committee elections the following Wednesday, which were held in the Student Union. Kay wasn't at the meeting so I sat next to two people who turned out to be current committee members. They encouraged me to stand for a role but I was unsure. I was making progress in my assignments but they were still incredibly demanding and I had limited reserves of free time.

The meeting was chaired by someone called Elena. I'd assumed that she worked for the Student Union because of the ease and confidence with which she led the meeting, until she mentioned that she was in the second year of a Modern Languages degree. The committee elections began with the major roles of Chair, Secretary and Treasurer. I listened carefully to the people who spoke and the vision they had for developing the scheme and marvelled at how busy students were also able to commit to managing a programme of national reach and significance.

After these roles had been filled, Elena announced that there were a number of roles coming up that would be suitable for first year students who were new to the university and hoping to dip their toes into Target Schools. The position that piqued my interest was one of the two 'Shadowing Scheme Training Coordinator' roles, a position that would involve training volunteers for the inaugural year of the Target Schools Shadowing Scheme. The plan was for dozens of students from non-fee paying schools to descend on Oxford to shadow a current undergraduate student for a day; sitting in on their lectures and tutorials and eating lunch in an Oxford hall. I remembered how reliant I had been on Mr Booth's son to explain Oxford's peculiarities such as its quads and tutorials, and the way in which ambition had gradually spread amongst the group.

When this role came around, I raised my hand confidently alongside a person sitting on the opposite side of the table. Two roles and two volunteers. I assumed that would be the end of it. But committee rules dictated that we both had to give a short speech about why we wanted to do the role and what we could bring to the position.

I spoke second and shared my experiences of attending a comprehensive school in inner city Birmingham and how important it was to debunk the myths that told certain people that places like Oxford were not for them. We were both elected unanimously and I immediately threw myself into the role, delivering training sessions and writing training manuals within a matter of days. By the end of the first term, balancing work alongside volunteering had become too much for my fellow training coordinator and I had to deliver two training sessions per week.

The coordinator of the scheme as a whole was also struggling to meet the expectations of organising a national programme and so I offered to take on more responsibility. I was really passionate about the mission of Target Schools and thoroughly enjoyed having the opportunity to share my story one-on-one and to bigger groups of students.

Paulette's advice helped me to hone my presentation skills. I spoke with confidence and poise, added natural points of humour and utilised my new secret weapon, a photograph.

The photograph had been taken when I was in Year 11 at Hamstead Hall but had been posted on Facebook years later. I was standing by the entrance to Top Playground when someone had taken a phone out of their pocket. I was reluctant to take part and wanted to get on with playing football, but Tobias had gestured for me to get in the shot. The photo showed 8 boys as they were; Paul being the comic, throwing gang signs with an opened tracksuit top showing a metallic chain. Also in the photo were Tobias, Ashley and Riyomi. And then on the edge of the photograph, towards the far left of the group, was me.

I would begin my talks by asking if anyone could see me in the photograph. The assembled students would smile and then point towards the tall figure at the end with his hands in his pockets who seemed somewhat out of place - my preference for playing football re-interpreted as an inner dialogue between fitting in and standing out.

The photo was a godsend for school presentations. Within seconds, students could understand my background, the school I went to and the person I was. I was able to forge a connection and the right to be listened to.

Fuelled by my interest in access to higher education, I volunteered to take part in the University of Oxford's *Wall of 100 Faces*[5].

The wall featured short videos submitted by a range of undergraduate and postgraduate students speaking about some aspect of living and studying in Oxford. My video (which on writing, is still available on the 100 faces website) begins with the typed words 'Daniel Stone, 1st year Economics and Management, St Peter's College'. I'm sat down with a graffitied wall in the background, a freshly-shaven head courtesy of the Cowley Road barber, wearing a red Nike t-shirt and a black Adidas hoodie with grey stripes and a red trim that unlike conventional jackets, opened across my chest in a V-shape.

My dialogue begins: "I'm a big, I'm a big, f-ff-football fan. I think th th that was one of the main things I was looking for when I first started ah ah aht Oxford University. To find a football team or find somewhere where I could kind of play football with other people. So I think every College, erm, like has their own individual football team so I remember like the first week kind of coming up to Oxford and finding a football team and finding it was a place where I could meet other guys and get to know them."

---

[5] http://www.ox.ac.uk/admissions/undergraduate/why-oxford/wall-of-faces

131

Football trials were at the very end of freshers' week. The St Peter's football pitches were leased from Hertford College and were a considerable walk away from the centre of Oxford. It felt good to smell the fresh grass and to see a full-size pitch with nets and green and gold corner flags.

After some passing and teamwork drills, the team captain Tom Langridge, gathered us into a huddle. He informed us that he had been impressed by what he had seen in the practice exercises and was confident that we had a good set of freshers who could help propel us up from the lower reaches of the lowest first team league. He told us the importance of working for each other and to enjoy the practice game. The final instruction was to order ourselves according to our position. The sole goalkeeper retreated to the far end of the pitch. The defenders were told to stand closest to him.

As the practice exercises were taking place, I had been sizing up my competition in the innate way that men are able to look at another man and know if they could take them in a fight. Similarly, I had been looking at those gathered for the trials and reasoned that my physical attributes and football brain would make me a natural fit as an offensive threat. Besides, I had always been frustrated by the defensive role given to me in Hamstead Hall and saw this as a new beginning.

So I ignored the call for defenders and midfielders and took my place as an attacker. It was a place that I never surrendered throughout my time at Oxford.

V

Oxford is often spoken about as a polarising experience. On the one hand there are many people who love their time at Oxford. They make friends for life, thrive in the often intense and persistently demanding environment of lectures and tutorials, and graduate from university as a more well-rounded and capable individual. But there are a significant number of people who at some point in their time at Oxford, do struggle. They may find the workload too taxing and cultural differences too polarising. And at times, especially at the beginning, I did struggle.

But I drew on the reserves of resilience that I had built up in my younger years. I thought back to my A level in Further Maths and the ways that I had found solutions to seemingly impossible problems. I recalled how I had adapted to the hyper masculine culture of Top Playground while maintaining friendships with people across my year group. I could also point to my experiences in Ghana, where I had formed strong relationships with people, despite obvious differences in culture and language.

I didn't put myself under pressure to fit perfectly into the Oxford ideal. I knew that I could tread my own path and go at my own pace, and that this would be OK.

By the end of my first term, I had firmly established a number of pillars that would sustain me throughout my time at Oxford. I had football, which once or twice a week would allow the pressures of study to be overtaken by the collective desire of 11 students to win a game. I had my faith, which provided a higher goal and a moral compass. I had the ACS to keep me rooted in culture. I had my activism to keep me rooted in hope. I had my academic ambition that kept me striving to learn and improve. And I had friendships that had extended beyond E&M to Alasdair, Adam, Dave and Afua who studied PPE, and a Biochemist, Richard Gallon, who was a god on Halo.

Even before the end of my first year, I was able to say the following words while being filmed on a graffitied playing field in central Oxford:

"I don't have any re-regrets at all about co-coming to Oxford University. I literally think it's the be-best thing tha tha that I could have done. I think just in terms of the people I've met here, erm, the experiences I've had, erm, ju ju just being able to be in a place where I, where I'm being challenged and I'm being stretched. And I don't think you kind of get that in any other university. Errmm, I think perhaps umm in an ideal world I would probably have a bit more free time [laugh]. Erm but apart from that I would say, yes, it's been brilliant and I've enjoyed like every second of being in Oxford."

DANIEL STONE

THE PRESIDENTIAL RACE

"I think the position of an activist and the idea of it has been hugely diluted and hugely romanticised. True activism to me is laying down your life for a cause." - Courtney Boateng, Taking up Space[6]

I was almost President.

The only thing standing between me and the title was an initiation event. A challenge. A spectacle designed for one thing and one thing only - public humiliation. Tim, the former Entertainment Rep counted down "3, 2, 1... Go!"

Sanjay lurched forward and grabbed the three Jacob's cream crackers and began to nibble at them ferret-like. I started eating it in a similar fashion but realised that my technique wasn't as efficient as Sanjay's. I changed strategy and shoved half a cracker into my mouth, followed by another half. Suddenly an unusual sensation filled my mouth. The crackers were absorbing the saliva in my mouth at an astonishing rate and I still had another one and a half to go! I shoved the remainder into my mouth, willing my jaw to chew and my oesophagus to swallow. But the saliva was completely gone and without

---

[6] Kwakye, C. and Ogunbiyi, O. (2019) *Taking up Space: The Black Girl's Manifesto for Change.* London: Penguin Books.

moisture, the task of deconstructing the small rectangles of cracker was becoming impossible. Sanjay had already moved onto the egg and spoon section of the race. I had to do something. I took a deep breath and blew out in a straight direction, fragments of dust-like cracker particles, shooting out across Chavasse Quad to gasps from the assembled crowd.

My mouth empty, I balanced the egg on the silver spoon and skipped in pursuit of Sanjay. He had just reached the far end of the quad and had bent over to pick up a water gun filled with an unidentifiable liquid, which he proceeded to fire in my direction. I rolled to pick up the other gun and turned to shoot back at Sanjay, when torrents of flour, eggs and water were hurled in our direction from the St Peter's undergraduates lining the length and width of the quad. At the final corner of the challenge was a 'dirty pint'.

The bar manager, Sam, had taken me to one side before the beginning of the race. He heard that I was teetotal and wanted to ask whether I'd require an alcohol-free version of whatever concoction he was able to fashion. I told him that alcohol was fine. The pint glass was full of a brown liquid, which itself was made out of several other fluids. I could see the distinct form of small cylindrical shapes floating in the glass. I tried not to give the contents any further inspection and began to drink. I downed the pint after a few seconds and looked over to Sanjay who had his arms held aloft.

I walked over to Sanjay and we embraced, our clothes seeping with egg yolk and flour. The JCR applauded their champions who had sacrificed their pride so willingly on the altar of collegiate spirit. Because this initiation was for the JCR. It let undergraduates know that their Presidents were not above them. And in their own way, it was an opportunity for the JCR to thank Sanjay and to welcome in a new President.

I

In truth, it had come as a surprise to many (me included) that I put myself forward to be JCR President. For those who were committed custodians of JCR matters, I was only a peripheral figure of JCR meetings who rarely held the floor for very long. My contributions, when I made them, were short and precise observations rather than long orations. For those who weren't as engaged with the business of the JCR, Presidency was viewed as a burdensome task that would lead to hours away from friends and redirected towards College meetings. There was also the surety that your academic work would suffer.

I was certain that I would run for a committee position. The four core roles were those of Secretary, Treasurer, Vice President and President. There were also individuals who represented St Peter's undergraduates in discussions on food, housing and student welfare, others who organised College sports and entertainment, roles for academic affairs and the Student Union, and a manager of Oxford's only student run bar.

In a previous meeting, we had written into the constitution a new position called 'Access Rep', which would work with the OUSU Access Officer to support university-wide access initiatives as well as introducing new activity within St Peter's. My initial thought was that I would stand for Access Rep, given the activities that I was already undertaking with Target Schools.

I only thought about running for President after reading one of Sanjay's bulletins. He announced that the position of JCR President would be the first committee role up for election. Second year students didn't usually stand because the time commitment required to be President was too much to balance alongside preparation for final year exams. The onus was on someone among the rank of first year students to put their name in the hat.

The first question I asked myself was: *Did I want to become President?*
It was a role that from afar was wrapped in prestige and influence, but at closer inspection was pre-packaged with commitment and responsibility. Sanjay carried out his role admirably and was an effective conduit between the College on one side and students on the other. But it was clear that Sanjay worked incredibly hard. I would often pass him going into the library at a time when I was heading to bed.

I was certain that I would be able to represent the undergraduates of St Peter's with integrity and commitment, but commitment alone was not enough. As well as being a conduit, the President was also a buffer against College diktats. It was a role fraught with difficulties, lined only with the faint possibility of being able to make a difference. And I wasn't sure that it was worth the hassle.

But the President was a figurehead, especially for the new students arriving at Oxford. The President could impact the culture of the College, for better or for worse. They could facilitate the introduction of new rules and dissolve old ones. Their words and opinions were transmitted weekly to the whole College, and people usually paid attention. The prospect of being able to make my contribution to a place that I now called home, convinced me that this was an important position and a position that I wanted.

Sanjay offered to meet any interested candidates one on one to answer any questions they had. I arranged to meet Sanjay in the living room of the 'Presidential Suite'; the room in St Peter's that had been reserved for the sitting JCR President. It was a large room overlooking the main College quad, with a large wooden desk pressed close up to the window. I had a number of questions for Sanjay: What did a typical day look like? How did he utilise his committee? What did he have to sacrifice to be a good President? Was it worth it?

As I listened to Sanjay, I began to grow in confidence that I could do it. I saw the opportunity to serve my College and my University and was thinking of ways that I could use the tools of policy, advocacy and personal example to make St Peter's an even better community to reside in.

But this enthusiasm was tempered somewhat when I remembered that the presidency was an elected position. It wasn't enough for me to know all of this within myself; I needed to convince my peers to vote for me. In my mind, my background was of little consequence. I was aware that I was an Afro-Caribbean male with brown skin from Handsworth in Birmingham, who had attended a school that no-one had heard of. But I knew that I was Daniel and that from the first day of fresher's week, I had treated everyone with respect. I believed, without question, that in turn I would also be respected and that if my ideas were good enough then I would reach my goal.

The first person who knew of my decision to run for JCR President was Arnault Barichella, a History student from Paris who was known for his unconventional remarks on political philosophy and the quality of English food. We were eating one of the English meals that he could tolerate, brunch, when he turned to me and said "Daniel. You would make a fine President."

I smiled and replied, "Do you know what? I'm going to do it."

Arnault grinned and slapped me on the back. He called over Dan and Mike who were heading in the direction of the brunch queue. "Daniel is running for President!" Dan and Mike looked at me in disbelief. Not necessarily at the fact that I was running for President, but because this news had been delivered to them by Arnault rather than hearing directly from their friend.

Over the next few days, they helped me to write my Presidential manifesto and to craft the speech that I would have to deliver at the Presidential hustings in the JCR. As the days passed, my confidence and passion grew. I came up with ideas that I thought could build on the collegiate atmosphere we had in St Peter's and I rehearsed my speech over and over again; writing it out word for word and analysing my gesticulations in my bedroom mirror. By the day of the hustings, I was ready.

I began the speech by telling my story. I never explicitly told many of my peers about growing up in Handsworth and how it had fuelled my passion for politics and for community. I spoke about Target Schools and the responsibility we have as students at one of the best higher education institutions in the world, both to support each other and to do what we could to 'give back'. I introduced my key manifesto points which centred on enhancing the St Peter's community and building our capacity to make a difference. Then I finished with my piece de resistance, an analogy to the namesake of the College, St Peter, who in the Bible had taken the audacious step of walking out onto the water to stand with Jesus. I urged my peers to be focused and to be brave, and that together we could make St Peter's a better place to learn and to live.

The applause died down and Jack Matthews raised his hand to ask the first question.

"What does OUSU stand for and what does OUSU do?" Jack was known around St Peter's and the wider University as someone who had taken a great interest in the Student Union, while most other students regarded it with at best apathy and at worst open hostility.

"OUSU stands for the Oxford University Student Union," I stated confidently. Jack smiled. "In a word, I would say that it does representation. It represents the views of students to the University and allows us to contribute to decision making. It also organises meetings and events like the freshers' fair."

Jack continued. "But why is OUSU needed when we have the JCR?"

"I think the JCR is great for College issues but there are some things that are done better together and across the University. For example, I am part of the Target Schools Committee - which is supported by OUSU - we have committee members and volunteers from most Colleges. It wouldn't be possible for one College to organise Target Schools. But I know that a lot of people don't understand what OUSU does. If I'm honest, there's a lot I don't know about OUSU but I'm keen to learn."

The next question was asked by Ollie, a first year French and Spanish student who was also a member of the St Peter's football and rugby first teams. Over the past term I had forced myself into the starting line-up after beginning the season on the bench. I played most games as an attacking right or left winger and had started to add goals and assists to my hard work and endeavour. "Hi Daniel. So we know that you like to play football and are part of the St Peter's first team. What would you do if there was a clash between a St Peter's football match and a meeting in College? Which would you choose?"

Around 60 St Peter's students were in attendance this evening, including Tom Langridge who hadn't paid much attention at all to my speech. He had been busy watching his beloved Derby County on mute while discussions about the JCR had continued around him. But on hearing a football related question, his gaze left the white and black shirted players to study my response.

I took a few moments to consider my answer. "Well... I do enjoy football," I started. "But I take seriously the role that I'm standing for so if there was a clash, I would have to choose the meeting."

"Nooooo!" Tom exclaimed. Part in jest but with a sincere frustration that he might be about to lose one of his best attacking options. I kiddingly shrugged my shoulders and scanned the room for the source of the next question.

The next question was asked by Sanjay. As President, Sanjay was responsible for writing and circulating regular JCR emails to keep the student population informed of ongoing disputes and upcoming events. Sanjay's emails tried to encourage students to attend the fortnightly JCR meetings, which took place on a Monday evening. These meetings were opportunities to discuss and debate College issues, vote on JCR policies and hear updates from our elected officers on the progress of their portfolio.

JCR meetings tended to be poorly attended. To entice people who didn't have a natural inclination to engage with matters of the constitution and political representation, the JCR committee would pay for Domino's pizzas to be delivered at the start of the meeting. Within seconds, the pizza boxes would be wiped clean. The empty sachets of sauce and the odd remnant of a pepper as the only evidence that pizza once stood there.

"Hello Daniel," Sanjay began in his usual warm manner. "How many JCR meetings have you attended since starting in St Peter's and what could be done to encourage more students to attend?"

I had expected the first part of the question but took my time to respond so that I could consider an intelligent response to the question of engagement and attendance.

"Around 2 or 3," I began, noticing looks of disappointment spread across the room. I paused for effect; pleased that I had the audience exactly where I wanted them. "Unfortunately Target Schools Committee meetings are also on Monday evening. So I come along to as many meetings as I can. Because we have the Shadowing Scheme beginning this year - which I would encourage you all to support - I've had to prioritise Target Schools. However I'm only on the committee until the end of this year and will be able to attend all meetings if elected."

Several students gave nods of approval and waited to hear my ideas for transforming meetings. "On the second part of your question, I think the introduction of pizza to JCR meetings has been great. But I think we could perhaps also try to make discussions more entertaining. We could maybe have set topics each meeting. So in one meeting we could look at 'access' and think of creative ideas to do with access. And in another we could look at 'food' or 'sport'." I could see a number of sceptical expressions on the faces of those listening and my voice trailed off: "Or not, it's just an idea I suppose."

II

In the end, I stood uncontested for the position of President. This should have made my election a formality but come Election Day, I was surprisingly nervous. As well as having the option to vote for me, undergraduates at St Peter's could also choose to *Re-open Nominations* or colloquially, they could choose to vote for RON.

The day before the election, I heard that there was a growing campaign for RON on the basis that if a President wasn't elected in the first round, then the rule that required the serving president to reside in the Presidential Suite would be annulled. While I respected the underlying democratic principles, I was determined not to face the embarrassment of losing an election to no-one.

Voting was done online - each St Peter's undergraduate was given a unique code that would allow them to log on once and register their preference. I woke up early on the day of the election and circulated a mass text to my friends in College, reminding them to vote. I messaged Kaylita and asked her to spread the word amongst her year group, and then I began to knock doors in Matthew's Block. Guy answered immediately. He said that he had voted and told me that I had nothing to worry about. The next door was Richard's. He took slightly longer to answer and when he opened up, he was in a dressing gown, bleary eyed and slightly annoyed that I'd woken him out of his sleep.

By the end of the morning I had canvassed as much of the physical and electronic campus that I could and was convinced that everyone who was going to vote had done so. All I could do now was wait.

Voting closed at 8pm that evening. The tally would then be counted, recounted and verified. At around 8.15pm I received a call from the returning officer, letting me know that I had been elected as JCR President by 69 votes to 17.

I was delighted to have avoided the ignominy of being defeated by RON and that in around six months' time, I would have the honour of being the St Peter's JCR President. However, it irked me that around a fifth of people had voted for another round of elections. Some of these people may have jumped on the RON bandwagon and it was also possible that Tom Langridge had voted for RON in a bid to keep me playing football and that Richard had used his vote as payback for my unwanted wake-up call; then there was Tendai, who somehow managed to mistakenly vote for RON when he intended to mark his preference for me!

But I also sensed that there was a group of people who were unconvinced my candidacy and who would need to be won over once I began my role in earnest.

Over the next few months, the remainder of the committee positions were filled. Dan ran for Vice President but was defeated by Jo Wilkin, a Geography student. Dan ran again and took the position of Food, Housing and Amenities Officer. Others of my close friendship group were elected to positions: Alasdair became Treasurer, Adam got the newly formed position of Access Rep and Tendai retained the role of OUSU Rep that he had won in a by-election a few months before. At the end of the elections, I was pleased with the chosen committee.

Although I wouldn't formally become President until the end of the academic year, I had a number of responsibilities to begin before the summer break. This included chairing the Freshers' Week Committee, which was under strict instructions from the College Dean to reduce the number of alcohol-fuelled activities and club nights. This followed an infamous incident on one of the club nights I skipped - involving white t-shirts and marker pens - which ended up making the front page of the Oxford Student Newspaper. We used the previous year's schedule as a template, making extra provision for welfare and events that were alcohol free.

I also used the time before the summer to organise one-on-one meetings with my committee. Although I was friendly with most people in College, I thought that it would be useful to hear the motivations and preferred working styles of those who had been elected. It was great to hear the plans Rimi Solloway had to develop Arts events in the JCR and to involve the MCR and

SCR in the Christmas panto; Alex Yudin wanted to boost attendance at College Bops (themed fancy dress parties); Scarlett was going to make recycling provision the focus of her mandate as Environment and Ethics Officer, and across the committee were individuals who wanted to use their time to improve a specific area of life at St Peter's. We had an excellent group of committed, skilled and intelligent people who I thought could achieve a lot together.

III

I arrived back in Oxford at the end of the summer of 2009, around 10 days before the start of freshers' week. I regularly checked in with the JCR and Freshers' Week Committees to confirm that we were on track to deliver our pre-arranged plans. And I was adjusting to life in the Presidential suite, which had been refurbished over the summer. The old desk overlooking the main quad still remained but around it were new oak-panelled furnishings, new flooring and new fittings. The bedroom and ensuite bathroom, which I was seeing for the first time, had also been renovated. The gold-coloured taps and white fixtures shimmered in their glistening newness.

100 new students arrived on campus at the beginning of October, expecting to be entertained, inducted and made to feel as if they'd always belonged as members of St Peter's College. I stood in the JCR wearing the same green Adidas trainers that I had worn a year earlier, a matching green polo t-shirt (the attire of the freshers' week committee) and the additional burden of responsibility. This was a big moment for me. It was the only opportunity I would have to make a good first impression.

I practiced my short address in my room until it seemed natural. When the moment arrived, I spoke confidently; welcoming the new students, introducing the freshers' committee and providing the itinerary for that evening's activities, which included dinner in the hall and a number of welcome games and activities in the marquee.

Years later, I would learn that what was a big moment for me, was in fact a huge moment for the new freshers, many of whom had arrived in St Peter's with nerves and anxiety. Some freshers who were in the JCR that afternoon would later tell me that when they saw that I was JCR President, they "knew they would be OK" in St Peter's.

These were people who because they had been educated in a comprehensive school or were the first in their family to go to university or due to their own self-doubt, questioned deeply whether they would ever fit in as a student at Oxford. I was proud to know that my presence had helped them to reach an answer that was always within their grasp, *yes, they would.*

Over the summer, the freshers' committee had been thinking of a creative response to the Dean's strict instructions to reduce the number of events featuring alcohol. This edict had included an order to reduce the number of club nights from four to two. The cunning solution that we had devised was to make a distinction between *official* and *unofficial* club nights.

Official club nights were those sanctioned and organised by the Freshers' Week Committee who would pre-purchase tickets for large groups of St Peter's freshers. Unofficial club nights would be orchestrated by the Committee but wouldn't carry our fingerprints as visibly. After all, the Dean couldn't stop 50 St Peter's freshers from exercising their human rights to leave the College and spill out onto the streets of Oxford. And if, by chance, the same 50 freshers happened to stumble across the same night club and party the night away with their friends, well, then it was a stroke of luck!

Freshers' week was a great success. We rebalanced certain activities to be less alcohol fuelled without losing their fun, the football trials had produced another draft of promising Peter's athletes and we had (un)officially kept hold of the four club nights. The Sunday of freshers' week, we received an email from the Dean, instructing Alex Y, Jo and I to report to his office first thing on Monday morning.

I knocked on the door.

"Come in!" A voice rasped from the other side.

Although the room was the same shape as many others in the staircase, it seemed to take on a stature not replicated anywhere else in College. The oak furniture seemed darker and the room always seemed to be cast in a deep shadow, even during the daytime. The book shelves displayed the Dean's passion and academic discipline; classical music and specifically the works of Wagner. Three chairs had been placed on the opposite side of the desk, facing away from the door. I shuffled forward and pulled back the middle chair. The Dean, flanked on either side by the two Junior Deans, hadn't blinked since we entered the room. His gaze shifted from me to Jo to Alex and back again. We took our seats, Jo to my left and Alex to my right. He still hadn't blinked.

"When we met at the end of May," the Dean began. "Did I n-not tellll you that you were only to have two club nights?" The Dean kept his sharp stare behind his spectacles.

"They weren't club nights," Alex began.

"Rubbish! Do you think I was born yesterday?" Our thinly veiled plan had become desperately exposed. "Did I make myself clear in May?"

We nodded like naughty school children in the head teacher's office. "But we have a responsibility to give new students the best…"

"Enough enough. I heard your arguments in May and you were given clear instructions that you have knowingly disobeyed."

I used the pause in between breaths to make my case. "But the students are going to go out anyway. Better under our supervision where we can get them safely to and from College than on their own."

The Dean paused. His stare unmoving and focused on me. "Did I or did I not give you clear instructions in May?" He paused. "You have intentionally disobeyed a clear instruction and there must be repercussions. I would be within my rights to suspend all three of you right now." He paused again and watched us wilt under the possibility of being suspended from Oxford.

The pause seemed to be interminable. I thought of the shame my parents would feel when I showed up a few days into the new term with my suitcase and all of my belongings. I thought of retelling the story of my suspension to family members and friends, and of their shock and disappointment that I had thrown away this opportunity.

I broke the silence. "I am responsible." The Dean blinked in surprise. "As President, I knew what was being planned with the unofficial club nights and I approved it."

I wasn't sure why I decided to do this. Perhaps I thought back to the lesson in empathy that had been taught by my mum or I could have been emboldened by my dad's view that taking the tough road was *what men did*? It could even have been the economist within me, who reasoned that it was more efficient for one person to be suspended than all three? Or the politician who inferred that as President, the buck always stopped with me? Whatever the reason, my instinct, in the moment, was to take responsibility.

The Dean looked at Jo and then Alex. "You can go."

Alex gave me a look of gratitude as he stood to leave. Jo touched me briefly on the shoulder as she turned to exit the room. And then I was left face to face with the Dean. He spoke at me for around ten minutes, repeating the instructions that he wanted to be passed onto the next Freshers' Committee with no room for misinterpretation or unofficial events. He ended our meeting by saying, "Not a great start to the year, is it?"

IV

That meeting set the tone for a number of challenging issues that would plague my presidency; the most contentious issue being that of accommodation. St Peter's often referred to itself as being a relatively *poor College* that didn't have the endowments, land or holdings of some of the older and more illustrious Oxford Colleges. Before my term as President had begun, College decided to sell one of its off-campus accommodation blocks in order to boost the amount of cash that it had in store for other purposes.

The accommodation block was in need of repair and renovation, and with increasing numbers of students choosing to live in private rented accommodation in their second year, it was never fully occupied. So from a financial perspective it wasn't a wholly unreasonable decision to make.

However, St Peter's promised - in its prospectus and online materials - to guarantee accommodation for all undergraduate students who wished to stay in College owned property throughout all their years of study. The sale of the accommodation block would mean that they were no longer in a position to make this guarantee. It was still highly likely that everyone who wanted to stay in College accommodation would be able to do so, but the total number of rooms no longer surpassed the total population of students and so there could feasibly be a shortfall.

The JCR was in an uproar about this decision, which they saw as a betrayal of the promises that had been made pre-application. Most students chose to air their concerns at the Monday JCR meetings (which experienced a sudden surge in attendance) and through the consultation form I had circulated by email. Some students also took me up on my offer to speak to them in person about their concerns.

I recall one student being in tears while he told me why it was so important for him to have guaranteed and familiar accommodation for his second year of study. He told me that he felt helpless but that he trusted me when I reassured him that the College would not be able to renege on the promises that they had made to students who had applied under these terms. At this time, I was seeing the College Bursar on almost a daily basis to argue on behalf of students. I was confident that should the demand from students outstrip the supply of rooms, then the College would step in.

At this point I was working long hours organising extra meetings and reading through papers while trying to find time to do my academic work. Late one evening, I received a lengthy email from someone in my year group about the ongoing dispute.

The message had begun politely before descending into a spiteful and vicious tone. The author was clearly misinformed and had jumped to some heinous conclusions. In her ignorance she had chosen to attack me, my motivations and my commitment to finding a solution. I was hurt and stunned. I didn't know this person well but the few times we interacted she seemed mild-mannered and friendly. It was apparent that the impersonal nature of a written message had given her license to be unreservedly malicious. I composed myself before responding with a calm and measured response that addressed her concerns and reassured her that I was doing all that I could to resolve this matter in a way that would protect the rights of students.

When I found myself running out of energy and patience, my friends and the JCR Committee would sustain me. I knew that there were a number of people who had chosen to unhelpfully spread rumours and pass judgment on what they considered to be my poor leadership, but there were many others who chose to stand shoulder to shoulder with me in the middle of a difficult situation. Jo led the charge to push back against the position taken up by the College Bursar and other committee members thought of creative ways that we could diffuse the toxic atmosphere that had engulfed recent JCR meetings.

The week of the vicious email, I was perhaps at my lowest ebb and had forced myself to go to a house party in Cowley. I had been doing some reading beforehand and arrived at the party after it was well underway. As I entered the main room, I could see a number of conversations drawing to an unnatural stop as people sent uneasy smiles in my direction. It was probably paranoia, but I was convinced that everyone in the room was talking about me and judging me and wishing they had voted for RON.

I got talking to Tom Stevenson, who was studying Medicine. By profession he could probably see how tired and worn out I had become. He told me that the undergraduates of St Peter's had voted for me and believed in me and that I had to continue to do my best. That brief conversation was the shot of adrenaline I needed.

Energised, I approached the dispute with new conviction. Within days, we had a number of agreements that guaranteed College-provided accommodation for any students who had applied to St Peter's while the promise was in place, introduced a new room allocation model and negotiated a low percentage increase in the following years rent, which reflected the trauma caused by the sale of the accommodation block.

On reflection, this had been a baptism of fire. At times my natural attributes - my calmness, and my pragmatic approach to problem solving - had been strengths that prevented issues flaring up even further. But these challenging issues had exposed my inexperience. I tended to internalise all of my pressures and frustrations and wrap them in silence. I didn't tell anyone about the email I received. I understood that the email had been sent in confidence and in all likelihood was driven by fear. It was my job as an elected representative to channel the will of the JCR into appropriate action. But I failed to see that this was a heavy emotional burden for me to carry alone and that I needed someone to confide in.

This person could have been Jo, my Vice President, who was capable, trustworthy and whose skill set balanced mine. She was naturally more tenacious than I was. I could be too accommodating and passive; naturally empathetic when the situation called me to be partisan. But I didn't have the foresight or wisdom to delegate and to involve Jo more within my world and my thoughts. Consequently I felt as if I was facing most situations alone, hoping that the intuition of people like Tom would provide floats when I found myself drowning.

V

The part of the role that I most enjoyed was being a trusted and recognisable figure to others in College. At Christmas, I had a guest appearance in the JCR Panto and was asked by the Dean to read a passage from Isaiah at the College Carol Service.

My public speaking skills continued to improve and I enjoyed crafting speeches that I thought would be relevant, engaging and pertinent for my audience. I was given another opportunity to test my skills at Halfway Hall, a formal dinner held in the second term of our second year, to mark the median point of our time as undergraduates at St Peter's. In my speech, I opened by saying that Nelson Mandela was halfway through his life when he began a 25 year prison sentence. To the delight of some of those gathered, I reminded them that in Istanbul in the year 2005, Liverpool had been 3-0 down to AC Milan at half time, only to fight back and win on penalties.

My point was that it wasn't where we were at halfway that counted, but where we finished. I implored my friends and peers to strive towards the goals they had set for themselves both in and out of the classroom, and thanked the JCR Committee for their support and dedication up to the halfway point of our term in office.

A further speaking engagement had been arranged for me by the St Peter's Christian Union. As the demands of Presidency set in, I hadn't been as diligent in my attendance of CU meetings but had told the current leaders, James and Sam that I'd be willing to support where I could. We agreed to organise an event called Pizza and President. I would share my story of faith and the CU would pay for Domino's pizza. When the evening of the event came, the 30-40 seats in the Latner Building were fully occupied. Some of the attendees were supporters from the CU and a number of my Economics friends had come to hear me speak. There was also a contingent of students who had heard about, or smelt, the free pizza and were distressed to learn that there was a talk attached!

Once I began speaking, everyone was silent and respectful. I spoke about growing up in Birmingham with my parents and three siblings and how church had always been a part of my life. I shared the moment, when as a child, I made the commitment to live my life as a Christian and what it meant to live a life that was illuminated by the bible and prayer. There were looks of disbelief when I spoke about the role that I believed God had played in allowing me to be in Oxford - the interventions of new acquaintances almost as miraculous as the audible voice. And I ended by advising those gathered to take the time to ask the question: "God are you out there and if so, what do you want me to do?"

Then before I knew it, I was back on the start line in Chavasse Quad, racing against my presidential successor, Rob Collier, who had won the first election that was free of the rule requiring candidates to live in the Presidential Suite. My year as JCR President had been a series of sprints that tested my endurance, my ability and my heart. As my fiercest critic, I was aware of my shortcomings and was silently ashamed that my best intentions had sometimes failed to produce the most effective results.

I learned that representation is a burden that can only be lightened by an unwavering commitment to sacrifice and selflessness. I served the JCR with all of my ability and strength, and for that reason, over the coming months and years, I was able to reflect on my presidential year with pride.

TEAM TED

"As long as the water is troubled it cannot become stagnant." - James Baldwin, The Price of the Ticket[7]

The president of Oxford University Student Union was called Stefan Baskerville. Stefan had studied PPE at University College but was now a full-time officer for OUSU. He was personable, smart and driven, and unlike most people at Oxford, had managed to retain an accent. His North London vernacular told stories of a grassroots movement that was delivering change through building relationships and having meaningful conversations.

I listened to Stefan's description with cautious optimism. Three years had passed since I joined the Labour Party and I was growing tired of political meetings that were painfully unproductive and irrationally partisan. Everything wrong in the world was the fault of the Tories and their rich banker friends while the Labour Party was above reproach. I saw this illogical attitude reflected in local meetings and in the national press. Politicians seemed to be hell-bent on cloaking the truth with skilfully unanswered questions and finger pointing at the opposition.

But Stephen promised that Citizens UK was different. So I, along with half a dozen JCR Presidents, took the 90 minute journey on board the Oxford Tube towards Central London. I spent most of the journey speaking with Tom

---

[7] Baldwin, J. (1985) *The Price of the Ticket.* New York: St Martin's / Marek.

who was the JCR President of New College, Martha who was the JCR President of St John's College and Alice who was the JCR President of Wadham. Being with the other JCR Presidents felt like my intellectual home; the place where my mind most preferred to abide and the arena where dreams of transforming society could roam free.

We exited St James' Park underground station and into the chill of the evening air. On the short walk to the Methodist Central Hall, we passed several police officers, on high alert for anyone who may try to disturb the peace. Walking past their purview were groups of school children, adults of different ages, creeds and colours, and stewards wearing purple Citizens UK t-shirts. Stefan seemed to be well known amongst the purple-clad brigade who came over to warmly shake his hand. He introduced us as leaders from the University of Oxford. A similar conversation unfolded when we reached the doors of the main auditorium, only this steward stayed with our group and showed us towards our allocated seats.

The Methodist Central Hall was perhaps the perfect setting for what was about to transpire that evening. Built at the beginning of the 20th Century as a monument to mark the centenary of the death of John Wesley (the founder of Methodism), the Hall was to act not only as a church, but to be a place for exploring social questions. Physically, the Hall stands opposite Westminster Abbey and metres away from The Palace of Westminster. Ideologically, its aim is to bridge the gap between religious dogma and political power.

I was impressed with how well organised the assembly was. It started on time and was chaired by a representative from a Pentecostal Church in West London and an Imam of an East London mosque. The assembly began with a roll call. All of the member institutions present nominated someone to walk onto the stage with a banner or placard representing their organisation. One by one, people came forward, and one by one, members of the audience stood to clap and shout their support. As the final name was read out, around 70 smiling faces stood proudly facing the audience as citizens of London. As others around me began to sit down, I remained standing. For all that I heard and read about multicultural Birmingham, this was the first time I had seen people from different communities sharing a stage, united under one banner.

Yes, I shared a primary school playground with people from diverse backgrounds, but our experiences outside of school were largely segregated according to culture or religion. Our parents rarely interacted outside of these restricted social circles and as their children, we inherited their community. I marvelled that Citizens UK had somehow managed to penetrate these walls of division and provide a passage for people to acknowledge their shared humanity.

The main order of business was to make progress on two citizen-led campaigns. The City Safe campaign aimed to provide safe havens on high streets for young people who felt in danger. Organisations or businesses with the purple logo in their window agreed to lock their front door at the request of someone in need of assistance.

While coverage of City Safe hadn't extended beyond London, the second campaign was already viewed as being an issue of national significance. The Living Wage campaign argued that the National Minimum Wage, the minimum hourly rate for employees, was not enough for anyone to live on, especially in a city as expensive as London.

The ammunition used by Citizens UK to drive home their message was the power of testimony: "I begin my first job at 2am," the Somali man on the stage began. "It finishes at 6.30. After, I leave and go home. I make my children breakfast and send them to school. This is the only time I see my children. Then I work from 9 to 1. Then again from 3 to 9. I work long days and I am always tired. My wife and I; we work very hard. But it is never enough."

The stories were honest, raw and emotional. I could hear the frustration in the strained voices of individuals who had endured hardship for years on end. The stories were real. They shed light on lived experiences that would otherwise have remained hidden. The stories were powerful. They compelled you to respond.

After the testimonies, a number of carefully selected London-based decision makers were invited to the stage to respond to specific questions related to the two campaigns. The personality-in-chief was the Mayor of London, Boris Johnson, who was over a year in office after defeating the Labour candidate, Ken Livingstone. It was surreal seeing Boris in person. His dirty blonde hair was as disorderly as it had seemed on TV and his mannerisms were as peculiar. He began a stumbling response.

"Forgive me, Mr Johnson but you're not answering my question. Will City Hall agree to pay all of its staff a living wage?"

"Thank you… Yes… Well, I was getting to that."

"Would you kindly get there then Mr Johnson." I turned to Alice and smiled. The moderator had found the balance between being both firm and fair and was keeping a politician on his toes, much to my amusement.

"Yes, I can confirm that City Hall will be a Living Wage Employer." There was an eruption of cheers across the auditorium. I was stunned. A politician had finally been forced to answer a question directly and it was a result of the power and determination of an organised group of citizens.

The moderator called the assembly to attention. "And Mr Johnson. Can you confirm that London 2012 will be a Living Wage Olympics, where everyone employed to work at the Games will be paid at least the living wage rate?"

"As you know, we are incredibly proud to be hosting the Olympic Games, here in London, in about two and a half years' time. It provides another opportunity to showcase the wonderful diversity within London and to put London and the UK on the world map for delivering excellent global events. This is a once in a generation opportunity for the people of London and a chance to leave a lasting legacy. On legacy…"

"Mr Johnson, we do have a strict agenda to stick to. If you could kindly move towards your answer?" I nodded my approval to the moderator's intervention.

"Yes, certainly… London 2012 will be the world's first living wage Olympics and will show the world that London is a leader in both the principles and practice of compassionate capitalism."

Following that response, the moderator allowed the din of the audience's cheers and applause to continue until it reached its natural conclusion. After

Boris, representatives from the police and industry were also brought on stage to publicly declare their commitment to paying their employees a living wage and to support the City Safe campaign. There was something enlivening about seeing traditional models of power being flipped on their head. Politicians who, arguably, had made a living out of avoiding the questions and concerns of their electors, now found themselves with no room to manoeuvre.

I could see that this was no accident. The questions posed were direct, closed questions that had been written in order to be answered. It was also clear that the questions and topics had broad support from across the organisations gathered that evening. It had been evident from the testimonies and the organic manner in which the whole assembly had enthusiastically shouted their approval of each agreed action.

At the end of the assembly, several leaders from a range of organisations gathered at the front of the auditorium to participate in an evaluation. It was led by the assembly co-chair from the Catholic Church who explained that evaluations followed every event organised by Citizens UK and were a useful way of gathering feelings and marking areas for improvement. We were asked to say one word to summarise how we were feeling at that moment. My word was 'hopeful'. Why? Because I had seen people power in action. It held politicians to account, it persuaded industry to think beyond narrow definitions of profit and it inspired and mobilised people to believe that they could make a positive difference in this world.

The final act of the evaluation was to grade the assembly as you would a class assignment from A+ to F. The person to the left of the co-chair began: "As we never score an assembly an A, I have to give it a B+." The B+ scores followed around the circle. When it was my turn, I also gave it a B+.

If I could have given it an A, I would have.

I

Before the end of my term as President, I attended two days of community organising training held in Oxford. The foundational principles and techniques of community organising were based on the writings of Saul

Alinsky[8]. We defined leaders as 'anyone who has a following' and power as 'the ability to act'. And we learnt about 'one-to-ones', which were conversations designed to unlock an individual's motivations, passions and driving interests. These conversations relied on sharing personal stories, as a means of building relational power and understanding the soul of a person. The critical point in a one-to-one was to discover what makes a person 'angry'. According to community organising theory, when people are angry about something they are driven and motivated to change it.

I could see why forming a relationship with someone based on mutual trust and understanding was an important prerequisite to working effectively together. But the concept of anger slightly troubled me. I reasoned that the people I knew who were driven towards social change; people like Paulette and Errol, were mainly inspired by compassion and selflessness. As I pondered this definition further, I realised that beyond Paulette and Errol, there was a larger number of people who could speak at length about the problems in society but who were doing nothing to address them. I understood that another emotion was required to turn best intentions into committed actions. If this burning passion was called anger, then I could understand why it was an essential ingredient for change.

My training meant that I became suspicious when a number of JCR Presidents and individuals connected to OUSU began to ask to meet up for one-on-one coffees. They were always pleasant conversations but often implicitly and sometimes explicitly, they would try to find out what about life at the University of Oxford was making me angry: What did I want to change and what was I passionate about?

The reason behind these questions was that we were months away from the latest round of OUSU elections and potential candidates were jockeying for position and for candidates to join their 'slates'. Elected OUSU officers fell into a number of different categories. The full time sabbatical officers included the OUSU President and five Vice Presidents. There were over a dozen part-time roles which students fulfilled while studying. Then there were NUS delegates who were elected to represent Oxford at the annual conference

---

[8] Alinsky, S. (1971) *Rules for radicals: A practical primer for realistic radicals*. New York: Vintage Books.

of the National Union of Students. Slates were composed of up to four Sabbatical Officer candidates, six part-time candidates and four NUS reps. The benefit of slates were that you could share the load of campaigning across the thirtysomething Oxford Colleges with a team of people with whom you had created a shared vision.

I was flattered by these conversations and the thought that I was being sounded out by my peers, but I had no intention whatsoever of running in the OUSU election. Although I had been careful not to fall too far behind in my degree, it had clearly been malnourished in a year where the prime focus of my attention had been on the presidency of the JCR. The intention was for my final year of study to rebalance my diary towards academic work. Nevertheless, I accepted the invitation to have coffee.

And the more I listened to people who were passionate about aspects of life in Oxford they wanted to change, the more my position began to soften. Their devotion was infectious and they had fully harnessed the power of story to explain why they were uniquely positioned to understand and address the problems they identified. I began to reflect on my own journey and realised that I had perspectives on life that were unlikely to be shared by many of my peers. Within the space of a fortnight, I had shifted 180 degrees: I began to think that I might want to do this.

My thought process was similar to the one that had led me to the JCR Presidency.

Could I be a good Sabbatical Officer? I thought that I possessed a good base level of skills and that my year as JCR President had taught me how to be a more effective leader and team member.

Did I want to be a Sabbatical officer? After a year spent balancing my degree with my presidential responsibilities, the idea of being able to develop projects and initiatives full-time certainly appealed to me. There was one of the Sabbatical roles in particular, Vice President (Charities and Community) that seemed like a good fit for my interests. I would have responsibility for the student fundraising society (RAG) and the Environment and Ethics Committee, and would support the fledgling Oxford Living Wage Campaign. But most importantly, I would have the opportunity to craft a vision for the community aspect of the portfolio, which was yet to define a clear strategic purpose.

Would I run...?

I was concerned about falling further behind in my academic work. My final exams were a matter of months away and there would be no retakes or second chances. With the election being held in November, I would lose most of the first term campaigning. But then again, this also meant that I would have the final two terms to learn and revise content. I took my time, waiting until the final week of term to make my decision.

When I texted Jack, he immediately rang back. "That's brilliant news Dan. I'm really delighted that you've agreed to run. You'll make a fantastic sabbatical officer." Jack Matthews had put himself forward as a campaigner manager for a potential slate. He was a sage on election regulations and would become our chief tactician.

"Thanks Jack," I beamed. It meant a lot to be validated by someone who had watched my entire journey as a student politician from the hustings to the handover race. "Where are the others?"

"We're over in New College at Tom's. Come round if you're free?"

Tom had decided to run for President and had filled the remaining sabbatical officer slot with Elena, the former Chair of Target Schools. Elena had returned from a year studying abroad and was running for Vice President (Academic Affairs and Access). I would be the third sabbatical on a slate that included a strong team of part-time officers; Alistair who was standing for E&E Rep, Sarah who was aiming to be the inaugural Chair of the Oxford Living Wage Campaign and Jacob Diggle who was standing for Academic Affairs Officer.

Over the course of a number of long evenings and demanding weekends, we crafted our broad vision into carefully worded policies that we hoped would resonate with the student body. We discussed tactics for the election, which was as much about values as it was about setting up social media accounts and building our supporter base: we were going to run a positive campaign that was going to inspire people to get involved with their student union. We began to rehearse speeches and held private question and answer sessions designed to tease out any important gaps in knowledge. As our ideas crystallised, we began to believe wholeheartedly in the version of Oxford we wanted to create.

And as we spent time together, we began to meld into a team. We were there to provide new sparks of creativity. We were there to make each other laugh. And even when we were too tired to be productive, we were there.

We entered the new academic year with confidence, with thousands of orange campaign posters, and with a new name for our slate: Team TED; named after its three sabbatical officers: Tom, Elena and Daniel.

II

The Presidential speeches were up first. Tom was running against Martha. Both were my friends and both were excellent candidates. At the invitation of JCR and MCR Presidents, they had spent the past fortnight touring College meetings and could probably recite their opponent's speech for them. I had been to a number of these events and thought that there was very little to choose between Tom and Martha. It was the same during the central hustings; the evening that was likely to attract the largest and most informed crowd.

Martha seemed more nervous than usual but hit her key policies - official minimum standards of academic provision across colleges and a career development fund - and answered questions with authority. Tom performed well in both sections and probably shaved it overall.

Next up were Elena and her opponent, Hannah Cusworth, who were both experienced and knowledgeable candidates. They gave in-depth answers to questions on academic feedback sessions, the Browne Review into Higher Education Funding and the likely impact of an increase in student fees on potential applicants, without skipping a beat. I gave the bout to Elena on points.

The other sabbatical positions were uncontested so the hustings moved to the final contested election of the evening, Vice President (Charities and Community). There had been murmurings that I would face competition for the role and in all honesty, I was hoping these rumours were true. Winning my JCR election against RON had been something of a hollow victory and I wanted the opportunity to test myself; to see how I would hold up when running against someone. When the candidates were announced, it was confirmed that I would stand against Nathan, a Chair of the Oxford University Labour Club (OULC). Nathan would command a network of politically engaged individuals who knew how to get people to vote. He had positioned himself as the anti-establishment candidate who was outside of the closed network of JCR Presidents. There was a strong possibility that I could lose.

Nathan spoke first and began nervously, saying that he wouldn't follow what some people had done by sharing his personal story but would instead focus on what people really cared about, policies. He stuck to his anti-establishment message, berating OUSU for not doing more to connect to students and for failing to prove its relevance. The audience was largely made up of OUSU officers and supporters who watched on with derisory expressions. I could feel the energy being expelled from the room as each critical phrase went by. The end of the speech was met with a polite pattering of applause and I waited to be called forward.

I was wearing dark blue jeans, my green Adidas trainers and an open turquoise cardigan that revealed my purple Adidas t-shirt with the fluorescent green trefoil, which I had given the mantle of my 'lucky' t-shirt. I looked out across the room and felt comfortable and confident. I knew what I was going to say and I knew how I wanted to say it.

"I'm going to speak about who I am," I began. "Because who I am has defined what I have done and why I am running to be the next Vice President for Charities and Community. I grew up in an inner city area of Birmingham called Handsworth. A few miles from Handsworth is another inner city area called Aston, where I went to church as a boy."

While preparing a speech, I had been unsure whether to mention my Christian upbringing in a crowd that was likely to have a majority of people who were atheists, agnostics or members of different faiths. But Jack had reminded me that if my story was going to come across as genuine, I needed to put all of myself into it.

I continued: "From time to time, my dad would take my siblings and me out of church and lead us for a walk around the local community. And he would ask us what we noticed. I'd see dirty streets, off licenses and poor housing; signs of poverty that were obvious in a place like Aston. But if we look, the signs of a broken and unequal society are all around us." I could feel the audience hanging on my every word.

I spoke about my time in Ghana and mimicked pounding fufu; my knees bent while I pounded the imaginary maize into submission. I used my work with Target Schools as evidence of my commitment to charitable activity and sewed in my key manifesto points: Taking the community beyond the college gates, holding the University to account and creating a culture of volunteering and giving. I thought that I performed well and was pleased that the room once again felt energised.

The first question was asked by Charlotte, the RAG President. "What's the best thing about participating in charitable activity?"

"I actually took part in a charitable activity with RAG a few months ago," I started. "I did the charity bungee jump despite being terrified of heights." Laughter. "I think the crane was about 180 ft. high." I stretched upwards. "I remember as the crane was going up and up and up, thinking what have I done? And then I got to the top and looked out - not down, but out - and could see across Oxfordshire. And then the operator ushered me towards the ledge and said that I'd have to jump head first after he'd counted to 3. So he said *1, 2, 3* and I jumped. And I began to scream and shout until my breath ran out. But I was still falling. And it was like my brain couldn't understand why I was still falling and hadn't hit anything yet! And then the rope pulled back and ohhh, wow."

I waited for the laughter to subside. "But I learned that charitable activity is great for all the reasons that Nathan listed about how you can give to a worthy cause and make a difference to people and the issues they support, but it's also great for the person taking part. You're stretched beyond things that you'd naturally experience or encounter. And do you know what, it can also be really fun!"

III

The polls opened the following Tuesday at 8am and would close on Thursday at 6pm. Our Election Day strategy was to take care of business at home before pushing for votes and turnout farther afield. This was where being part of a slate could give you an advantage. Tom pushed for Team TED votes in New College, Elena canvassed Wadham, and of course, I drummed up support in St Peter's.

My Economics friends were great. They helped me to go door to door to remind people to vote and sent out text messages to anyone they had a friendship with, both within St Peter's and further afield. My wider network was also brilliant. The ACS not only voted but also passed on election fever to their friends and acquaintances.

By the end of the first day, we had exhausted all of our personal contacts and networks. The focus was then on eking out those possibly decisive votes from students who were either undecided or ambivalent. We picked up our assault through social media and stepped up face to face campaigning. We had a rota for standing outside popular Colleges and lecture halls, hoping to convince students to vote. Lectures began at 9am and we would campaign through the day, visiting any meetings or events that we were invited to. They were long, tiring, exasperating days.

Most students seemed unaware that an election was going on despite the countless emails, posters, newspaper advertisements and social media posts. I couldn't understand why they didn't care about the raft of changes we were hoping to bring to Oxford.

It came as a relief when Thursday finally came around. The election results were going to be read out late on Thursday evening in the OUSU building. I sat on one side of the room surrounded by the other members of Team TED. The Martha 4 OUSU slate took up the opposite length of the room with the remaining independent candidates and OUSU officials stood unevenly wherever they could find space.

There seemed to be an invisible, impenetrable force field surrounding the two slates. We didn't speak to each other or make eye contact. The other slate was the enemy; the only thing that stood between us and our dreams of transforming Oxford.

We sat in the room for what seemed like hours while the final votes were verified. Conversations within teams ground to a standstill. People had begun to stretch out on the floors; others had gone to other rooms in the Student Union, looking for a quiet place to retreat, free from leaflets and chatter.

AFTER OXFORD

Sometime after 9pm, the Returning Officer entered the room with the results. She began by announcing the results of the NUS reps, then the part-time officers. As the results were being declared, Jack was furiously trying to decode what these results could mean for the upcoming sabbatical officer positions. It was difficult to draw too many conclusions - the results had been tight and neither slate was decisively on top.

The uncontested sabbatical results were read out first. RON had lost both elections to Seb Baird for VP (Welfare) and Yuan Yang for VP (Women).

My results were up next: "For Vice President (Charities and Community). Nathan Connolly, 683 votes. Daniel Stone, 821 votes. RON, 43 votes. Daniel Stone is elected Vice President (Charities and Community)."

Tom slapped my back and I hugged Elena. Nathan came over to shake my hand and wish me the best for the role. I smiled momentarily at Jack before turning to hear the next set of results.

"For Vice President (Access and Academic Affairs). Hannah Cusworth, 947 votes. Elena Lynch, 878 votes. RON 56 votes Hannah Cusworth is elected Vice President (Academic Affairs and Access)."

A jubilant shout came from the Martha 4 OUSU sofas. Silence and conciliatory hugs from Team TED. For months we had planned and campaigned as if victory was our predestined outcome. We hadn't entertained the idea that we would fail. I hugged Elena. I could see that she was upset. Exhausted. Fearful.

"For President. Martha Mackenzie, 1483 votes. Tom Scott, 1246 votes. RON 121 votes. Martha Mackenzie is elected President."

I could barely hear the end of the announcement above the noise of the cheers surging from one half of the room. On our side there was only deflation. I slumped to the floor, unable to keep myself standing any longer. As I looked up, I could see members of Team TED in tears. I got to my feet and walked over to offer conciliatory words; we had fought a valiant and honourable race and had lost narrowly to a strong team.

After a few moments, we crossed the divide and offered our congratulations to Martha 4 OUSU, before slinking off into the night to assess what went wrong, to dream of what might have been and most importantly, to sleep.

In the immediacy of the result, my victory was bitter. Completely and utterly bitter. Over the past few months, I had willingly given more and more of my time, energy and self into pursuing our collective dream for the Student Union. We created a narrative for why Team TED had been formed and why it was essential to the future of Oxford. I internalised this narrative and it had given me an unparalleled confidence. But now it was forever lost.

MYTHICAL 8TH WEEK

"Think lightly of yourself and deeply of the world."
Miyamoto Mushashi[9]

The summer of 2010 began with an event in the Houses of Parliament. My dad didn't want to attend: London was too far. It was a weeknight. What was this event anyway? By the end of the evening, his son had been named the *Number one black student in the UK.*

The journey to Parliament had begun several months earlier with a phone call.

"So, how much do you know about Rare?" I'd received an email a few days earlier saying that I had been nominated by a friend for Rare Rising Stars, an annual search for the best black students in the UK. The person on the call had introduced herself as Esther.

"Not much to be honest!"

Esther laughed and explained that Rare helped talented young people from diverse backgrounds get good jobs in top companies. The purpose of Rare Rising Stars was to celebrate diverse talent and reverse negative media stereotypes. Nominations were anonymous and would be shortlisted by a

---

[9] Musashi, M. (1974) *A Book of Five Rings*. New York: Overlook Press.

panel of judges. The top scorers would be invited to attend an awards evening in Parliament. "So, tell me about yourself."

I began in Handsworth with tales of my upbringing. I journeyed to Ghana and then settled in Oxford. At the end of my story there was an unnatural silence. "Are you still there Esther?"

"Yes, just writing! That was brilliant - thank you Daniel."

I hadn't expected to be shortlisted and I certainly didn't think that I would be invited to Parliament. I was convinced that I hadn't achieved anything remarkable. What I thought to be my most outstanding accomplishment to date - getting into Oxford - was a feat that I shared with thousands of other young people every year. My assumption was that Rare had invited the top 20 or top 25 nominees in order to hold suspense on the night; I was content to be one of the dozen or so invitees who made up the numbers.

I met my parents just outside the barricade leading into Parliament. After walking past the armed guards, we were asked to pass through a security check. Bags checked, pockets emptied and photo taken, we entered into the grand lobby of the Palace of Westminster; the area where BBC reporters usually stood to tell the nation of the day's breaking political news. Today we occupied this space.

Rare Rising Stars 2010 was hosted by David Lammy MP who opened proceedings and explained that this evening was the end of a year-long search to crown the top ten black students in the UK. He reiterated the selection process and stated that the awardees would be read out from the person who received the 10th highest score to the 1st.

As the award winners were read out, I thought it less and less likely that I would get an award. These were incredible people who had started charities, businesses and social enterprises, and who were making a real difference in media, enterprise, student politics and sport. I felt privileged to hear these inspiring achievements and was already thinking of people I wanted to speak to after the close of proceedings to get their Facebook details or contact number.

AFTER OXFORD

When the biography of the person in third position was read out, my dad turned to me and said: "Never mind Daniel. You know we're proud of you." I smiled. I was having a great evening.

In second place was Melba Mwanje, who studied at St Catherine's College in Oxford. I'd met her briefly at a number of ACS events; she had a really calm and friendly manner and I had no idea that she founded a charity based in South East London. After the applause died down for Melba, the biography began for the number one rising star:

"Our number one star was raised in Birmingham and was state school educated." I turned to my parents who were looking back at me in amazement. "He admits that studying at Oxford 'was a huge shock to the system,' but rather than letting the change in environment faze him he saw the opportunity to encourage open-mindedness and diversity amongst his peers…"

The introduction continued, describing how this individual had worked with his community in Birmingham, volunteered in Ghana and held positions of leadership in Oxford and St Peter's College. I couldn't believe that they were talking about me. My parents were still open-mouthed. Esther was on the raised platform still reading through my biography. I could see people in the audience nodding along and pointing at seated young men who they thought might be Daniel.

In anticipation of what was to come, my mum leant over and adjusted my tie so that it sat neatly above the top button on my shirt. I straightened the arms of my jacket as Esther proclaimed: "Please welcome forward our number one Rare Rising Star, Daniel Stone."

The room burst into rapturous applause. I hugged my parents, re-straightened my jacket then strode forward to collect my award. As I walked towards the stage, guests on either side of the aisle were looking up adoringly at me, sending affectionate smiles in my direction. It seemed surreal to be awarded for something that for me, was just living. I shook the hand of David Lammy MP and Raphael Mokades, the founder and Managing Director of Rare. I was handed a framed certificate that read: *This is to certify that Daniel Stone has been acknowledged as one of the ten most outstanding black students in the UK in Rare Rising Stars 2010.*

DANIEL STONE

I

Around the time of the OUSU election, life was good.

I became a BNOC (Big Name on Campus). My comments could often be found on the outer pages of the Oxford Student Union newspaper. The rapper, Drake and singer, Rihanna were high in the global music charts meaning that I finally had some good music to listen to on a night out. I was comfortable on the dance floor and had developed a friendship with many of the club promoters, which meant that I could get free entry without queuing.

I found more time to play football and went on several impressive runs of scoring goals in consecutive games. In one match, I scored a hat-trick; but then also managed to stumble over my feet and missed an open goal from about a yard out. At the start of every game I would confidently rifle through the kit bag for the number 10 shirt, safe in the knowledge that my teammates would have it reserved for me. If the decisions taken during my first term in Oxford had been to ensure my survival in an unfamiliar environment, I now felt that I belonged and was thriving.

But I saw my newfound privilege and power as an opportunity to champion change. I was acutely aware that there were people around me who found Oxford to be a harsh, uncompromising and prejudiced place. During my second year, I joined the OUSU student-led Campaign for Racial Awareness and Equality. I first became aware of CRAE when a room of largely white students voted down the request of the CRAE co-chairs and members to be renamed The Black Students' Campaign. I decided to attend the next meeting in a show of solidarity. I ended up running a campaign.

The 100 Voices Campaign would seek to record the experiences, good, bad and otherwise, of 100 Black, Asian and Minority Ethnic students at the University of Oxford. Armed with my dictaphone, I spoke to friends about their experiences of being asked inappropriate questions, being put in inappropriate situations and being called inappropriate things.

I was not surprised that the broad carnival of cultures and ethnicities that I had taken for granted in Birmingham was somewhat narrowed in Oxford, but I was astonished by what people didn't know - or often more disconcertingly - presumed to know. I often found myself on the receiving end of racial and cultural stereotypes held by individuals whose primary references to black culture came from the Fresh Prince of Bel-Air.

Not all of these stereotypes were negative. Quite a few elevated me to a status of 'cool' that I could never have dreamed of during my years at Hamstead Hall. But like all stereotypes and generalisations, they relegated me to a lesser version of the person I was.

I knew that Oxford needed to change. I felt it instinctively and now we had evidence.

I had the opportunity to present our findings to the Pro Vice Chancellor (or PVC) responsible for issues of equality across campus. He began our meeting by saying that there was "no racism" in Oxford. By the end of our 45 minutes together, he had been forced to revise this position and to acknowledge that prejudice was rife.

We presented the interviews as anonymised extracts written up into a formal report with four key themes and recommendations.

Two of these themes, *lack of diversity in the student community* and a *culture that struggles to welcome differences in race and ethnicity* illustrated the ways in which the composition of the student body had fostered a sense of discomfort among many BAME students. A third theme highlighted the failure of curricula to capture the diversity of *non-Western thought, people and culture*. The fourth showed the ways in which the lack of diversity had created a *sense of social isolation among BAME students*. Our argument was that the institution needed to acknowledge and challenge the structures that reproduced prejudice, and to offer support to students who found Oxford to be an unwelcoming place.

In the Afro-Caribbean society I found an invaluable support network, a group of fellow agitators and a collection of amazing friends. My JCR responsibilities had prevented me from being present at many ACS events in my second year and I had declined the opportunity to run for a position on the committee, which was ably run by a number of my friends: Janeen, Daphne, Naomi, Afua, Marcel and Cherish. At the start of my third year, I was able to enjoy their company more often. We'd dance together in the r'n'b room in Lava Ignite, celebrate birthdays and watch films featuring actors like Tyler

Perry and the Wayans Brothers. I loved the noise, laughter and freedom that my friends from the ACS brought to my life. They were also fantastic allies during my OUSU election campaign. They would text messages of encouragement and support and were some of my most proactive canvassers. I'd get text messages from mutual friends saying that *Janeen was telling everyone in Trinity to vote for Dan and Team TED* and *how did I know Daphne?*

That question always made me smile. I wondered how societies of people largely brought together by their race or ethnicity were viewed by outsiders. My friends in St Peter's would be surprised when I seemed to know and acknowledge every black person I saw in Oxford. Some of these people were students who I knew from the ACS but there was a significant number of people who were complete strangers.

Nodding in their direction acknowledged their presence and them, mine. After my victory in the OUSU election, I remember seeing more forceful nods of acknowledgement as I walked the streets of Oxford. My brown face on orange Team TED posters had clearly not gone unnoticed.

II

By December 2010, the posters had come down. I had my election victory but I was staring up at a bewildering mountain of work, unsure that I would be able to scale it.

I was also paying the price of choosing pragmatism over passion. Development Economics - which tried to answer questions related to the growth of emerging economies in places like Africa and Latin America - should have been the module I was most looking forward to studying. Books on the economics of slavery and contemporary African states had sparked my interest in Economics as a discipline, but the spread of marks in final exams was relatively narrow. Most people got middling 2.1s and very few people ever got 1sts. Accounting, on the other hand, had much greater variation. Yes, some people did very poorly but it was possible to score well in accounting exams because it was an objective mathematical subject.

In an effort to guarantee a high 2.1 and possibly even push for a first, I had chosen to study Accounting. It was a huge mistake.

After a nightmare module with an absent and substandard tutor, it was a certainty that I would be at the lowest end of the scoring distribution. I reasoned that my expected poor performance could be so bad as to put my overall 2.1 in jeopardy. A cloud of worry would descend whenever I opened my accounting textbook. I thought back to my Further Maths A level and told myself that I would eventually understand the content. But my optimism was fading with each passing day.

From January 2011, I cut down my non-academic activities as close to nil as I could go. I still attended church, which I found to be a calming influence at a time when I was feeling increasingly anxious, but I rarely went to Christian Union meetings or midweek groups. I relinquished the remaining posts I held on student committees and only went to ACS events or nights out when it was for a very special occasion. I would even skip football matches unless I achieved all of my academic objectives for that week (which also included catch up reading and revision).

When the exam timetable was released, it provided news of a horrendous schedule of examinations. I would have eleven 3-hour exams in the space of a fortnight and on some days I would have one in the morning and another in the afternoon. I began covering the walls of my room in revision notes and kept notes on my bedside table so that I could read them before turning off the lights to mark the close of another long day.

During this time I relied heavily on my Economics friends. Tendai, Richard, Dan, Mike and I were now sharing the top floor of the St Thomas Street student accommodation alongside Jo and Scarlett. Ali and Adam were on the floor below and never too far away from our shared kitchen and communal space. 'Finals fear' had gripped us all.

Put simply, this was a fear of failing:

It was the fear of working so hard to get into Oxford only to leave with a degree considered to be substandard. It was the fear of the graduate jobs that would suddenly become unavailable because the numbers on our CVs read 2.2. It was the fear of being classed as lower ability. It was the fear of conversations with friends at Oxford and loved ones at home, who with eager expectation would ask us how we did in our degree. We all felt it and we all wanted to help each other escape it.

We did this directly through sharing course notes, insightful perspectives and relevant references. But more important to me was the indirect support: The afternoon breaks playing FIFA, the evenings watching films and the knowledge that I wasn't alone in my feelings of inadequacy.

My room in St Thomas Street was next to Tendai's. Tendai had become one of my best friends. He was a regular DJ at St Peter's College bops, where he would blast out tracks like Wiley's *Too Many Man* and Ludacris' *You's a Hoe*, which were played for their ridiculousness rather than for any musical or misogynistic purposes. Whenever Tendai discovered a new song that he loved, he would play it loud and on repeat, and would sing at the top of his voice: *I done shot a man down. In central staaa - tion, in front of a big old crowd… ohh ohh oh oh.* His other favourite was *beautiful people… owwooww don't you know, don't you know.* Those songs being *Man Down* by Rihanna and *Beautiful People* by Chris Brown.

I also turned to music as a source of relaxation and would regularly listen to one particular song to help settle my nerves at the end of a taxing day. I would load YouTube, press play and the smooth melodies and riffs would begin:

Now the skies could fall
Not even if my boss should call
The world it seems so very small
'Cause nothin' even matters at all

See nothin' even matters
See nothin' even matters at all
Nothin' even matters
Nothin' even matters at all[10]

---

[10] Hill, L. and D'Angelo (1998) *Nothing Even Matters*. Ruffhouse Records, Columbia Records.

Of course, my final exams mattered greatly and I knew it. But D'Angelo and Lauryn seemed to capture a greater truth. Pressures would come and go through life. The things that were most important to me had been there before Oxford and would be there when I graduated. Regardless of my results.

With this in mind, I agreed to take out 3 days to attend a Christian Conference in Exeter College. The conference was a matter of weeks before the start of my exams so it didn't make much rational sense to lose time that could have been spent revising; but I felt that it was important for me to be there. I was feeling spiritually and emotionally drained. The pressure of the exams were looming large and even with D'Angelo's wisdom and the support of my friends, I was failing to find peace.

In the first evening, a student from the University of Cambridge called Flick had gone into the chapel and started to play a worship song on the piano. It would be fair to say that I have an average voice but I decided to sing along. As I sang out, I experienced something supernatural. My arms were stretched out in a 'T' shape and I felt something physically pass through my stomach and hit the person who was standing behind me. He immediately doubled over and began singing joyfully.

When I went back to my room in St Thomas Street that evening, I could barely stand. I eventually collapsed to the floor where I remained for around 30 minutes, surrounded by a feeling of joy, peace and affirmation. I still don't understand what happened in this moment and why I've been unable to replicate this experience since.

But in a time of desperation and loneliness, something was there.

With my spirit revived, I now felt ready to face my final exams.

III

My first exam was a 3-hour Microeconomics paper. That morning, I dressed in the mandatory sub fusc attire - a dark suit, white shirt, black bow tie and a black undergraduate gown, which resembled a long buttonless jacket with missing sleeves. On my right lapel was a white carnation flower to symbolise the fact that we were sitting our first exam. I took the familiar walk down the High Street towards Examination Schools, but was too lost in my memorised diagrams and references to engage with the world around me. I paid no attention to the tourists reaching hurriedly for their cameras, the Oxford residents going about their daily commute or my fellow students who looked pensive about what lay ahead. This was the beginning of the end and my time of reckoning.

The Great Hall had been transformed for the examination period. Lecture-style seating had been replaced with rows and rows of individual desks. I located the desk that had been allocated to me and immediately began to undress. I took off my gown and placed it on the back of my chair. I unclipped my bow tie and shoved it into my suit jacket, which I then placed over my gown. I loosened the top button of my shirt and rolled up my sleeves. I sat down and took a pen out of the transparent pencil case. Then I waited for the instructions to commence writing. I would repeat this ritual a further ten times over the next fortnight.

The most difficult aspect of the Microeconomics paper was the time constraint. In three hours I was expected to answer four mathematical based economics questions, each with their own parts (a) - (g), along with three essay questions. The exams were designed to give truly exceptional students an opportunity to shine and show their ability. In exams like Strategy and Macroeconomics, I could feel intelligent connections and inferences flowing from my pen. In other exams, such as Microeconomics, I knew that I was unlikely to trouble the highest tier of marks. My strategy was to remain calm and pick up as many marks as I could using the knowledge I had.

But I had no plan for Accounting.

My 22nd birthday was the day before the Accounting exam. I spent my birthday revising, memorising and generally struggling to make progress. I entered the examination hall certain that I lacked the knowledge required to gain what in my mind, was a respectable mark. As I worked through the questions, my fears were confirmed. I told myself to keep going; a few marks could swing my final degree classification in either direction. At the conclusion of the exam, I had the scant consolation that the worst three hours of the examination period were surely behind me.

AFTER OXFORD

On the morning of my eleventh and final exam, I walked to Examination Schools wearing a red carnation. I felt overwhelmed by the fact that I was so close to completion. So close to having my life, an enjoyable life, back.

At half past twelve we were instructed to put down our pens. It was over... I sat in my chair, my hands holding the back of my neck and breathed a deep sigh of relief. I had completed my education at Oxford. I had completed a 17-year marathon through formal education. I would never have to sit another exam again!

As I exited the Examination Schools, friends from Team TED and the ACS were waiting to greet me. A paper hat was placed on my head and a Hawaiian plastic garland was wrapped around my neck. I was so happy and so exhausted. Out of the Economics group, only Ali and I finished that afternoon. We spent the evening in a daze; unsure of what to do with the vast oceans of free time that were now at our disposal. I spent the next day pulling my revision notes off the wall and packing away my revision folders, with the dependable voices of D'Angelo and Lauryn Hill in the background.

IV

By the end of the seventh week of the summer term of 2011, all final year exams had been completed. We now had seven days before our parents would descend on Oxford to remove our belongings from St Peter's College for the final time. We dubbed this seven day period 'Mythical Eighth Week'. It was mythical because for most of our final academic year, we questioned whether it actually existed; whether there was indeed life beyond and outside of exams and revision. And then having got to eighth week, we didn't quite know how we got there: How we made it through the three hour exams and the awkwardly worded questions. And now that eighth week had begun, there was a realisation that we did not have much longer to enjoy this special time of our lives; when we were able to walk across the hallway to speak to our friends.

Eighth week then became our final opportunity to enjoy Oxford; to try new things and to repeat those activities we loved. In the evenings, we went to student club nights and ate out in the city centre. During the daytime we played football and went punting.

Punts were similar to Venetian gondolas and had to be steered by a trusty and reliable hand. Tom Lloyd, who joined the 'Economics Boys' in third year (even though he studied Geography), had given himself the title of Admiral of the Oxford Waterways. A title he wore proudly until Mythical Eighth Week, where his punt got stuck and he fell head first into the water below.

In that week we had sentimental moments such as a farewell meal that we ate around the table of the kitchen in St Thomas Street. But we also had ill-advised moments such as the decision that Dave, Richard and I made to take part in the Atomic Burger Challenge.

I became concerned when the staff at Atomic Burger asked us to sign a disclaimer before the food arrived. We were also given blue plastic gloves to handle food that was deemed to be hazardous for skin, yet somehow suitable to be swallowed. When the plate arrived, I saw that three large chicken burger patties had been stacked using pizzas as the base, the top and the 'bread' in between. Around the tower of pizza and chicken were fries. Lots and lots of fries. The entire plate had then been covered in a pungent orange sauce that I could smell was going to taste hot. The whole plate was designed to resemble a volcano with the primary resemblance being the heat. We began to eat.

The sauce was intoxicating but I kept chewing and swallowing and stuffing more fries, chicken and pizza into my mouth. After a few minutes of eating, I decided to dismantle the tower from the top down. Around halfway to the ground floor I hit a wall. My chewing became slower and the sauce seemed unbearable but I kept going. Another chicken burger was consumed then another pizza. On and on and on I went until the plate was cleared. My reward was an Atomic Burger t-shirt with the word 'Winner' written on the back. I spent the remainder of Mythical Eight Week with a warm sensation in my stomach that made it uncomfortable to eat and sleep.

In that final week in Oxford, I reflected a lot on the three years that had gone by. I had made some great friends and met some incredible people. I had pushed myself socially and academically. I had taken positions of power and influence that were beyond anything I had the capacity to dream of. Through my work with Citizens UK, I was developing a better understanding of the world around me and how to be an advocate for change. But through all that I observed in Oxford, I sensed that the world that was being reproduced through higher education was still alien to the promise of the world as it could be.

Oxford was reflecting the priorities of society as a whole, which elevated financial gain and individualism above all else. In a few months' time, most of my classmates - some of the most intelligent, gifted and principled people I knew - would begin jobs in the City of London. Of course our economy needs financial services and the talented people to lead them, but it was a concern that other sectors would seem to be so unattractive to people who could have used their time and skills to do anything they wished to.

Years later, I read Michelle Obama's autobiography, *Becoming*[11], in which she told her own story of balancing the practicalities of pay checks with the desire to pursue a career with meaning. I was struck by her description of her husband, Barack Obama, who "believed and trusted when others did not. He had a simple, buoying faith that if you stuck to your principles, things would work out." These words articulated better than I could, the approach that I had committed myself to. I would stick to my principles in the firm belief that they would not let me down.

My uppermost principle was to use my time to serve worthwhile causes. I resolved that the purpose of the organisation and the content of the role were much more important than the resulting salary. But I also knew that I needed to be purposeful and strategic in my approach, and to consider the doors that may be opened or closed tomorrow as a consequence of the decisions I made today. I knew that the University of Oxford brand was valuable but it was not a master key. I would still need to prove myself to a world that was unfamiliar with the notion of intelligent black men.

Because people still reacted in disbelief when I told them that I was studying at the University of Oxford. *The real one? Really? Did I mean Oxford Brookes University?* One person even had the nerve to try to catch me out by making up the name of a College to see if I would correct them. Perhaps for the first time I understood what my dad meant when he said that I would have to work twice as hard. Because implicit within this line of questioning was the incredulity that someone who looked like me, sounded like me and who had my background, could have studied at Oxford.

---

[11] Obama, M. (2018) *Becoming*. New York: Crown.

While the odds were undeniably against me, these people failed to realise that my background - which instilled within me character, discipline and determination - had given me a chance. And sometimes one chance is enough.

V

My first job after graduation was as a sabbatical officer with the Oxford University Student Union. My fellow sabbaticals were the three triumphant candidates from Martha 4 OUSU - Martha, Hannah and Seb; Yuan Yang who stood as an independent candidate; and Jim O'Connell, who had won a by-election for the post of VP (Graduates).

Over seven months had passed since the election results. Seven months that had been monopolised by my degree. In that time, the bitterness that I felt in the aftermath of the result had eased but nevertheless, I was grateful when Martha asked if I'd like to meet up for a coffee before our roles formally began. It was great to resume our friendship after a year of being on opposing teams.

My first few weeks in OUSU were reserved for handover meetings with my predecessor, who was also called Daniel, introductory conversations with a range of internal and external stakeholders, and team building activities with the other sabbatical officers. One such activity was the Margerison-McCann Team Performance Wheel. Following the assessment, we began to call ourselves 'The Perfect Team'. Between us, we covered every segment of the Wheel (I was a 'Controller-Inspector'). Conforming to type, I placed the performance wheel alongside the Gantt chart that was proudly fastened to the wall behind my desk.

I was settling in well. The partisanship of the election campaign was behind us and natural friendships were forming across the whole team. We were pushing on with the business of championing reform for our respective portfolios while seeking to build trusting relationships with the new cohort of JCR Presidents.

I was so engrossed in my new role that when results day came, it was something of a surprise. For some undeclared reason the Economics and Management results had been delayed and I had given up my daily ritual of logging into the online portal to see if they had finally been published. It was a Friday morning when Martha, who sat in the desk next to mine, turned to me and said "the E&M results are out."

I opened the internet browser and typed in my student ID and password. The home screen looked identical as the days and weeks before except for a new icon towards the left hand side of the monitor, which read 'final examinations'. I clicked on the button and there in writing were the numbers 2.1 and the text 'upper second class'.

I had made it through the rigours of the University of Oxford and in a few weeks' time, my parents, siblings and grandma would join me in Oxford for my graduation ceremony.

The other Economics and Management students in my year at St Peter's were (from left to right): Tendai, Dan, Una and Mike.

Above: The annual JCR photograph (2008-09) Left: During and after the Presidential race with Sanjay Nanwani. We put on quite a spectacle much to the delight of the JCR!

Right: With one of the St Peter's porters John, who would welcome everyone who came into the College (I'm wearing my lucky t-shirt!)

Far right: I came as a dove to the Noah's Ark 'bop' courtesy of the artistic skills of Richard Gallon.

Halfway hall marked the midpoint of our time as students at St Peter's. As JCR President, I was required to give a speech.

The Afro-Caribbean Society was the source of some of my best friendships and a vital support network. The outcome of Rare Rising Stars 2010 was a surprise; I enjoyed meeting the team from Rare after the ceremony in Parliament.

Mythical 8th week: With Dave and Richard before and after the Atomic Burger Challenge, and attempting to punt.

Graduation day with the 'Economics Boys' (from left to right): Mike, Tendai, Dan, Adam, Alasdair, Dave and me.

The OUSU Sabbatical Team (minus Yuan): Hannah, Seb, Martha, Jim and me.

With Tom and Elena; the T and E in Team TED.

AFTER OXFORD

DANIEL STONE

RETURNING TO THE CLASSROOM

"To lose faith in the system is to place self before service."
- Identity Economics, Akerlof and Kranton[12]

His name was Anton. He was in his mid-twenties and was therefore slightly older than me. At around 5'11, he was slightly shorter. He had a broad smile and a gold tooth towards the left of his mouth. When he spoke, he used a combination of London and US slang. He used his words to produce rap music, which told his story of reformation and salvation. He was smart and streetwise and curious as to why a graduate from the University of Oxford was seeking to work on gang crime issues in his community.

The first time we met was over a coffee. I had started working part-time as a community organiser based in the Centre for Theology and Community. I was on a one year contract to develop the City Safe Campaign within institutions based in an East London community. One of the local Pentecostal churches called 'A Radical Church' - or ARC for short - had identified Anton as one of their emerging leaders. Using the recommended structure of a one-to-one conversation, I began by sharing my story, beginning with my upbringing in Birmingham.

"Yeah, I heard Birmingham is a madness. What are the two main crews called again? Johnsons and..."

---

[12] Akerlof, G. and Kranton, R. (2011) *Identity Economics: How Our Identities Shape Our Work, Wages, and Well-Being.* Princeton University Press...

"The Burger Bar Boys," I replied. "Although apparently they've changed their name."

"Yeah, it happens - gangs change their names a lot but it's the same people running them though. When I was inside, there were bare man from Birmingham. Birmingham is as crazy as London."

"Nah!" I smirked. "It's OK. I mean, if you're looking for trouble, you can find it. But anything can happen to you in London at any time."

"True... Do you know Lady Leshurr?" Lady Leshurr was a female rapper and grime artist from Birmingham. In 2011, she hadn't yet hit the mainstream charts but would have been idolised among the UK rap community.

"I've heard of her, but I don't really know her stuff."

"You're from Birmingham and you don't know Lady Leshurr?!" I was being mocked now and could see the full glint of Anton's tooth as his head fell back in laughter. I remained silent and hoped that the conversation would move on. "So how long are you here for? A year, yeah?" I could hear the scepticism in his voice.

"Yeah, I'm here for at least a year. But whatever we're able to build over the next year can be continued by people who live here," I said with a confidence that hid my doubt. "So, I guess the question is, what can we do together in the next year? And what makes you angry?"

It seemed that Anton was angry about quite a lot. He didn't know his father and was angry about having to develop his own concepts of manhood without a role model or guide. He was angry about the lack of opportunities that had been presented to him after finishing school and that a life of crime had been the most economically viable option. He had spent time in prison where anger and violence were the going currency. He was now angry that promises of support and employment after prison had not materialised. However becoming a Christian had channelled that anger towards wanting to make the most of his life. He told me that he enjoyed writing music and was going to use that as a way to make money and transform lives.

Anton wouldn't strike you as being a typical churchgoer. But then again, ARC wasn't a typical church. ARC's leader, Pastor Peter Nembhard, was himself a reformed prison inmate. Losing two and a half years behind bars at the age of 16 had set Pastor Peter on the road to salvation. He now did everything with an unabated passion: sweat would run down his forehead as he worshipped God during Sunday morning services and when he took up a role as striker in the after church football match.

Pastor Peter was genuine, warm and knowledgeable about the challenges and temptations of a life of crime. Traits that endeared him to Anton and many of the young people who became members and leaders at ARC.

One of the female leaders was called Keisha. In our one-to-one she told me how the influence of gangs had always been visible in her family and in her neighbourhood. She decided to follow in the footsteps of older siblings and join a gang. Her primary responsibility was to carry contraband for the male gang members; the rationale being that the police were less likely to stop and search females. Keisha now worked full time for the Borough Council and had ambitions to start a charity designed to teach entrepreneurial skills to young people.

With Anton, Keisha and four others, I now had a strong base of leaders within ARC who were all motivated by a desire to make a positive difference in the lives of young people.

I began meeting with other institutions in the area. I met with the Imam of the local mosque to discuss issues in the Muslim community. They were also concerned by the number of young people who were being drawn away from faith and into gangs. The Imam pointed to difficulties in the formal education system as being the root of the problem: "Without education, young people cannot get the fast cars and nice clothes they see on TV." I'd heard this argument before; that drugs and gangs were perceived as the most likely route to the flashy lifestyle youngsters saw on billboards and social media.

There was a similar story in the local Baptist Church, whose Pastor was mournful about the state of modern families: "What many young people are seeking, and often finding in gangs, is belonging."

AFTER OXFORD

The Anglican Church didn't have many young people but they empathised with the issues that they saw in their local primary school, where children as young as 6 were being used to transport drugs and other paraphernalia.

In addition to faith leaders, I spoke with school leaders and representatives of youth organisations who all agreed that something needed to be done, and that it would take the effort of the whole community.

I knew that City Safe could never be the solution to the broad range of social, economic and interpersonal reasons that explained why individuals choose to join gangs, but it was a start. And the hope was that by getting people to work across religious, ethnic and social lines to achieve something as simple as getting a shopkeeper to post a purple sticker in their window, you would liberate them to formulate long term plans, together.

On a bright Saturday afternoon, around 40 people from the communities and institutions that I had spoken to, met outside the McDonald's opposite the Baptist Church. Although the numbers were fewer than I hoped for, it hadn't gone unnoticed that many different sections of this East London community were gathered together, all wearing matching purple t-shirts. We walked down the high street, speaking to store owners and members of the public on our way. Almost all were willing to join the City Safe campaign and had the purple sticker to prove it. The 'small wins' were infectious. People were smiling and cheering and energised about the work ahead. They were standing shoulder to shoulder with people who shared the same passion and the same anger as them, and were proud of it.

While the cheers continued, I was concerned. I knew that people would soon grow tired of small wins and want significant and tangible change.

I

During my year in OUSU, community organising was the primary tool used by a group of students to campaign for the University of Oxford to become an accredited Living Wage employer. Over the summer I hatched a plot with the chair of the Living Wage Campaign, Sarah Santhosham. We decided that our starting point would be to collect stories. Without testimonies, the university could dismiss our requests as the figment of a liberal imagination, when we knew and sensed the reality of the hardships faced by people who were being underpaid for the services they delivered.

We agreed that before term started, I would try to find at least one person who was willing to go on record. We decided to focus on buildings owned by the central university (rather than individual Colleges) and to seek out cleaners who were likely to be on the lowest end of the pay scale. We reasoned that cleaners would work through the night and finish early in the morning. So over the space of about a fortnight I had a number of very, very early starts.

The first day I arrived at 7am. I waited outside for over 30 minutes before I realised that I had probably left it too late. The second day I arrived at 6am to see that most of the cleaners were already walking away from the library. I tried to speak to someone but they were in a hurry and spoke very little English. I was buoyed by the fact that I was getting closer and arrived at the library the very next day slightly before 6am, and waited. At around 6am, a middle aged woman exited the building followed by two of her colleagues. They were initially hesitant as a young man with a hoodie and large coat (to keep me warm in the cool morning air) strode towards them.

"My name is Daniel." I spoke slowly as I assumed that they too would not have English as their first language. Sarah had the brilliant idea of translating the basic idea of the Living Wage campaign into Spanish text, which I handed to the three women as I spoke. They read it carefully.

"Li-ving wage?" One of the other women began. "What this is about? More pay?"

I nodded.

"No, you get us in trouble."

With that, she dragged the arms of the two other women with her and began to walk away.

The first middle-aged woman looked back with hope and desperation in her eyes.

AFTER OXFORD

The next day was Saturday so I decided to wait until the next week before going back to the library. I arrived at 5.50am on Monday morning. The cleaners came out one by one but the woman I was looking for wasn't among the group. I returned on Wednesday. At about 6.03am she walked out with her other, less vocal colleague. After a few words in Spanish, the woman left her colleague and walked over to me. "I have a son. I no want any trouble. But it is hard." Tears started to roll down her face as she spoke.

We walked around the corner to avoid the possible gaze of her supervisors. For the purposes of this account, I shall call her 'Maria'. We exchanged contact details and I told Maria that Sarah would contact her to arrange a time to meet. Within the next week, Sarah had met with Maria along with a member of the campaign who spoke fluent Spanish. Her story was heart-breaking - she had lost her husband and was working several low paying jobs to provide for herself and her son. She finished most days hungry and tired; the definition of someone who was paid a wage that wasn't enough for her to truly live.

With Maria's testimony, we were able to get a front page story in the Oxford Student Newspaper, which we used to promote a protest that we had organised in the following week, to be held outside the Social Sciences Library - We reasoned that it was where we likely to find the most sympathetic and socially minded students and academics.

The article generated more testimonies; more stories of hardship and hardworking people who were forced to strive endlessly just to make ends meet. The press activity also caught the attention of the senior leaders of the University, specifically the Pro Vice Chancellor who months earlier had claimed that there was no racism in Oxford. Sarah and I were invited to a meeting, along with Hannah O'Rourke, who was another student leader of the Oxford Living Wage Campaign.

We prepared thoroughly for the meeting and presented economic arguments in favour of paying staff a living wage and data produced by other Russell Group universities who had become accredited living wage employers. We knew that convincing Oxford that they were falling behind accepted best practice in the sector would be an effective line of attack. We repeated the content of the testimonies that we had collected from people who were employees of the University of Oxford and reminded the PVC of the responsibility of universities, especially those with the history and heritage of Oxford, to be vanguards of betterment within society.

189

The PVC responded positively; he said that it seemed entirely sensible that the University should pay its staff a living wage especially given the example shown by other higher education institutions. He took a copy of our documents and said that he would arrange to meet with a representative of the Living Wage Foundation to look into the feasibility of implementation.

The PVC was true to his word and the meeting was arranged around a month and a half later. The University had done its homework before the meeting and shared a diagram, which proved that the majority of directly employed staff were paid a living wage; the problem was with contracted cleaners. We weren't going to allow the PVC to pass the blame so easily and stressed that they could make it a requirement that any third-party contracts had to prove that they were paying their staff a living wage. The PVC explained that this sort of decision would need to go through a series of internal committees but that it was a proposal they would bring forward.

I was midway through my final term as an OUSU sabbatical officer and no progress had been made. We had provided Maria and many of her colleagues with a lifeline, and I was desperate for our progress not to be lost in a fog of bureaucracy. We wrote another article in the Oxford Student Newspaper using some of the stories that we'd held back. I also sent an email to the PVC warning that some members of the committee were fishing with the national press to see if they were interested in writing a story based on the information we had found. This wasn't entirely true but I knew that negative national press coverage was the University's kryptonite and that we needed to leverage anything we could to our advantage.

We were soon in the PVC's office again. He explained that discussions would be taken forward but that these things took time. Thankfully, Sarah and Hannah would both be in Oxford for at least another year and would be able to continue the fight after my year in OUSU had finished. A month or two after I left Oxford, Sarah sent me a text message to say that the University of Oxford had become an accredited living wage employer.

It seemed to me that the campaign worked because there was a centre of power for us to push against. Yes, the centre was relatively complex, inaccessible and resistant to change but it had an embodiment in the form of a PVC and university committees. We could devise strategies for bringing our cause to their attention and for making it in their interest to at least consider our request. Ultimately it was a finite problem that started and ended with defined processes in procurement and budget setting.

But the issue of gangs was different. There was no definable source of power. No one person or committee who could decide to make gang violence cease. Opposing gangs would require mankind to oppose ourselves: our own greed and individualism, our failed families and our idolisation of the rich and powerful. Yes, police and education systems could and should do more, but any attempts to point the blame for why people choose to join gangs would see our fingertips pointed squarely at our own chests.

II

I worked in East London for three days of the week. The other two days, I worked for Rare. On first viewing, Rare was unremarkable. It was based on the fourth floor of an office block near Farringdon, which seemed to be shared by an eclectic mix of tech start-ups, graphic designers and modelling agencies. The old lift would strain as it brought its passengers towards the upper floors of the building, but it was easier than taking the calf-busting journey up four flights of an increasingly narrowing staircase.

The office itself was open plan. Around a dozen or so desktop computers sat efficiently opposite or adjacent to one another to maximise space. To the right was a medium sized meeting room with a glass front and a smaller room perched next to it. One of the best features of the office was the balcony, which looked out onto the backs of other small businesses; the computers, manikins and artwork giving a clue as to their respective occupants.

But inside this office, I saw magic take place. Rare usually worked with university students or recent graduates from underrepresented or disadvantaged backgrounds. *Rare Candidates*, as they were known, often came to Rare uncertain about their future career or in need of support to navigate treacherous assessment centres. Whether it took weeks, months or years, Rare would support their candidates to land their dream job. Portraits of smiling diverse faces lined the walls of the office as a permanent reminder of what was at stake. When someone gained a Training Contract or job offer, a cheer would erupt, filling the whole office with the sound of success.

Rare was founded by a warm hearted, straight-talking, charismatic man called Raphael Mokades who was uncompromisingly driven towards excellence, improvement and success. Monday update meetings were quick fire rounds of key facts with no waffling. Raph would rattle off an efficient stream of information about client meetings and company strategy without pausing for breath, oblivious to the wry smiles of his colleagues. As a lone spoke in a relatively flat organisation, Raph was my line manager. He demanded that both the content and presentation of my work was immaculate; free of grammatical errors and directing the eye of the reader to the most important information. I enjoyed Raph's leadership style; it helped me to raise the quality of my work to the standard expected by the private sector and before long, I was producing work that was returned with only minor corrections.

Raph understood that *people* are an organisation's most valuable asset, and so the usually opposing forces of high performance and high hilarity somehow coexisted at Rare. The three words Raph chose to define the working environment at Rare were fun, food and flexibility. The balcony acted as the perfect location for annual team BBQs, monthly team lunches (in the summer) and daily conversations with colleagues. Christmas parties were epic and usually began with a team building activity that involved forging ourselves into a human pyramid or swinging off high ropes. After a large meal, the office would divide into two teams, ready to do battle unto death in the annual quiz. It took the whole Christmas break for wounds to heal and for enemies to once again become colleagues.

The programme I managed at Rare was called Target Oxbridge. Its founder Naomi Kellman, had been in my ACS friendship group at Oxford. Target Oxbridge was a response to the underrepresentation of people from African and Afro-Caribbean heritage in the universities of Oxford and Cambridge. While the population of people of African and Afro-Caribbean descent in the UK was 3%, they made up barely 1% of the Russell Group Universities and a much smaller percentage of students in Oxbridge.

In 2011, the Prime Minister David Cameron had brought the underrepresentation of black students at Oxbridge into the national spotlight when he revealed that "only one black student had been admitted to Oxford in the previous round of admissions."[13] He was mistaken, in that one 'Home Afro-Caribbean' student had been admitted - there were a larger number of Home students with African heritage. But nonetheless, this provided momentum for programmes like Target Oxbridge, which sought to give black students the confidence and knowledge to gain a place at the UK's top higher education institutions.

I loved working with young people who were hungry to fulfil their potential but I was hesitant about representing a programme whose eligibility criteria was based on ethnicity. All of my sessions would begin with the picture of me outside Top Playground, with my hands in my pockets, looking really out of place. Pupils would marvel that the boy in the photograph studied at Oxford and was the same young man who was now standing before them.

A stream of questions would follow: *What was Oxford like? Was the work difficult? Did I meet Emma Watson* (A reference to Harry Potter and the fact that Emma Watson studied in Oxford for a year). The pupils hung unto my every word; entranced and inspired.

But then the moment in my presentation would arrive where I introduced the Target Oxbridge programme: the mentoring, guidance and trips that successful applicants would receive. And the eligibility criteria.

This was usually fine when the school had planned ahead and given me a room of academically able African or Afro-Caribbean pupils. It was much more awkward when the room had a high proportion of pupils who weren't eligible either because of their ethnic background or because their predicted grades were too low. The predicted grades scenario was tough but fair; if pupils didn't stand a realistic chance of making a strong application, the only compassionate thing to do was to tell them. But it was much more difficult to tell someone that they couldn't apply because of the colour of their skin.

The best part of me believed in a world where people were encouraged to dream freely regardless of their ethnic background and I was concerned that my actions were reinforcing a way of thinking that I wanted to have no part of. For many of these young people, I was a role model; a living and breathing embodiment of what they hoped to attain. They had been inspired by my story, but in return I only had something to offer those who were rich in melanin.

---

13   https://www.independent.co.uk/news/education/education-news/cameron-in-row-with-oxford-over-black-students-2266447.html

Rare wasn't immune to soul-searching regarding its eligibility criteria. It had been criticised by a vocal minority for adopting a focus that was too narrow; *what about white working class kids? Surely black children born into middle class households were more privileged?*

I discussed these thoughts at length with Raph, and the more we spoke, the more I realised how complex and largely subjective disadvantage is. Rare had drawn a line in the sand but over time, and as it built its credibility, this line was pushed further and further into the deeper crevices of inequality. While on this journey, any person who had found a job, success or purpose, was worth cheering.

The affection that colleagues at Rare felt for their candidates began from the very first conversation. Before any formal training or development began, successful applicants were first invited to take part in an activity designed to find out what made them 'tick'. A number of statements were read out and the respondent had to give a number between 1 and 5, where 1 was low priority and 5 was high.

"I am motivated by money."

I paused, "2". Money wasn't a motivation but it also wasn't completely irrelevant. It was correlated with quality of life and how my skills and time were valued.

"I like working with numbers."

"5" - no hesitation.

"I value helping others."

"5"

The statements were read out by Raph's younger brother Dan, who also worked at Rare. Dan was a larger-than-life, sparkling character with a sharp wit. He spent around two-thirds of the year working for Rare and the rest of his time in Vegas or writing a book. He was wonderfully observant and would see strengths and insecurities in people that few took the time to notice.

"Can you tell me one moment that you're most proud of?"

I paused. I considered giving 'getting into Oxford' as my answer or the award given to me by Rare in Parliament. But I knew that my proudest moment had been in November of the previous year.

I had been invited back to Hamstead Hall as the guest of honour at the annual awards evening. The hall was full of parents, pupils, teachers and governors. My parents were also present as a show of support. In reality, having them in the audience made me incredibly nervous! It was the first time that I would speak in front of them and I felt more hesitant than usual. I began shakily. My mouth became really dry and I fumbled with the water bottle as I took off the cap. But I soon found my stride.

"There was a Teenager in Glastonbury called George Garret who changed his name to *Captain Fantastic Faster than Superman Spiderman Batman Wolverine Hulk and the Flash Combined.*" I took a long gasp of air. "You see, not all change is positive. So how will you ensure that the changes you make in the final few years of school or going into sixth form or university, will allow you to GROW?"

My speech had taken shape over a few weeks. I had quickly identified the four key points I wanted to make in the speech, then edited and crafted them into an easy to remember acronym.

"Be GENEROUS: You will grow when you discover that you have something to give." I spoke about the time that Paulette encouraged me to share my story with the group of young people at an event in Villa Park, and that years later, I met one of the girls who had been in the audience and who was now a student at Cambridge.

"Be ROOTED: You have to determine what is important to you." I told the story of my decision to take a gap year and the difficulty of opposing my dad.

"Be ORGANISED: I have lost count of the number of well-meaning, ambitious, hardworking, capable young people who miss out on opportunities in life because they're not organised." I was honest about the discipline that it took to stick to revision timetables and that employers expect professionalism as a minimum requirement.

"Be WISE: Wisdom will call to you from many different places. From your teachers, the things you've read or seen, from your parents. When it calls, listen. Why? Because wisdom will tell you to get back up after you've suffered a setback of a failed application. Wisdom tells you to plan for the long term and to work hard. And wisdom helps you in those really tough decisions in life – when you're thinking about studies or relationships or jobs. Wisdom won't let you down."

After the academic awards were four special awards. The first two awards, the *Richard Wright Awards* were awarded to individuals who had achieved outstanding academic or sporting feats. The *David Brown Community Award* was presented to someone who had been a good citizen or had a positive effect on their local community. Both awards were named after past long-serving head teachers of Hamstead Hall.

Then for the first time, a student in Year 11 was given the *Daniel Stone Award*. The award was presented by Mr Farah, who had taught me Maths in Sixth Form. He explained that I would be the perfect ambassador for this award, not only because of what I achieved but the manner in which I achieved it. I wasn't proud or boastful but was always mindful of the students and teachers around me.

As Mr Farah spoke, my eyes welled with tears. I felt so incredibly proud. To see a lasting legacy to my time in Hamstead Hall; to see good character honoured alongside other measures of success; and for my parents to be witness to this.

Dan had a smile glued to his face while I told the story. When we went back into the office after our conversation, he announced: "Guys, guys! You know that 'what makes you tick' question about your proudest moment? I asked Stoney (as I was affectionately known). And you'll never guess what he said?"

Everyone waited silently in expectation.

"He's got a friggin' award named after him. Yeah! The Daniel Stone Award!"

In all my time at Rare, I never lived that down!

Dan actually ended our meeting by giving me a really deep and challenging question to think about. "Why are you here? Why aren't you out there, doing what you're passionate about?"

Dan didn't want me to leave Rare of course, but he was pushing me to be more confident. He knew that I knew what mattered most to me, but that I wasn't pursuing it. I didn't give him a direct answer at that moment but I pondered the question over the coming months.

I wasn't motivated by money or 'status careers'. I wanted to make a difference. But this also meant that I grew frustrated by mediocrity. I knew that if I was going to really make a difference, I needed to think, act and be better than I was.

IV

Work in East London was becoming increasingly frustrating. People would miss planning meetings despite their assurances that they would attend. I was growing more distant with Anton who I found to be unreliable. I arranged for a professional contact to have a meeting with Anton to talk through some of his budding business ideas. He didn't show and I was forced to make an embarrassing apology to someone who I had only recently met.

Then in early 2013, Target Oxbridge achieved its first three successes. Kalm, Alex and Nkisu were given offers to study at Oxford. I was invited into the London studios of the BBC but would be speaking to regional radio shows across the country in the regular two hour slot on a Sunday evening that usually featured content targeted at the African and Afro-Caribbean community. After church in the morning, I spent the whole day with Anton and his friend, eating, playing FIFA and talking about future plans. They were smoking weed. I declined. I said my goodbyes in the late afternoon and caught the underground into Central London.

I met Andre from Rare and Kalm and Alex, in a cafe across the road from the BBC studios. Andre briefed us on the key points that he wanted us to discuss during the interviews: the purpose of the programme, the support successful applicants could expect to receive and the focus on developing the potential of young people, whether that led them into Oxbridge or another top Russell Group university. I was struggling to keep up with Andre as he spoke. I felt drained and unusually lethargic. I ordered a drink and hoped it would jolt me into life. I wasn't myself as I left the cafe nor when I entered the live recording studio nor when the red light turned on and I was asked to give my name. The interviews were awful. My brain wasn't functioning! I remember including the word 'potential' in almost every sentence of every answer. Many of my responses seemed flat and impersonal. And then at one point, I told the female radio presenter from Liverpool to "let me know" when she was next in Birmingham.

The next day, I listened to the recording of the interview that had been posted on the BBC London website. A ten minute conversation had been edited down to around 30 seconds of usable tape.

A few months later I was in conversation with a friend who had spent a weekend in Amsterdam. He told me about smoking weed and eating marijuana cakes and how it had left him feeling lethargic and zoned out. I thought back to my interview car crash and realised that I had been passively smoking weed all Sunday afternoon, and had gone live on radio, stoned!

Despite the challenges of the project, I enjoyed some successes working in East London. We organised a successful anti-knife crime concert and I delivered fortnightly community development workshops to a dozen Year 8 students in a local school, culminating in a visit to Oxford at the end of the school year. But I was unhappy and unsettled.

I found out that Keisha was pregnant with Anton's child. Anton sensed my disappointment and feared my judgement and our relationship deteriorated. And I was becoming increasingly disillusioned with the vision of an organisation who would parachute me into a community for a single year when I could see that it would take at least ten years to build the strength of relationship required to form bonds of trust.

They knew, and I knew that I would be unable and unwilling to give that.

It felt like the right time to return to Birmingham. The only problem was that I didn't have a job or much of a plan. Initially I was OK with this. I figured that I was employable and that it would only be a matter of time before I found something.

But then I began telling people about my plan to relocate. A question would immediately follow: *What have you got lined up?* Or something to that effect. When I replied with the word *nothing*, I would detect an expression of hurt and/or surprise. For my current employers it was a look that said: *Are we that bad that you would leave with nothing to go to?* For friends and other well-wishers it was a reaction of concern: *How can you not have a plan?* With each conversation I began to feel an increasing amount of shame and insecurity.

My first idea was to set up a black hair shop - despite having no links with suppliers, no experience managing a business and no real interest in, or knowledge of, black hair. But I knew that there was demand.

From Birmingham to London to Manchester, black hair shops provided an essential service to the black community but also produced the very worst in customer experience. Black hair shops are predominantly owned and staffed by men from South Asia. Most would have at least half a dozen employees in what was a relatively small shop, who in my mind were given clear instructions to make every customer feel as uncomfortable as possible. They would watch your every move in the belief that a single blink would lead to oils, creams and combs suddenly disappearing into the pockets of wily black people. The environment of black hair shops - in which customers were treated like criminals - had been a source of disgruntlement for decades.

In addition to the commercial rationale, I believed that hair shops were an important meeting point for the community, from which renewed solidarity and community-based initiatives could spring. A number of years earlier, during a summer break from university, I drafted some plans with my local barber shop in Handsworth to turn their first floor area into a homework club.

My barber understood that his shop was a place where parents and children felt safe, and that safety could be developed into engagement.

So when people asked *what I had lined up*, I would say that I was going to open a black hair shop. There were still looks of surprise but these were usually followed by the words *sounds interesting* or *tell me more* or *good luck*.

I gave my default answer to Tim Thorlby, a former consultant who now worked at the Centre for Theology and Community. Rather than giving a textbook affirmative answer, he adjusted his glasses and asked if I'd ever run a business before? I said no. He asked if I knew anything about the black hair business. I shook my head but said that I had started to read some useful books on supply chains. He asked me to write a business plan to consolidate my ideas on paper and to see if the figures added up. I began to prepare the document and quickly realised that I wasn't interested in doing it.

However, writing a business plan helped me to think creatively and commercially, and before I knew it, I thought of a new idea. My plan was to work with secondary school children in Birmingham offering careers advice, university application support and motivational workshops. I would charge schools a fee to deliver the content and/or would follow the Rare model of charging corporate clients.

I came up with the name *The In Sight Project* as the focus of my intervention was to show young people what was possible and who they could become, and then I would help them to get there. I wrote a business plan with estimations of the numbers of schools, students and clients I would need for the business to be financially viable.I registered as a CIO with Companies House and drafted a constitution that outlined my mission and goals. And then I began organising meetings with local schools and touting for business.

I did have some early successes. Two secondary schools invited me in to deliver day-long workshops. I delivered hand written letters to recruitment and social responsibility leads of the big graduate employers based in Birmingham and received some warm responses. I even had the chance to pitch for some seed funding in a Dragon's Den style competition where I finished in the top 4 (only the first placed applicant was given financial support).

But after a few months I realised that my idea was doomed for failure. There simply wasn't the critical mass of more able students in the schools I was engaging with to make my business plan stack up. Schools also didn't have the budgets or available space in their timetable to employ me for the number of lessons or workshops that I would need to deliver in order to make a living. My estimations had been widely inaccurate and had exposed my inexperience.

My intentions were good. I knew that as a young man who was willing to give back before I took for myself, I was communicating a powerful and necessary message. But the reality dawned on me that this present version of Daniel was ill equipped to help. I didn't know enough about the challenges I claimed to want to fix. I hadn't disciplined myself in the study and research of these issues. I didn't know how to manage complex projects in the real world or how to truly work collaboratively. I hadn't tried to work with people like Errol who had knowledge and experience of working with schools.

I was unwise and I was naive. I had followed my heart but had disengaged my mind.

But through this experience, I was learning some very important lessons. Working for charities, even those designed to tackle injustice, could be unfulfilling. I needed to think more carefully about my future employment decisions. And I still needed to GROW.

DANIEL STONE

RETURNING TO LONDON

"We corrupt a good, an activity or a social practice whenever we treat it according to a lower norm than is appropriate to it." - Michael Sandel, What Money Can't Buy[14]

The palm of my hand hovered over the pan. I could feel that the oil was hot. I picked up a coated chicken leg by its ankle joint and lowered it in. The oil burst into life, covering the chicken in golden bubbles. I hurried and dropped in another three legs, then a further four thighs; being careful not to allow one to cover the other.

While they cooked, I began the next batch; tossing the chicken in the pre-prepared seasoning and flour. After a few minutes I used a spoon to lift out the golden brown pieces of fried chicken and placed them into a dish for further cooking in the oven. It would stay here for at least 45 minutes.

I pushed open the kitchen's folding doors and walked out into the corridor. The golden tinsel was in place over the door frame and running along the stairs. Gold and silver bells adorned the photo frames and paper decorations spiralled down from the ceiling.

---

[14] Sandel, M. (2013) *What Money Can't Buy: the Moral Limits of Markets*. New York: Farrar, Straus & Giroux.

AFTER OXFORD

The playlist that Joanna had created on Spotify was humming in the background. The Christmas offerings from Boyz II Men, Destiny's Child and Chris Brown would wait until our guests had arrived. For now, we were enjoying the serene tones of Michael Buble.

The living room table was placed against the far wall. It was covered in a red tablecloth and was full of food and drinks: crisps, sweets, chocolate treats, hard dough bread, cake, salad, coleslaw, and plastic plates and cutlery.

"How's the chicken going?" Selina inquired.

"Yeah, it's almost done. I'll put some more on later if we need it."

Selina smiled. "This is going to be so much fun!"

For the past year, I had lived with Selina and Joanna in South East London. Our abode was a spacious three-bedroom house that was directly opposite the home of the Reverend Les Isaac, the Managing Director of the charity that I now worked for. Ascension Trust was a Christian organisation, founded with the purpose of equipping churches to serve their local communities.

There was a quick turnaround from job application to job offer, and Les offered me the spare room in his house while I found my feet. It was really enjoyable living with Les, his wife Louise, his son Jake and his daughter-in-law Tinu. Their house was always alive with conversation and laughter. Les drove to work on most days and so we would be together on the daily commute, listening to the radio and discussing politics, leadership and current affairs. One of Les' passions was to see young people advancing into positions of leadership, where they could use their perspective on the world to translate services and activities into a language that resonated with their generation.

Over the course of the past year, 'Les Isaac' had become my default answer to the question 'who is your hero?' Or 'who do you most admire?' I struggled to answer these questions honestly in the past. But in Les, I saw a skilled and experienced leader who had a genuine and deep compassion for people. I saw this compassion engulf senior leaders in the religious and secular world, as well as young people, the homeless community and the disenfranchised.

One Saturday morning I accompanied Les to Ascension Trust's office in Brixton. It was a rainy day and as we approached the office, we could see a line of around a dozen people queuing outside the building next door. Les could see that the building was closed and immediately opened the door at Ascension Trust, welcoming the dozen people in for tea and biscuits.

The house my sisters and I now lived in was owned by Les' neighbour called Jackie. Jackie decided to move back to Guyana for one year that would turn into two, three and eventually an indefinite relocation. She wanted to find reliable tenants to rent the house while she transitioned abroad. If such tenants couldn't be found, then the house would be left vacant.

On my first visit to the house, I had been impressed with the magnitude and orderliness of the place. There was a large living room with a sofa set facing a TV and a window with blinds that looked out onto the neat front garden. The dining room was also very big with a large extendable wooden dining table, which had a protective covering to prevent scratching or staining. From the dining room you could walk directly into the back garden, which had a beautiful green lawn bordered by plants on either side. The house looked immaculate and Jackie stated, sternly, that she expected both the interior and exterior of the house to be maintained.

The tour continued upstairs with a decently sized bathroom with a shower and bath. There were two large bedrooms with their own king-sized bed and walk-in wardrobes. We then entered the third bedroom; although 'enter' was perhaps an overstatement. The bedroom door barely swung back before it hit the single bed. I craned my head around the door and saw a small single wardrobe standing adjacent to a chest of drawers. I knew that Selina and Joanna would never agree to staying in this room and that I would have to accept these limitations in order to make the deal work. And I would do it because, as my dad taught me years ago, that was what men did.

But I was delighted to have the opportunity to live with my sisters. I hadn't lived for an extended time with my family since before university. Joanna had grown so much - she was funny and stylish but also couldn't be bossed around so easily, which was annoying given that we needed her to do her fair share of housekeeping and cooking.

Selina and I would have to call regular 'house meetings' where the agenda would focus on issues such as taking the bins out (which usually were done by Selina and I), gardening (which I almost exclusively did on account of the garden shed having spiders) and re-establishing the cleaning rota (which had been agreed at the previous house meeting but which subsequently had not been followed).

But the positives of living with Selina and Joanna far outweighed the negatives. It was great having people at home after a long day at work, even just to while away the hours watching box sets like Breaking Bad and How to Get Away with Murder. Dramatic moments always seemed to be amplified when watching them unfold on a sofa next to one of my sisters. "What did Annalise just say?!" "No way - Hank!" "I am the one who knocks..."

"Who did you invite?" Selina asked.

"Just a few people - no more than twenty," Matthew smirked.

"What? You don't even live in London!" Jo screamed, playfully hitting out towards Matthew, who grabbed her arms and playfully pushed them to one side.

"I know people, OK." That was an understatement. While most people collected stamps or bottle tops, Selina, Joanna and I had reached the conclusion that Matthew collected friends. Matthew had recently relocated to Manchester where he was working as a Pastoral Care Manager for a secondary school, but he still had an entourage of London-based friends.

Joanna was in London working at the accounting firm KPMG. It was always surreal seeing my little sister return home from work with her professional business attire and smart laptop case. I would picture her walking around Canary Wharf with its glass-fronted skyscrapers and being in meetings with corporate clients. I knew that she would be able to hold her own but the culture must have seemed so alien to her at times.

Selina had spent time at a Bible College in Doncaster before moving to London to study towards a Master's degree in Theology, Politics and Faith-based Organisations at King's College and while working part-time for the Centre for Theology and Community (CTC). Despite some of the frustrations I experienced as a community organiser, I had no hesitation recommending CTC to Selina. It was perfectly aligned with her interests and Angus, the

Director of CTC, was a good man who sometimes found his ambitions tied by a lack of funding.

The doorbell was ringing at regular intervals now, and I retreated to the kitchen to prepare a fresh batch of chicken. I returned to the party around 30 minutes later to see Joanna talking to some of my friends from university.

"Here he is!" Dave exclaimed. I put the plate down and gave Dave a hug followed by Alasdair, Dan, Dan's fiancé Jade, Adam, Lloyd, and Tendai. The fact that I greeted Tendai differently to my other university friends was becoming something of a running joke. It was true that my other friends got a standard hug; where bodies faced together and one arm reaches over the shoulder of the other person at a diagonal. With Tendai, the greeting would begin with a coming together of our right hands, almost as if we were about to commence an arm wrestle, the top of our bodies would then be pulled slightly towards each other and then our grip would be released.

"Should've known we'd find Stoney with the chicken," Dan remarked. "We'd always see your brother in the kitchen in a vest with a tea towel over his shoulder, a large knife in his hand and the severed carcass of a chicken in front of him."

I laughed. The accusations were true. When I was a student, I could easily stretch a whole chicken across five or more days of poultry-based meals.

Most of the 'Economics Boys' were also London based and the majority worked in finance. The only exceptions were Richard who was about to begin a PhD in Newcastle and Mike who was working for a dairy company based in Denmark. For those of us living in London, it was easier to maintain regular contact. St Peter's had recently entered a team in an 11-a-side league that met every Sunday on Hackney Marshes. Most of our early games were long, hard slogs as a team of largely spindly Oxford graduates lined up against players who were our technical and physical superior. But with the addition of four or five new players, tactical discipline and our patented never-say-die attitude, we soon became competitive in games and began to pick up points.

For those not based in the capital, there were usually a number of occasions throughout the year where we would gather as a group. Richard's family home was in Whitby, Yorkshire and we organised regular weekends away into the heart of the Yorkshire Moors that usually included a messy night out in either Middlesbrough or Newcastle. But my favourite times with the Economics Boys was the time we spent abroad.

Dan did a fantastic job of organising successful overseas trips in some of the most unlikely holiday destinations, which included Montenegro, Estonia and Albania. I missed the first two trips but made the journey to Albania with Dan, Alasdair and Mike. When our plane landed we struck up a conversation with an Albanian who correctly guessed that we were foreign and wanted to know who we were visiting in Albania. When we told him we were there on holiday, he laughed aloud.

But Albania was a resplendent country with lush mountain ranges and lagoons with majestic blue water. Its natural beauty coexisted along symbols of its chequered past, such as the bunkers dotted along many of the mountain ranges and public spaces, that would have provided a final line of protection for civilians seeking to escape captivity or death during the Balkan Wars and subsequent Civil Wars. There was also a very clear mafia presence and influence. Middle aged gentlemen would lounge around in expensive beach-side restaurants, taking brief meetings and driving away in expensive sports cars.

Throughout the holiday, I was given no option but to be aware of my blackness. The staring began in the airport from children and adults alike. It wasn't malicious, it was the sort of disbelieving stare when you witness something for the first time. I could see the cogs in their minds turning: 'I've heard of these people with brown skin and its true!' After a few days I became accustomed to, but also increasingly tired of the staring, especially from adults who I assumed would know how to act with more grace.

In response, I decided that I would put on a bit of a scene for the local community so that legends and myths of the brown-skinned man would endure centuries after I returned to England (perhaps a slight exaggeration). So one morning I decided to go for a run along the main strip leading away from our hotel. I weaved in and out of lamp posts and ran backwards for about 800m, smiling to people as I went. The sun was hot and at the end, I was dripping with sweat.

I showered before meeting the others for breakfast in a local cafe. The waiter who served us said that he had seen my impressive running during the morning and had told his colleagues about it.

I

"Let it snow… Le-et it s-n-ow."

"O-ut-side it's cold."

"But the fi-re's blazin'. So ba-by le-et it snow-ow. Le-het it snow-ow." The Boyz II Men track was in mid-flow with a brief interjection from Josh who had tried and failed to reach the high notes on 'outside'. I applauded the attempt.

"Shut up Stoney!" Josh teased, reaching to give me a playful shove.

I jumped out of the way and hid behind Tanisha, a bubbly, creative person who had recently joined Rare as an intern. "Oooi, you two," Tanisha chuckled. "Watch it. I'm holding a drink!"

I stopped running around Tanisha and put my arm around Josh. "Bro, is it time?"

"Man thinks it's time yano." Josh replied in a mocking South London accent.

We looked around the room and saw Mark talking to Kieran and Carlton. Mark was the long term boyfriend of Kura, one of the Directors of Rare. He had a contagious and permanently cheeky smile and was a great beatboxer. It must have been the mischievous grin on Josh's face but as soon as we approached, Mark cupped his hands and began the grime beat. That was the queue for Josh and I to start.

"Rare! Rare's gonna get u dere! Rare's gonna get u dere! Rare, where?!"

The verses were still a work in progress but we were pretty confident about the flow of the chorus. And the chorus is all that matters on a grime track anyway.

In the summer I reduced my working hours at Ascension Trust from full-time to two days a week, with Selina taking up the parts of my job that I vacated. I returned to Rare on a part-time basis with the aim of fulfilling the vision of the In Sight Project; to give underrepresented and disadvantaged children at school and college, the opportunity to engage meaningfully with universities and employers.

At Rare, I had everything to launch this programme with the quality and scale it needed to fly. Rare had corporate contacts; they had designers who could produce snazzy learning materials; and most importantly, they had a pipeline, meaning that students who engaged successfully with our school programmes could be supported into university and beyond. I drafted a proposal for a programme that would begin with mass engagement in Year 9 before gradually filtering people according to their area(s) of interest. I then began making enquiries to a number of Rare's corporate clients and to companies who I thought may be interested in partnering on this scheme. Most ended at this stage with polite rejections that were usually based on a lack of resources or 'pre-determined strategic priorities that would not be reviewed for at least another 18 months'.

During this time, Rare received an invitation to pitch for a national diversity programme. We were given less than a week's notice to submit an application and to prepare our pitch. In reality we were probably a bad fit for the programme. They wanted scale and an organisation with partnerships throughout the UK. Rare was still predominantly London focused, geared towards quality rather than huge quantities, and was only starting out on its pre-university journey. But it was an opportunity that we had to go for. In the presentation, my pitch felt flat and I responded poorly when asked to justify why the total number of people we expected to engage with was in the hundreds rather than thousands. Raph was diplomatic: "Things could have gone better," he said. "But business is primarily about knowing what to chase, what to leave and what to allow to come to you."

A few months later, a law firm was in the process of reviewing their strategic priorities, which now included a stronger commitment to working with pre-university students. We were invited to pitch at their UK head office in the centre of London. I learned from the previous pitch and brought a better level of confidence and energy into the room. I also felt that we were a much better fit for what the law firm wanted.

They wanted a quality programme that would really develop young people and give them the skills and knowledge to gain employment in a top profession. Although they had ambitions to work beyond London, they were realistic and had given us the target of working with 8 schools in three regions of the UK. We were successful and in partnership, launched a programme that included tailored support and mentoring, writing exercises and mock trials, work experience, and university visits.

While I loved my work at Rare and Ascension Trust, I was missing the critical reflection that came with academic study. Both organisations required me to be constantly in the mode of 'doing'. I was rushing from event to pitch to training course to meeting to event, without having an opportunity to stop and think about the bigger questions: why is this even necessary? Are there theories and practices that would help me to become more effective at what I do? Are my actions deconstructing a failed system or just perpetuating it?

My desire to find more comprehensive answers to these questions, and the intervention of Bernardine Evaristo led me to consider further study. As a seventeen year old, Bernardine had encouraged me to reject my place at Warwick and reapply to Oxford. She now offered me another timely piece of advice: "Pursue further study. Get a Masters Daniel!"

That night, I began to research masters courses. Initially I was overwhelmed by the breadth of available courses but began to think of criteria that would help to narrow my options. First, I wanted to study at a reputable institution in London - as that was where I was based for work. Second, the course had to be part-time so that I could pay for it using my earned income. Third, it needed to use numerical skills. And finally, it needed to be of relevance to my future career goals and help me to understand the issues that I most cared about.

The requirements of the final criteria were unequivocally fulfilled by Education. I was convinced by the ability of Education to transform individual lives, diverse communities and entire nations. As a near-universal right, it was the most efficient and most effective way of setting people off on a good course in life. In the words of Nelson Mandela: Education is the most powerful weapon you can use to change the world.

So I began to search for Masters level part-time courses in Education and came across UCL's Institute of Education, which offered a range of courses linked to understanding practical educational issues and the ways in which they intersected with social constructs such as gender and race.

The Masters programme that caught my attention was in Educational Planning, Economics and International Development. The course description had emphasised its practical application, agility to suit the schedule of part-time workers and vibrant classrooms full of students from across the globe.

I began the part-time Masters programme in September 2014 alongside my jobs at Ascension Trust and Rare.

Lectures were three hours long on Tuesday evening. I would finish a full days' work at Rare then jump on the London Underground, alighting at Euston Square and walking the final few minutes to the IoE. It was often a struggle finding time within a busy week to fit everything in. My classroom and assignment readings were usually completed during my daily commute and at weekends. I would rush to gain a seat on the train so that I could comfortably flick through a print out of an article or a book borrowed from the university library. But the programme was thoroughly enjoyable and the course description had largely proven to be true. Modules and assignments did emphasise the use of practical models that prioritised process and theories of change. And classrooms were diverse and international. Most of my classmates were experienced teachers or people who worked in Ministries of Education in countries such as Brazil, India, Kenya, Nigeria and China. Group discussions were fascinating and often reflected the unique frustrations and opportunities of these environments.

I wanted the focus of my assignments and readings to be based in Africa. I held fond memories of the warmth of the Ghanaian people I encountered as a teenager; despite - or perhaps because of - their material lack. I believed that other societies could offer valid philosophical viewpoints that the West had forgotten or chosen to ignore.

In my initial Masters assignments I began poring over texts from African authors, looking for something that would ring true. I found it in the concept of Ubuntu[15], which is translated to mean *I am because of who we all are*. It was a philosophy that was championed by Nelson Mandela and Archbishop Desmond Tutu, but had roots centuries before, not only in written texts but in the lived experiences of people who had chosen to recognise the common humanity of their neighbours and the bonds that would force individuals to identify with something greater than raw self-interest.

It stood in contrast to the mantra of western societies, perhaps most succinctly captured by Descartes famous maxim, *I think therefore I am*. Both phrases seemed to define an individual's identity and the truth of their existence, but whereas one offered an individualised interpretation of events, the other stated the central importance of being defined alongside others.

I was progressing well in my studies and achieving my goals at work. Both Les and Raph were often astonished at how much I was able to achieve in the two days that I was based in their respective organisations. I set myself high standards that did not wane simply because I was working part-time. At the end of each day, my head would hit the pillow in my claustrophobic room in my rented house in South East London, and I was tired.

But I was fulfilled.

II

I dimmed the light in the living room and dialled up the music to full volume. Joanna and I purchased a speaker from Argos a few days ago. It seemed like an exorbitant expense at the time, but it was now filling the room with sound and the gentle shudder of the bassline.

Empty plates and cups now lined the fireplace and table as our guests took their place on the dancefloor. People organised themselves into parallel rows

---

[15] Waghid, Y. (2014). *African Philosophy of Education Reconsidered: On being human*. Oxford: Routledge.

Chaplin (2006). *The Ubuntu Spirit in African Communities*, Managing Director, South Africa Ubuntu Foundation.

and as the song began, they started the familiar routine: Two steps to the right. Two equal steps to the left. Two steps back (being careful not to step on the feet of the person standing behind you). Lean forward. Lean back. Turn. Repeat. "It's like candy!"

A few guests were looking on - wondering whether they'd missed the pre-party instructions for a coordinated dance. But the majority of my family members and friends from the Oxford ACS, work and church were moving in step; smiling, laughing and enjoying each other's company.

A few months before *Christmas at the Stones*, we wondered whether it would be worth it. Our weeks were already overflowing and hosting a party would take time to organise. We would have to pay for food from Brixton, drinks from Crystal Palace and speakers from Argos. And then after all that, what if nobody came?

But as I danced and ate with some of my closest friends, I knew that none of these things were ever a valid excuse. I couldn't put a price on friendships and the importance of providing a place for people to gather, even if it was only once a year. I had been truly blessed to know incredible people from different walks of life, and that in and of itself was worth a celebration.

One year later, in December 2015, *Christmas at the Stones II* doubled as my leaving party. I was going back to Birmingham. Again. But I was returning with a self-assuredness that simply hadn't been present years earlier.

Towards the end of the evening, I paused the music while we watched the Anthony Joshua vs Dillan Whyte fight on pay-per-view. As the two pugilists went toe to toe and blow for blow, I looked out across the room. In a few days' time this house would no longer be the place that I called home. Selina and Joanna would stay but I would move back into the home of my childhood on Westbourne Road in Handsworth.

In between rounds, Adam stood next to me: "So what are you going to be doing for work in Birmingham?"

"Well, my Master's will take me from January to September," I began, holding my pause for a moment longer. "Then after that... We'll see."

213

RETURNING HOME

"Out of a mountain of despair, a stone of hope." -
Martin Luther King Jr. [16]

I found out that my mum had cancer in 2012. It was during my year in OUSU, when I was living and working in Oxford. My brother, Matthew, had messaged to say that mum had been rushed into hospital. She had been complaining about pain in her legs for a couple of weeks, and her GP had been unable to offer a clear diagnosis. She'd woken up one morning unable to move. Thankfully, Matthew was still at home, so he was able to dial 999 and stay with my mum until the ambulance came. He called me that afternoon to explain how he and my dad had sat my mum up on a chair and carried her down the stairs.

"Blood cancer?! What do you mean…?" I was speechless. I knew that there were forms of cancer that could be removed, or at least controlled through treatment, but blood cancer sounded serious. Really serious.

"I know bro." Matthew replied dejectedly. "It's mad."

"How's mum doing?"

---

[16] King, ML., Jr. (1963) *I Have a Dream*. Lincoln Memorial, Washington, D. C.

Matthew inhaled. "It's tough. But you know mum."

I took a train to Birmingham the next morning. My mum was sat on the sofa when I walked through the front door. She gave me a huge smile, and a warm hug, and told me she was alright, in the sincere and yet dishonest way that only mothers can. Her true emotions broke through as she recounted the tale of events with painful candour: the throbbing pain in her leg, calling out to Matthew, and grabbing the chair so tightly that her knuckles began to hurt.

"Oh well Dan... Maybe God can do something great through this."

That evening my dad, brother, two sisters, grandma, and those of my mum's siblings who were able to come, gathered around her bed and prayed. Over the coming days, we told my mum's closest friends, colleagues, and the members of Mount Zion Community Church. We prayed for her with all of our strength and hope.

Once my siblings and I had grown old enough to make our own way to school, my mum had decided to leave her teaching assistant's role at St. James', and train to be a primary school teacher. She attended courses at Handsworth Community College to gain the qualifications in Maths that would make her eligible to enrol onto a degree level course. At the age of 40, she had begun a degree at Birmingham City University that would allow her to fulfil her ambition of becoming a teacher with a specialism in English. She would come home each day with assignments, textbooks and funny tales of her classmates. Most were in their late teens or early twenties, so in a very different stage of life. Nevertheless, Mum was able to build some incredibly strong friendships.

She would laugh at the fact that she had been to the cinema, or eaten lunch with women the same age as Selina: "You two could have been good friends Sel," she would tease. My mum spent most time with a woman called Tomar, who was about to get married and hoped to, one day, start a family of her own. The two friends would speak about faith, and raising children, and would spend evenings working together on coursework.

After four years of hard work, my mum graduated with an upper second class degree, and the right to be a teacher. Two weeks before her graduation, Matthew and I had gone shopping to pick out a brand new shirt and tie for the special occasion. We had gone into a specialist tie shop to see what they had on offer. It was the sort of establishment that would watch, in a peculiar manner, as anyone wearing anything but a tweed jacket dared to cross the threshold. The sight of two teenagers in tracksuits clearly unnerved them, and the eyes of the two sales assistants followed us as I felt the soft silk and examined the price tag of a tie with broad navy blue and light blue stripes. The figure next to the pound sign was considerably more than I had budgeted for - in fact, it was almost three times as much. But this was a proud and historic moment for our family. I handed over the money to the assistant in the bow tie who thanked me for my custom.

When the name Millicent Janet Stone was read out in Birmingham's International Convention Centre, a loud cheer was heard from our row. On the large screen at the front, our mum responded with a wide smile in our direction, before refocusing, and shaking the hand of the University Chancellor.

Finding work after graduation was difficult for Mum. She often found herself up against applicants who were twenty years her junior. Although she had experience on her side - including raising the four of us - schools were inclined to favour younger candidates who had more working years ahead of them. After each interview she would come home and say "If it's meant to be, it will be." As the weeks and applications went by, it became more difficult to maintain this optimism.

It was at this point that a family friend asked my mum if she'd considered supply teaching. Supply teaching was not the preferred option for most qualified teachers. Work was unpredictable: it involved waking up most mornings unsure of where you'd be working, what you would be teaching, and if you'd even have work at all. Once in the classroom, you'd be faced with a set of unfamiliar young faces, who would assume that the presence of a supply teacher equated to the absence of discipline. For many supply teachers, not having *your class*, and instead being a temporary feature in someone else's domain, was a constant source of frustration, and a nagging reminder of what was so *close* to being theirs. But the pay was decent, and it would be an opportunity for mum to maintain and practice her skills, so that she was ready if the right permanent teaching opportunity came around.

I never observed one of her lessons, but I know that my mum was a great teacher. I saw the love and care she felt for her students, whether they were hers for a fortnight or a day. Mum would come home after a long day's work and enthusiastically tell us where she had travelled, and the students she had met, and she would pray for them that evening.

"You should hear some of the things that teachers call their pupils in the staff room," she remarked to me once, an impassioned look on her face. "When I went to school this morning, the head teacher singled out one of the boys in front of the class, warning me to 'Watch out for this one'. To begin with, he was messing around a bit, you know, as a lot of boys his age do. But I just called him to one side and said 'Malachi, you're not naughty, you're a good boy.' You should see how he changed for the rest of the day!"

My mum realised that for permanent teachers, it was easy for familiarity and cumulative bad behaviour to breed contempt. But as a supply teacher, with a fresh outlook on students, she had a precious opportunity to rewrite the narrative that had been bestowed upon these children.

Around this time, I met Tomar for the first time at a church event. She told me that she'd been off sick for two or three days a few months back, and had been really anxious about returning to the classroom, wondering if the behaviour of her pupils would have regressed. At the start of the day she asked the class how their supply teacher was.

"She was really nice Miss. She was like you."

"What was her name?" Tomar had asked.

"Mrs Stone."

I

I spent the rest of the week in Birmingham and returned back to work on Monday morning. Martha was the first person outside of the bubble of church and family who I told about my mum's diagnosis. As the words left my mouth, tears followed behind. It was as if the reality of things had finally hit home.

217

Up until that moment, cancer had been something that affected other families. Now it was here: in my family; in my home.

In those early years of mum's illness it was difficult supporting from afar. She had spent the best part of her life caring for my siblings and me, and now I desperately wanted to care for her. As a family, we were only just beginning to adjust to the cyclical ups and downs that accompanied the regular blood tests and fortnightly hospital appointments. At the beginning, the downs far outweighed any glimmers of hope. My mum was forced to take time out of work while she went through treatment. She decided to shave her head, rather than waiting for clumps of hair to fall out one piece at a time. We were told that the cancer was terminal and that treatment would only serve to delay the inevitable. It was a crushing blow that I struggled to see how we could recover from.

After a while, though, things began to look up. My mum responded well to her treatment, and was given the all-clear for at least the next few years. With things returning to normality, she successfully secured a role with the Christian charity, Birmingham City Mission. She drove to schools around Birmingham, delivering whole-school assemblies based around stories from the bible. BCM used a creative method of communication, where staff painted characters and objects onto a canvas as they spoke. This meant that the teacher had to learn the story and explanatory text off by heart. My mum would spend hours practising with us all, reciting the stories and tracing her brush strokes until she perfected it.

But downs were just around the corner.

The cancer returned in two years, and mum was back to her regular visits to City Hospital. Again, she responded well, and we took a leap of faith, planning a family trip to Malta in the spring of 2015 to give my mum something to look forward to. A few days before the flight, she contracted an undetected infection, which surfaced after we'd landed in Malta. She spent the entire week of our holiday in a Maltese hospital.

In unerring line with her character, she was able to find the funny side:

AFTER OXFORD

"At least I can say that I've been to Malta!"

When I moved back to Birmingham at the start of 2016, I was returning at what would be the start of another downward turn. My mum had felt acute pain in her back towards the end of 2015, and had gone for a scan at Queen Elizabeth's Hospital in Birmingham. In January 2016 the results confirmed our fears: the cancer had returned, and only a matter of months after the latest clear reading. The cancer was now viciously attacking my mum's spine, meaning that she was no longer able to stand straight. I remember accompanying her to an appointment with the consultant, who showed us both a scan of the damage that had been done to her vertebrate. My mum acted bravely during the appointment, but afterwards, standing together in the corridor of City Hospital, I hugged her and we wept.

My Master's degree provided a welcome distraction from the heartache of seeing my mum's worsening condition. I had an assignment due at the beginning of February, and I would then begin my dissertation: a twenty-thousand word submission on a topic that was yet to be decided. Compared to being in paid employment, I had an abundance of free time, but I was mindful of the need to use this time productively. After returning home for Christmas and New Year, Joanna and Selina had returned to London and Matthew had gone to Manchester.

I spent the first week of January transforming my bedroom from a cluttered jungle into an ordered oasis. I cleared everything out from under the two single beds in the room, discarding objects that were obsolete and packing away anything with material or sentimental value. I cleaned everything and set up a working area that looked out onto Westbourne Road. I then drafted a detailed daily schedule to begin on the following Monday.

I set my alarm for 7:00am, and would begin the day by jogging to Handsworth Park. While in London, my annual income had been just enough to cover my living costs, which were primarily rent, transport, food and my Masters. I had savings, but was keen to reduce all non-essential expenses, which included membership of a gym. My gym was now the children's play area in Handsworth Park, vacant because of the early hour. I pushed myself to traverse as many rungs of the monkey bars that I could without falling, and did press-ups on benches and dips on the playground roundabout, before running back. In the first few weeks, I would be astonished when fellow joggers would greet me with a "Good morning!"

"That would never happen in London…" I said to myself, while continuing my route around the cricket pitch, and towards the duck pond.

It felt comforting to be back in a place where I felt like a visible part of a visible community.

I'd usually return home at around 8:00am to find my mum in the front room sat in a bright red dressing gown, eating breakfast and watching the news. "Been running?" She would say, with a huge grin on her face.

"Yes, mum. Morning," I grinned back, puffing. I was usually out of breath, having run up Westbourne Road's steep incline to arrive at our front door.

She was still smiling widely. "Where did you run to?"

"Just to Handsworth Park." Deep breath. "I ran around the cricket pitch, and the pond." Breath. "And did some exercises in the play area."

"Ooooh – you're fit Dan! Fancy taking me on one of your runs one morning?"

"Sure - we can go now if you're ready?!"

She was laughing now, so strongly that she was almost as breathless as me. "After my breakfast," she joked.

I assumed that these questions would only keep up for the first day, but every day, like clockwork, my key would turn in the door, and my mum would ask me whether I'd been running and where I'd gone. This was her way of telling me that she was proud.

After my daily exercise routine I allotted myself 30 minutes to shower, get ready, make breakfast and eat breakfast. The coordination required to achieve this should not be sniffed at. I put the oats and water on a high heat while I gathered my clothes for the day. On my return to the kitchen, I mixed my porridge and left it to simmer on the stove. As I exited the bathroom, after my 8-minute shower, the porridge could be put on the side to cool. I applied lotion to my skin and pulled on my clothes. By now, the porridge was 'just right', and I wolfed it down in the remaining minutes. Poetry in motion.

Following breakfast was my 'devotion' time, which was the term given to time spent in prayer, meditation or reading the bible. During my time in London, I largely neglected time spent developing my faith. My days were full to the brim, and I had become a slave to prolonged working hours and lengthy commutes. Now, I was in charge of my time, and could structure my days according to what was most important to me. The Masters was necessary, and gave me a long-term goal to work towards, but I wanted time for God, for exercise and for family to be the central pillars of a successful day.

From 9.00am I would have 30 minutes for 'life admin', which included responding to emails and checking social media. From 9.30am to 5pm I would work on my Masters, with an hour-long break for lunch scheduled at around 1pm. Being at home meant that I could spend this hour with my mum, who would always begin by asking how my work was going.

Unless I'd had a particularly productive, or a particularly unproductive morning, my default response was "Yeah, it's going well." I had given my parents a broad overview of what I was studying, which would probably need to be updated every two to three weeks, and certainly not on a daily basis. Besides, I wanted to focus my attention on the daytime TV programmes that I would watch with Mum, like Father Brown and Judge Rinder. She would laugh out loud at the latest issues people had chosen to expose to the nation: "Imagine talking your business out on TV!" We'd discuss the case, and what judgment we felt should be passed. Judge Rinder tended to side with us.

At 5pm, I would spend more time reading the bible, or would listen to Christian sermons or podcasts on topics like social change, prayer and personal mind-set. I particularly enjoyed the structured and well-reasoned sermons of Tim Keller, who would break down complex subjects clearly and articulately within three bullet points. At such a time of personal uncertainty, engaging with these concepts helped to keep my mind from resting in a place of despair.

At 6pm it was dinner time. I treasured these moments with my parents. I noticed that my relationship with them was very different compared to when I had last lived at home, at the age of 18. Then, my parents were figures of authority and order. Now, I began to see them both in a completely different light, as the warm, funny, faithful and, in some ways, broken people, who had loved me so dearly all of my life.

Growing up, I struggled to build the depth of relationship I wanted to have with my dad. We've always been very different people. He's compulsive, whereas I rely on rationality and structure. Now, I began to see him as a cultured and complex man. He achieved perhaps more than even he himself could have dreamt: he had a wife, four children, owned a house. Despite his younger years being a time of limited opportunity, he had built a home life full of books, music and conversation. I realised that at a different time, and in different circumstances, he would have thrived in university.

We would have the odd moments alone to talk. He told me of the pressures of being a young man and a husband, and struggling to find work with a baby on the way. He spoke about the strain this had placed on his mental health, and the way in which family and faith had helped him to find peace, a home and a job. I could see that these more recent strains were weighing heavily on his mind. More than anyone, my dad absorbed the pressure of wanting to do something to help with my mum's illness, to make things better. I would hear him praying early in the morning and late at night. He found information on alternative medicines and natural remedies that soon became staple foods in our household. I sensed the futility, but I also knew that hope was the only currency worth having in times as seemingly desperate as these.

II

In February, I handed in my final assignment, and my thoughts turned to my dissertation. Following my research into Ubuntu, I had done some reading into different forms of community-led education in Africa and discovered School Management Committees. SMCs were a means of providing community input for the governance of schools. A number of international organisations had provided funding for SMCs to be rolled out in a range of developing countries, meaning that there was a rich variety of theoretical and evidence-based literature, and Ghana was one of the countries involved in early pilot projects.

I made plans to fly out to Accra, Ghana's capital, in the beginning of April, to stay there for a month. I would spend the first week with Bishop Mike Royal and his wife Reverend Viviene Royal, who I knew from Mount Zion Community Church, where Mike had been an Associate Pastor from 2003-2005. Accommodation for the later weeks was generously offered by friends of Reverend Les Isaac, Reverend Sammy and Florence Adjepong, who regularly hosted him during his trips to West Africa.

By the time of my flight, I had broadened the focus of my dissertation to look at models of inter-school collaboration between government-funded public schools and wealthier private schools, where governance and SMCs could be one possible avenue of partnership. Sammy and Florence ran a high-performing private school in Accra, whose clientele were mainly the upper-middle classes. They agreed to be interviewed for my research, and to put me in touch with other private school owners in the region. Mike was a trustee for a private school in a rural area of Ghana that charged minimal fees, with the aim of providing affordable, high-quality education to families in local villages.

It was surreal being back in Ghana. It looked reassuringly similar, and yet also strangely different. Shopping malls had sprung up everywhere, and more cars streamed down the carriageways. I was hoping that my return to Ghana would prove that I had not lost the best parts of myself since leaving school; that I was still the person who loved to play football, learn new things and contribute to the community.

I spent my first evening in Ghana playing Ludo with Viviene; Eric, her brother; and Amy, Eric's fiancé. Ludo is a board game, usually played by children, that has the simple aim of getting your four counters around the board to the safety of your 'home' zone. But this version of Ludo was brutal. Every ejection was met with ruthless whoops and chides, which I couldn't help but participate in.

The next day, Mike, Viviene and Eric were busy attending to a family matter, so they dropped Amy and I off at a local hotel. The hotel was willing to let non-guests lounge by their pool, with the mutual understanding that a steady stream of food and drink orders would follow. Amy and I spent the whole morning and early afternoon sipping fruit smoothies and nibbling on snacks while discussing education, left wing politics, social reform and music.

Eric was a DJ, and Amy was a professional singer. I'd woken up that morning to hear her soulful voice echoing around the house as she was making breakfast. I remember being transfixed by the emotion in her voice as she sang Sam Cooke's *Change is Gonna Come*. Each phrase exuded new feelings of hardship and pain and hope.

The next morning, Mike and I left for Takoradi, a smaller city towards the west of Accra. We'd left at 5am, because Mike was going to preach at the church we were visiting in the morning. As Mike was doing all of the driving, I felt it was my duty to fill the four hour journey with stimulating topics of conversation. We both felt that a leave vote in the upcoming EU referendum was possible because there were many people who blamed Eastern European migration for a perceived downturn in their communities.

I mentioned to Mike that I had applied for a role at the University of Birmingham just before departing for Ghana, and asked him about his own experiences in choosing a career path. He laughed: "The secret is not to choose." He went on to explain that he was holding senior part-time roles across four organisations in Birmingham, London and Ghana. All the roles had been built on his passion for education, and his commitment to faith, but he had put no further restrictions on what was possible. I resolved that this was an approach worth emulating and considered which two or three passions would form the central pillars of my career.

When we arrived, we were welcomed by David, who Mike had said would take me to visit the local schools during my stay in the church compound. The compound was situated in the middle of a rural village. The road into the compound was covered in red dirt that climbed and descended in uneven mounds, making the ride an incredibly bumpy one. On the journey through the village, Mike seemed to have his car horn permanently pressed inwards. Every few yards he would see someone he recognised and the horn would be accompanied by a wide smile and a wave. Often the horn was directed at startled stray chickens; on hearing the blaring noise, they would flap out of the road and away to safety.

AFTER OXFORD

Brick huts lined both sides of the jagged pavement, some of which I noticed doubled as both homes and places of business. Women sat outside these dilapidated buildings sewing, plaiting hair or frying eggs. It felt surreal to be confronted with such stark material poverty only hours after I had lazed around by a hotel pool in metropolitan Accra. Yet the two realities seemed to coexist without fuss or clamour.

The church had been sponsored by donors from the UK and mainland Europe, and provided accommodation for the Pastor and his family, as well as a place for the community to gather on Sunday. David took Mike and me into the living room of the church leader, Pastor Joe. He embraced Mike warmly and shook my hand. We had a brief conversation, where I told him about my educational background, and the research I was doing in Ghana.

"Ah! God is *good-oh*. You must share." I knew that *sharing* was an invitation to speak to the congregation. Mike said it was a great idea, and that he would introduce me at the beginning of his sermon, so I willingly agreed.

The service took place in a large room that looked out onto the main entrance of the compound. The window slats had been opened, to allow in some fresh air, and three or four fans had been placed at the front of the church. Mike and I sat towards the left of one of these fans, although it made little difference to the stifling heat. The congregation began to enter, and I recognised some of the people we had passed on the road, except that the women were now wearing head wraps and traditional Ghanaian dresses, and the men colourful shirts and smart trousers.

Once the singing began, it was if someone had inadvertently ripped open a giant bag of Skittles. The rainbow of multi-coloured dresses and brightly coloured shirts, jumped and danced around the room, caring little about increasing levels of perspiration generated by their energetic claps and shouts. During one song, I attempted to jump along with those sitting behind me, but I began to feel self-conscious and slightly light headed, and swiftly returned to my default motion of rhythmic clapping with my two feet planted firmly on the ground.

After the singing had finished, Mike was called forward to speak, and, after thanking his hosts, he introduced me, and asked me to come forward to share my story with the congregation. Most people in the villages spoke the regional dialect, Twi, meaning that both Mike and I were required to use an interpreter.

"Greetings in the name of Jesus."

The words that came out of the mouth of the interpreter in translation had a more passionate manner than I had perhaps intended. The congregation responded "Greetings," in unison and in English.

"My name is Daniel." My speech had to be delivered in short bursts for the translator. I dutifully paused after each clause.

"I am from the UK. From a place called Birmingham. I am from an area in Birmingham that people sometimes look down upon. They say it is no good. That only trouble comes from there. But that is not true. God has been with me. God is with all of you. He took me from this same area in Birmingham. To one of the best universities in the world. The University of Oxford. God can do good things for you too."

Even before the translator had begun relaying my message, there were noises of approval and surprise from the audience when I said the name *Oxford*. I was genuinely astonished that the reputation of Oxford would travel so far, and to a place that had very little contact with the world of higher education. I wondered what other words would have engendered a similar response. Barack Obama? Manchester United? Why, and how, had Oxford entered their purview?

I ended my speech by talking about my Masters (although Educational Planning and Economics didn't translate very easily into Twi) and the research I was hoping to conduct in Ghana. I was awarded a rapturous applause as I took my seat. I glanced up with a smile at the congregation, but internally I was riddled with feelings of guilt.

I wanted to deliver a speech that was uplifting, and I was conscious that it received a positive response from the audience, but I was also aware that messages of achievement could be poisoned chalices in the context of poverty and limited opportunity. I wasn't convinced that what I had said was objectively right or truly honest, but I hoped that the translator had allowed my words to give meaning and relevance to the listeners in whatever context they faced.

I stayed in the church compound for the next three days, where I had long conversations with Pastor Joe and his family. We spoke about education, politics and football, and enjoyed long walks in the Ghanaian countryside, where we tended to vegetables and livestock. I was sad to leave behind this tranquillity for the noise of Accra, but had to make headway with my research.

Back in Accra, I was now moving into the home of the Adjepong's. My first few days there were spent alone with Sammy, the father of the house, while his wife Florence was abroad in Jamaica. Their son, Kofi, and younger daughter, Primrose, were also away; and their eldest child, Naomi, had moved in with her husband, and was expecting her first baby. Those few days with Sammy were great. We would end each day glued to the News Channel, which was keeping us informed of the strange happenings in the US primary election race. The business tycoon Donald Trump had decided to run as a candidate for the Republican Party, but both Sammy and I agreed that his campaign was a publicity stunt that would soon run out of steam and credibility.

Like many Ghanaians, Sammy had a driver. Chuku would transport Sammy around Accra, while he took phone calls or replied to emails. If I needed to travel somewhere, and Chuku was free, he would take me; but for most journeys I would take a taxi. My first few trips were a Russian roulette. Some were comfortable, and the drivers would charge me a fair price. Other drivers would try to charge an extortionate rate, with cars that struggled to accelerate beyond 30mph.

Eventually, I met a driver who was stationed around the corner from the Adjepongs', and on whom I could rely. His name was Prince, and he became my regular driver. Whenever I was planning to go out somewhere, I would message him the night before, and let him know what time I wanted to be picked up in the morning. Invariably, he would be late. I would call to ask how far away he was. His response was always "Five minutes," which meant forty-five by most other measures of time. I adjusted my text messages to request pick-up at least thirty minutes before the time I actually had to leave, and our relationship worked fine from thereon in.

Sammy warned me that it would be difficult to gain access to government schools. There had been a recent exposé of public schools in Ghana, carried out by an undercover journalist. Consequently, schools were now deeply suspicious of outside visitors, especially those who made it known that they were there to ask probing questions. In light of this, my interviews were progressing better than I ever dreamed would be possible: within the first three weeks of my trip I had surpassed the target I set myself, of getting interviews from ten schools. I had even been able to get into three government schools, after following up on a contact given to me by a friend in the UK.

The teacher responded to my first email, but hadn't replied since. Nevertheless, I turned up at her school on the date I had mentioned in my email. I was able to make it into the heart of the school without being stopped, and told a staff member that I was looking for Miss Ansah. He pointed in the direction of a classroom without any further inquiry. Miss Ansah was surprised to see me, but she was hospitable. After I explained the purpose of my research, she not only allowed me to interview her, but also gave me personal introductions to the head teachers of the schools located in adjacent compounds. An unexpected, but very welcome, turn of events.

While visiting the schools, I saw first-hand the immense disparity in wealth and opportunity that characterises the Ghanaian education system. Private schools that charged the highest fees had facilities rivalling the best schools in the UK: fully furnished IT suites sat next to technology-driven classrooms with interactive whiteboards. Even more impressive was the breadth of their curriculum. Schools were educating their pupils in the importance of enterprise, leadership and critical thinking, from the earliest years of primary school upwards.

In contrast, government schools, and some poorer private schools, were shockingly underfunded. Classrooms were dreary and unprotected against the elements. In Miss Ansah's school, wooden tables and chairs lined up in rows facing a single blackboard. She told me that there had been a heavy downpour last week, and that the school had been forced to close for two days. Some owners of the best schools, such as Sammy and Florence, used their position of influence to push for reform in public schools, and to help local schools and their pupils where they could; but it was clear that Ghana's education system was failing to deliver for its citizens.

AFTER OXFORD

My speedy progress meant that I had two full weeks to enjoy freely before returning to England. By now, Kofi had returned from his time abroad, and was hosting his friend Bernard, who was of Ghanaian heritage, but had been born in London. Kofi and Bernard had studied at university in the UK together, and both had an entrepreneurial spirit and a knack for making money. Kofi had already launched a luxury shoe business, and Bernard had come to Ghana in search of a business opportunity. The three of us became inseparable for the remainder of my time in Ghana.

Our time as a trio began in a really wholesome manner. TEDx Accra happened to fall on one of the weekends I was in Ghana, and we decided to attend. I got to observe fascinating debates on pan-Africanism and millennials, and was surprised by the numbers of people in my generation, and who were born or educated in the UK, but had chosen to return to Ghana. Many of these millennials I heard speak were liberal and socially minded people, who had been raised in a context where they were underrepresented minorities. Their experiences had led them to identify, in one form or another, as oppressed. But in the Ghanaian context, they had power afforded to them by their education, their wealth and their networks; and whether they liked it or not, they were now part of an elite class.

One gentleman, who I guessed was around thirty, stood up to share a story.

"Before I moved back to Ghana, I paid for my car to be shipped over to Accra by Ferry." Some audience members had already begun to shake their heads: they knew what was coming next. "I paid good money for it to be transported so that I could drive it in Ghana, it was a nice car. Then I get to the port, and the guard is looking confused. He says there has been some mistake with the shipment, and my car has gone missing, but he is sure, very sure, that he can find it."

Despite being relatively new to Ghana, I had been stopped enough times by Ghanaian police to know that this was code language for: You look like someone who has money, give me a bribe.

"So I asked him how much, and he said 500 Ghana Cedis." The head shaking was accompanied by dismayed sighing. "When I came back to Ghana, I made a vow that I would never take a bribe, and that I would never pay a bribe: otherwise I would be just as bad as those people we call corrupt. So I told him no. He said OK, 300 Ghana Cedis. But I refused to pay. To this day, I have not paid the bribe, and there is probably a customs official somewhere in Accra driving around in my car."

I laughed wistfully, admiring the storyteller's conviction. But it also got me thinking. How do you transform a society whose norms have become crooked? The storyteller had stood by his principles, but in return had forfeited his car, and, while noble, his actions were a drop in an ever-enlarging ocean.

Other speakers from various countries in Africa spoke about Ghana's burgeoning arts scene, and the economic potential for Africa given the rise of solar energy. At the end of the TEDx week, I was full of hope for Ghana's future.

The following week, I decided to re-encounter the darkest depths of Ghana's past. My initial response to Kofi's suggestion of going to Cape Coast Castle had been one of reluctance: it was a long journey, and I recalled the callousness of the place, and the way in which it had stirred up deep and uncomfortable notions about the need for mankind to dominate all that it deems to be inferior. But I was interested to see what emotions and thoughts still awaited me behind its walls.

The castle was just as soulless the second time around. Seeing the large gates, the church in the courtyard and the door of no return; I was forced, once again, to reflect on the nature of humanity. Perhaps we had progressed, but I could see, both in Ghana and in the UK that many of the structures designed to dehumanise and disenfranchise others because of their race, gender, economic status and other features of their personhood, were still firmly in place.

In a room within the castle, an artist was selling paintings and sculptures. I felt drawn to a painting that was mostly green. A darker shade of green made up the shape of a dozen tree trunks that reached up to a paler green sky with a yellowy-green sun. All around were luscious plants and grass: a vision in green, all except for the centre of the canvas, where a woman stood in a parting between the trees, clothed in orange. I stood transfixed in front of the painting for about five minutes. When the artist noticed me, he came up to offer me a price. As is customary, we settled at around half what he'd quoted.

After leaving the castle, we went to the restaurant with the crocodiles that I had visited as a teenager. On that occasion, they remained statuesque for the duration of our visit. This time, Bernard and I paid a waiter 20 Ghana Cedis to gently prod the crocodiles from a safe distance until they wiggled into life. For another 20 Ghana Cedis we could hold a baby crocodile and take photos. Not even crocodiles were impervious to the power of money.

On the flight back to the UK, I reflected on how much the way I related to Ghana had changed. I had gone from a naïve volunteer to someone who was able to perceive more of Ghana's many shades.

Studying Economics provided me with a way of articulating these observations in the language of supply and demand: Economics explained why the Ghanaian equivalent of Sky Sports had around a dozen sports channels, the majority of which were dedicated to showing the English Premier League, the European Champions League and the NBA. Economics allowed me to critique the system that permits one person to be educated in the highest-quality classrooms, while another hadn't received textbooks that term. Economics could also shed light on why prostitution was on the rise in a country that, to an outsider, seemed to have a church on every street and street corner.

But Economics did not provide many realistic solutions. There weren't many people I met in Ghana who were ready to leave their car at the port in return for justice.

III

I had seen more of the world and its people. I was thinking in new ways, and this forced me to change the ways I perceived myself and everything around me. Included in this revolution was the way that I interacted with life in Birmingham. I would occasionally bump into people from Mount Zion

Community Church, usually when in the process of going about our daily lives, or occasionally when I would visit the church with my family.

The conversation would usually begin, "Daniel - good to see you! Are you still in Oxford?"

"It's good to see you too, and no, I graduated around five years ago."

"So – you're back in Birmingham?" (This was code for "Why haven't I seen you in church?")

"Yes, I've been back for almost a year now."

"Ah." Here it comes. "So - why haven't I seen you in church?"

My answer would vary, depending on my relationship with the person I was speaking to. My default response was that I was going to a church in the centre of Birmingham. Most inquirers were happy to hear that I was still going to church, even if it wasn't the same congregation as in my childhood. For those who I could joke with, I would say that I had converted to Islam.

For the few who had the wisdom and willingness to engage in a discussion about the reality of Black Pentecostal Churches, I would say that my childhood church spoke in a language that I could no longer relate to or tolerate. It was of a different generation and a different nature.

For decades, Black Pentecostal Churches had relied on the noise of climactic singing and bellowed preaching to stir the soul into experiencing God. Education had taught me to filter these experiences with questions and reasoning, but I found that many churches were unwilling, or ill-equipped, to tailor their Sunday morning encounters to suit people eager to rebalance their experience of church: away from the commotion, and towards considered, and sometimes critical, reflection.

But I also struggled to settle in churches that, while intellectually challenging, reflected the priorities and lived experiences of their leaders, who were predominantly white and middle class.

From my experience, the soul of oppressed peoples has a history soaked in hardship and frustration, longing and hope, which affects all aspects of our outlook on life, the way we worship, and the manner in which we pray. Certain churches were simply unable to get beneath the surface of life to reveal its injustices and disappointments, and the prayers of desperation and anger that emanate towards God as a consequence.

Although I was yet to find a settled community through church, I had been able to regain some of my childhood friendships. I lost contact with Chris while we were studying at universities in different parts of the country, but I was now becoming an active participant in the exciting steps he was taking into marriage and fatherhood.

Chris had asked me to be a groomsman at his wedding. We spent a Saturday morning, along with the other groomsmen, trying on our light grey suits and attempting to decide the best combination of waistcoats, handkerchiefs, ties and cravats. In the afternoon, at Chris' stag do, he was dressed up in a cow outfit, and made to endure a game of paintball where all participants were aware of the three rules of engagement: avoid getting hit, shoot the other team, and show no mercy to the guy in the cow-print overalls. After a night on the town, I called a taxi to take Chris and I home. We spent the journey laughing about the day's events and reflecting on the crazy fact that one of us was on the verge of getting married.

Richard Singh from Hamstead Hall was now a successful businessman and avid reader, who would always end our conversations by asking when I was going to join his enterprise. On one occasion I patiently listened to his pitch about ACN, a direct sales company that had an ethos of developing and empowering the people who sold its range of products. I politely declined Richard's offer to join, but didn't hide my admiration for all he had achieved and become. I also had brief encounters with Paul and Tobias, who I would bump into from time to time in the gym or in bars. Seeing friends, no matter how briefly, was a constant symbol of belonging. Birmingham held my history in its people and in its places.

I had come back to Birmingham with the belief that I had choice. Perhaps I was part of the first generation in my family who had been given this honour and burden. My grandparents had taken whatever jobs were available, and my parents, while having a wider array of options, by no means had the luxury of trading pay for job satisfaction.

Looking for jobs, I had come across a two-year graduate scheme offered by the University of Birmingham. It gave successful applicants the opportunity to rotate around a variety of internal departments, working on interesting projects and gaining access to senior members of the university through mentoring and project work.

I had very little interaction with the universities in Birmingham growing up, but my time in Oxford had shown me that higher education institutions were influential, and had facilities, skills and capital that had the potential to greatly benefit the communities on their doorstep.

The eligibility criteria stated that applicants needed to be former students of the University of Birmingham. I emailed the programme coordinator, who confirmed that I was ineligible. I despondently returned to the university's jobs website, hoping that I would see another role that would fit the bill. The University of Birmingham Careers Network were advertising for a Widening Participation Internships Officer, who would shape and lead activities designed to help students from less privileged backgrounds improve their chances of getting graduate level jobs after university. I completed my application before my trip to Ghana, and interviewed three days after I returned to the UK.

The position seemed to be the perfect amalgamation of all of my previous roles and interests: the careers-focused work I had done at Rare, my experience working in schools with students from disadvantaged backgrounds, and my time in OUSU where I came to understand the inner-workings of universities. In my presentation to the interview panel, I used a photo from a private school in Ghana to illustrate the work they had done to develop the leadership potential of school pupils. I also showed the photo of me on the Top Playground of Hamstead Hall School, authenticating my own identity as a member of the widening participation community.

IV

Outside work, my mum's health had taken a turn for the worse. The cancer returned again and was slowly deforming her physical body, but, miraculously, never came close to touching her soul.

AFTER OXFORD

What I saw in the last few months of my mum's life reflected perfectly the wonderful person, and mother, I had always known. Even in the face of excruciating pain, she was an example of kindness and selflessness: she never wanted to inconvenience nurses and doctors, and showered them with smiles and upbeat stories about her children. But I couldn't help but notice that her language was beginning to slip into the past tense. She would talk about the good life she'd had and how much her kids and family had meant to her.

The final conversation that I had with my mum was on Friday 3rd November 2017. It had been her birthday three days earlier, on 31st October. I'd come home from work to hear that she'd been rushed into hospital because she'd had difficulty breathing. The doctors who had attended to her noticed, from the date of birth written on her patient profile, that it was her birthday. My mum had jokingly asked whether - as a birthday present - she'd be allowed to stay at home. They had laughed, but declined.

I drove to hospital with Matthew that evening. I'd bought Mum her favourite treat from Greggs - a cinnamon bun - as a poor substitute for her real birthday cake, which was waiting at home. Matthew had sent out a text message to my mum's friends, family members and former colleagues, to remind them that her birthday was coming up, and we had been flooded with gifts, cards and messages. Matthew and I sat at her bedside, opening card after card, in which people had written their support and encouragement, told my mum of the difference she'd made in their lives, and given their prayers for her recovery. Mum was visibly frail, and in pain, but after each card she would smile, say how nice the message was, and then signal for one of us to open the next one.

The University of Birmingham had given me permission to work from home on Fridays to support my mum and family. This particular Friday, I had finished an urgent piece of work in the morning before going to hospital. I arrived at midday, and went to my mum's bedside, where she was lying down with her eyes closed.

I held her hand. "Mum?" Her eyes opened slowly and she said, smiling, "What are you doing here Dan?" Mum had insisted that we shouldn't miss work or put our careers on hold to look after her, so her statement captured a range of emotions: surprise and weariness, concern and delight. "I've finished my work for the day, and wanted to see how you were getting on." She smiled.

At this time, she was too frail to type text messages without great difficulty, but she hated leaving messages unanswered. She asked me to type out responses to my sisters, her siblings and other friends who were still awaiting a reply. Most responses were brief, something along the lines of: "I'm fine, and will be out on Monday."

I'd only been there for around half an hour when one of the nurses arrived with my mum's lunch tray. "See how the Lord provides." It seemed like every word my mum uttered required energy that she no longer possessed. "You've come just at the right time." She skipped the main course and asked for the jelly. I helped mum up on her pillow and began to feed her.

I talked about the jelly that she would make for us as kids in the summer holiday, in a mountainous mould that would be spooned out in disorderly blobs onto our plates, alongside a scoop of vanilla ice cream.

I talked about the house we were trying to rent, so that we could give my mum somewhere more comfortable to stay once she got out of hospital.

I spoke about work, and my fears that I wasn't yet fulfilling my potential, and the disappointed or deflated look that sometimes came across people's faces when I told them I was working at the University of Birmingham after leaving Oxford, rather than in a law firm or an investment bank.

My mum listened patiently, her eyes warmly studying my face as I unloaded my frustrations. Again she smiled: "That's a great thing about you Daniel. You don't care what other people think or say. You'll keep doing what you know to be right."

Towards the end of my hospital visits, I always asked my mum if she wanted me to read her a passage from the bible, or listen to a song. "Play some music," she said today.

I pressed play on Spotify, and a Fred Hammond song began to play. My mum closed her eyes and smiled as the lyrics of the song passed by:

When the battle makes me weary

It seems that I've lost ground
It's so hard to hear Your voice Lord
With distractions all around
I try to lift my hands, to give You praise
But then a spirit of heaviness
Tries to shield Your face, so I'm saying breathe
Breathe into me oh Lord, the breath of life
So that my spirit would be whole
And my soul made right
Breathe into me oh Lord, day by day
So that my heart is pure before You, always, always[17]

At the end of the song, my mum called for the nurse, and I had to leave to go to a house viewing.

"I'm sorry to leave you mum. When you come out, you'll have a nice big house to stay in."

My mum smiled vacantly, her eyes struggling to stay open. "Don't worry Dan. It was just nice to see your face."

I kissed her on the forehead, and went to the house viewing. At just after 9pm that evening, my mum passed away.

I drew back the curtain around her hospital bed and held her hand again. "Mum..."

V

The weeks after my mum's passing were an emotional roller coaster. I was in the throes of grief, along with the rest of my family, having lost the woman who had brought me into this world. But we also had to plan a funeral service for approximately 600 people that would take place towards the end of November, and many evenings were taken up with dozens of visitors coming

---

[17] Hammond, F. (1996) *Breathe Into Me Oh Lord.* US: Benson.

to our house to pay their respects. Seeing friends and family lifted my spirits, but I was emotionally exhausted.

On the morning of the funeral, I walked down the stairs from my bedroom in Westbourne Road to find some of my aunts, uncles and cousins in the living room. They were dressed serenely in black.

Some already had tissues and handkerchiefs ready for what was set to be the most difficult of days. The cortege was waiting outside with a casket viewable through the transparent windows, the words 'MILLICENT', 'SISTER' and 'MUM' written in capitalised wreaths on three sides. Many of our neighbours had stood outside in the crisp autumn sunshine to send us on our way, their presence conveying all that needed to be said. It was surreal, sitting in the front car with my siblings, Dad and Grandma: a position that we had never expected to be in, at least, not so soon.

We planned the service to be a celebration of my mum's life. We sang some of Mum's favourite worship songs, and heard from people who had known her, or had worked alongside her. My mum's siblings gave a joint address, and my grandma sang an old Christian hymn.

In the weeks leading up to the funeral, my grandma had been concerned that she might become overwhelmed by emotion and unable to sing. But on the stage, next to her eight children, the lyrics of *The Pearly White City* came out clear and strong:

> *There's a holy and beautiful city*
> *Whose Builder and Ruler is God;*
> *John saw it descending from Heaven,*
> *When Patmos, in exile, he trod;*
> *Its high, massive wall is of jasper,*
> *The city itself is pure gold;*
> *And when my frail tent here is folded,*
> *Mine eyes shall its glory behold.*
>
> *In that bright city, pearly white city,*
> *I have a mansion, a harp, and a crown;*
> *Now I am watching, waiting, and longing,*
> *For the white city that's soon coming down.*

Then Millicent's four children - my siblings and I - were invited forward. Selina began by speaking about our mum as a woman, a confidante and a friend. Matthew shared the odd moments when he'd managed to get on the wrong side of my mum, a difficult task that could only be achieved by persistent nagging and misbehaviour, but how she was always a woman of incredible love and warmth. Joanna told of my mum as a teacher, and a champion for her pupils, children and friends.

I used my time to talk about the Millicent that I encountered and loved. I reflected on the fact that she had always managed to find time to talk to neighbours on the way to St James. I remembered the conversations that I overheard from my bedroom window while doing my Masters dissertation, where she gladly offered counselling, advice and prayer when her friends were going through tough personal struggles, despite her own ongoing battle with illness. I spoke about Millicent as my mum: a mother of faith, humility and love.

My dad ended the family tributes with three W's, told through a series of funny stories that encapsulated my mum perfectly: her Worship, her Work ethic and her Wonder.

As the casket was lowered into the grave, people around began to sing soulful songs of heaven, hope and glory. Then, once it had reached its final resting place; Matthew, my dad, Uncle Howell (my mum's brother), Uncle Gary (my dad's brother) and I picked up shovels and began to throw dirt on top.

When we grew tired, my cousins, aunts and uncles took the shovels and continued the work. Then other family members, including my grandad, took their places. Then some of the congregation from Mount Zion Community Church. Then my mum's friends. Then former colleagues. Then some of our childhood friends, Chris and Richard. Then some of my friends from Oxford who had come to the funeral: Josh and Tendai, Daphne and Janeen. Everyone did their bit, shovelling, and lifting the dirt, until the grave had been filled.

This was community.

Because of Oxford, my community now included people like Dan, Adam, Alasdair, Dave, and his fiancé Safa, who had driven up to Birmingham in the days prior to the funeral, and more who sent their condolences through flowers and cards.

Because of Oxford, I was more aware of my capabilities, more effective in my reasoning and more confident in my future.

But I also realised that the most important things that defined me were mine before Oxford, during Oxford and after Oxford.

Faith in God, and in the ability that He has imparted within me to think and to learn; Hope in the potential of humanity to serve our planet and its inhabitants better; and Love of truth, meaning, friendship, family: the things that truly matter in this fleeting thing we call life.

So; faith, hope and love, these three. And the greatest of these is love.

I was enchanted by Citizens UK and their ability to mobilise people from different backgrounds in the pursuit of change. Working at Ascension Trust reminded me of the importance of service. It was a pleasure leading volunteers around the UK who wanted to make a difference in their communities.

I loved my time at Rare: I built great friendships, worked on important programmes like Target Oxbridge, and learned how to meet the high standards of the private sector.

A number of alumni created the Oxford Black Alumni Network to connect graduates and inspire the next generation.

I've had the opportunity to travel to some great places. Albania was an unexpected delight and Ghana will always hold a special place in my heart. Kofi, Bernard and I spent a day on the beach, playing football and sharing our hopes for the future.

I graduated with distinction from my Master's degree in Educational Planning, Economics and International Development. Soon after, I began work at the University of Birmingham.

I moved back to Birmingham in January 2016; it was surreal living back on Westbourne Road after so many years away but it was great to be somewhere I belonged.

I've been able to keep in touch with many of my friends from university. Left: The 'Economics Boys' on Dan's wedding day. Right: More of the gang at Dave's wedding in Italy.

Left: In Portugal with my siblings. Above: With Matthew and Chris.

My mum was a wonderful person who devoted her life to equipping my siblings and I to become the people we are today. I dedicate this book to her.

EPILOGUE – TAKING AMRIT

"Love is the force that transforms and improves the Soul of the World." - Paolo Coelho, The Alchemist[18]

I didn't believe that I was capable of the deep emotions of love that are frequently paraded on our TV screens, written into our novels and sometimes projected into our longings and aspirations. I am not a man of emotional highs and lows. I am not a woohoo type of person, neither am I someone who easily gets in moods. I'm a steady-kind-of-guy.

Unbeknown to most people, my spiritual journey has taken me to a place where I am no longer convinced by the exclusivity of Christian faith.

Most (but not all) major religions begin with the concept of an infinite and uncontainable God; who was before anything else was, who is the 'I am' and the source of all creation. Most (but not all) major religions have then claimed that through their texts and practices they have been able to monopolise a relationship with this infinite being.

I think it's natural for people to want to do this. As people, we sometimes crave certainty more than truth. We're desperate for God to be in a shape and size that we can control. And most (but not all) religions are desperate for God to be recreated in our own image: to be black or female, to fight for 'our people' and to be a champion for our cause, to give wealth and health,

---

[18] Coehlo, P. (1993). *The Alchemist*. San Francisco: Harper.

prosperity and long life, as rewards for following the path taught by our religion and our religion alone.

This approach must lead to division. Rather than emphasising commonality, most (but not all) religions separate people into those who are following the 'true' path and those who are misguided or deceived. Whole communities and cultures are built around religious practices meaning that someone's perception of God becomes woven deep within the fabric of their personal identity.

It now feels like I have gone through a process of detangling. In doing so there has been an inner conflict between the Daniel I believe I am, and the Daniel that others think I am, or hoped that I would become.

Religion has been for me a place of comfort and a source of community. I believe in God and am confident that there is at the very least, partial truth in Christianity. But I am also losing the will to stand for something that I don't wholly believe in. As someone who was raised to read and understand the bible, I am clear that I am not living a 'Christian' life driven by biblical priorities such as evangelism and the saving of souls.

I believe that what unites people of faith is greater than what divided us, and that submissive practices like committing our lives to Jesus, the Muslim declaration of faith called the Shahadah, and the Sikh baptism of 'taking Amrit' are all pointing us in the same direction of acknowledging and surrendering to our creator.

Amrit is also the name of the first person I fell in love with.

I met Amrit while working at the University of Birmingham. Amrit worked in Careers Network and sat on the desk next to mine. We would begin each morning with the same rhetorical question "Y'alright Amrit?" "Y'alright Daniel?" On such simple things was a strong friendship built.

We would talk and laugh together about things inside and outside of work. We began to arrange lunches individually and as part of a larger friendship group. Amrit lived in Handsworth Wood and would give me a lift into Handsworth on Fridays to mark the end of the working week. I always knew that Amrit was a special person. She had an incredibly warm and genuine heart, and was secure enough in her views to be straight-talking. We had a similar sense of humour and an almost identical perspective on the world driven by the strong moral principles passed down from our parents.

And then unexpectedly and in the words of Mrs Potts from Beauty and the Beast, 'there was something there that wasn't there before.' We began to catch each other's eyes in meetings. Our conversations during the Friday car trips revealed more of Amrit's character. And the more I saw and heard, the more I was drawn to her.

I didn't know how to respond to these growing feelings. We were from different cultures and religions. I knew that many Sikhs, especially those from older generations still adhered to the social hierarchy of the caste system meaning that I, as a black man, would never be accepted by many in Amrit's community. I sensed growing feelings in Amrit but without speaking, we agreed not to allow these feelings to surface.

I generally thought that I had a good handle on things. However towards the end of my time in Careers Network, I could sense my emotions getting the better of me. During a game of badminton, I wagered that the loser should have to give the winner a kiss on their right cheek. I won the game comfortably but never received my prize!

As my mum's condition worsened Amrit was one of very few people I chose to confide in. I recall one afternoon where the pressure and heartache of the whole situation became overwhelming. It seemed like I had stared blankly at my laptop screen for hours on end before leaving work at the end of the day. I was waiting at the bus stop and felt exhausted. It was as if all my energy had left me. I could barely stand and was desperate to shut out the world. I called Amrit. I said that I'd been having a rough day and was hoping that we could talk on the way home. She had already started the journey to Handsworth Wood but turned around her car and met me at the bus stop. Just speaking to Amrit lifted a weight off my shoulders. There was nothing that either of us could do but just being with her made all the difference.

I successfully applied to the University's Graduate Management Trainee Scheme and from early 2018, I only rarely saw Amrit. It seemed like we had successfully put an end to what we were feeling. Then I did something that still confuses me to this day.

AFTER OXFORD

I was on the bus heading into work when it came to mind that I hadn't seen Amrit in a while. I sent her a WhatsApp to ask if she'd like to have lunch today or later in the week. Amrit replied to say that today was fine. It was only later on in the morning that I realised that 'today' was actually Valentine's Day! I decided not to cancel but to go ahead with our lunch. Then in the beautifully direct and loving way that Amrit can, she asked me to explain myself. Why had I invited her to lunch on Valentine's Day?

She said that she felt and knew that a lot had gone unspoken between us, and that she'd had feelings for me and that she didn't know what to do with them. I remained largely silent. For the remainder of the afternoon I pondered my next step. I had hurt a friend in the past by declaring feelings that were true but that I'd been unable to follow through into a relationship. I had to be certain that I would be able to pursue things with Amrit, or I reasoned, it wasn't worth starting anything at all. I thought that the cultural and religious differences would be too significant for us to overcome, so I took what I thought was the right and difficult choice. I called Amrit that evening and told her that I had overstepped the mark at badminton - and that it was nothing more than that.

I thought that would be the end of things. But my answer hadn't given Amrit the closure she desired. There were still feelings that needed to be explained away. So she asked if we could meet to talk about things in more depth. This time, rather than trying to control the outcome, I was honest. I told Amrit that I liked her but that we were both aware of the differences between us. Things would probably be easier with my family but Amrit confirmed my fears about the way that her family would respond, especially her dad. It would break apart her family. We decided to end it but agreed that it was good that we had chosen to be honest.

And then in the following weeks, I began to think. I thought about my own journey of faith and whether the decision I had made was based on what I truly believed or on the expectations and reactions of others. I decided that the fundamental beliefs of Sikhism - belief in one God, in virtuous character and in the oneness of humanity - were the parts of Christianity that were the core of my faith. I thought about Martin Luther King Jr and his famous words that urged us to judge people based on the content of their character rather than race or any other superficial characteristics. Perhaps subconsciously, I also thought about Walt Disney: Princesses who married Street Rats and Beasts who turned into Princes. Was an unhappy ending really inevitable? There were people all over the world who had defied culture and religion in pursuit of love.

And then I began to think about who I really was and who Amrit really was. When we stripped away race and culture and all of the things that we had been socialised into. What would we find if we removed all of those things and were left with 'the face we had before we were born'? When I considered my soul and that I had been created by God without these man-made laws and structures, then my path became clear. I truly believed that Amrit could be the person whom my soul loved, and that I would regret it for the rest of my days if I didn't at least see what might have been possible.

An evening after work, I asked Amrit to meet me in Handsworth Park. I told her that I knew the challenges we faced but that I wanted us to try. Amrit asked me to tell her why I liked her and without hesitation I listed all of the qualities I saw in her: her character, her approach to life, her self-awareness, her honesty, her level-headedness and her beauty. Although we were yet to embark on a formal relationship, our time as friends meant that I knew the core of who Amrit was. After we'd both spoken for a few minutes, we had a moment of silence to take in everything that we'd both shared. My soul felt completely at peace. I could have sat there next to Amrit for hours.

The first people I told were in my immediate family. My siblings were glad that I had found someone that I felt for so deeply but queried what this would mean for my faith and my future. My dad's initial response was a question: "Is she Christian?" When I said that she wasn't, he continued: "Well... Your mother and I have brought you up in a certain way. But you're a big man now!" A few days later he comforted me with the simple phrase: "Love has no rules."

Amrit was more cautious about telling her family. It was likely that some of her family members and closest friends would stop talking to her, at least for a while. Even if we were able to sustain a relationship Amrit feared that I would be made to feel unwelcome by a community who would never bless our union. There were also unresolved issues about how we would raise children and how I would be integrated into a culture that was far removed from the English-speaking British Caribbean experience.

The questions and fears became too much for Amrit and she called it off, saying "I feel as if I'm breaking my own heart in saying this Daniel. But we can't do this."

And so it ended.

For love was not able to conquer discrimination, prejudice and unwritten tradition.

At least not for us.

Acknowledgment

I would like to thank my family and friends; as this story is as much theirs as it is mine.

I would like to thank the countless people whose words and example have inspired me: my teachers and tutors; my employers and colleagues; my mentors and role models; and the heroes and heroines of the past whose lives touched me through print.

I hope that my honest words and experiences will serve to inspire others and to remind us all that the most important things in life can't be written on a certificate.

I would like to thank my editor, Lorna Darknell, who allowed these honest words to be conveyed more clearly to the reader.

And in breaking with tradition, I would like to thank myself. This book was mostly written on my commute - on the top deck of an often noisy bus. Daniel, well done for persevering.

AFTER OXFORD

To contact the author, email: afteroxfordbook@gmail.com

Printed in Great Britain
by Amazon